BEING WITH

BEING WITH

Book 2 COURSES FOR LIVING

Exploring life and faith together

Samuel Wells

CANTERBURY
PRESS

© Samuel Wells 2025

First published in 2025 by the Canterbury Press Norwich

Editorial office
3rd Floor, Invicta House
110 Golden Lane
London EC1Y 0TG, UK
www.canterburypress.co.uk

Canterbury Press is an imprint of Hymns Ancient & Modern Ltd
(a registered charity)

Hymns Ancient & Modern® is a registered trademark of
Hymns Ancient & Modern Ltd
13A Hellesdon Park Road, Norwich,
Norfolk NR6 5DR, UK

All rights reserved. No part of this publication may be reproduced,
stored in a retrieval system, or transmitted,
in any form or by any means, electronic, mechanical,
photocopying or otherwize, without the prior permission of
the publisher, Canterbury Press.

The Author has asserted his under the Copyright, Designs and Patents Act 1988
to be identified as the Author of this Work

Scripture quotations are from the New Revised Standard Version of the Bible,
Anglicized Edition, copyright © 1989, 1995 by the Division of Christian Education
of the National Council of the Churches of Christ in the USA.
Used by permission. All rights reserved.

British Library Cataloguing in Publication data

A catalogue record for this book is available
from the British Library

ISBN: 978 1 78622 694 5

EU GPSR Authorised Representative
LOGOS EUROPE, 9 rue Nicolas Poussin, 17000, LA ROCHELLE, France
E-mail: Contact@logoseurope.eu

No part of this book may be used or reproduced in any manner for the
purpose of training artificial intelligence technologies or systems.

Typeset by Regent Typesetting

Contents

Being With Resources QR Code   vi
Preface   vii

1	Being With Church	1
2	Being With the Bible	27
3	Being With Baptism	55
4	Being With Your Significant Other	66
5	Being With Child	77
6	Being With the End of Life	107
7	Being With Yourself	138
8	Being With Creation	157
9	Being With the Other	184
10	Being With Being With	213

References and Further Reading   239

Scan the QR code below to access the Being With resources:

- Access to the live training, an essential to helping with the delivery of Being With.
- Support videos.
- Downloadable resources including advertising posters, postcards and banners.
- The latest ever-growing online resource library.
- Monthly update emails.

being-with.org/book2/

Preface

The original Being With course was a group at St Martin-in-the-Fields for exploring faith that Sally Hitchiner and I created. The group first met in January 2020. It went online in lockdown and further groups proliferated during the pandemic. It spread back in-the-room as conventional meeting patterns resumed in 2022. Since then it's been practised both in-the-room and online. Two books, *Being With: A Course Exploring Christian Faith and Life: Leaders' Guide* and *Being With: A Course Exploring Christian Faith and Life: Participants' Companion*, were published in 2022. James Fawcett began as Head of Being With in 2022. With dedication, skill and imagination he has built an international network of trained leaders and participating congregations such that many thousands of people new to, returning to, re-evaluating and seeking enrichment in faith are now 'graduates' of the original Being With course in many countries, particularly the UK and the US.

The Being With course arose from four sources. One was a longstanding sense that churches across a broad spectrum of theological and liturgical traditions are generally less attuned to what's involved in bringing people to faith than evangelical ones, and generally need to up their game in this area. Another was my theological exposition of 'being with', beginning in 2011 with the publication of *Living Without Enemies*, and explored in several books, the best known of which are *A Nazareth Manifesto* (2015), *Incarnational Ministry* (2017) and *Incarnational Mission* (2018). 'Being with' began as a way of reimagining mission, but has expanded to become a project for reinterpreting the whole of Christian theology, as fully articulated in *Constructing an Incarnational Theology* (2025). A third was Sally Hitchiner's extensive background in leading and promoting enquirers' courses and her energy and imagination for how such a culture could be translated into a different setting. And the fourth was the particular culture of St Martin-in-the-Fields in central London, a community where faith and action have long been held close together, and where initiatives that have benefited the wider church and world have long found fertile soil. While this volume bears my name, I want to give great credit to Sally, without whose inspiration there wouldn't be a Being With course and movement, and James, who has with great skill organized, garnered funds for, extended and empowered the movement.

Once a significant number of people had participated in the original Being With course, two impulses came simultaneously. One was to make the course available far and wide. The two original books sold exceptionally well, and another more detailed book has been published to succeed them. The other impulse was to create a follow-on course for those who'd enjoyed the original course – and in many cases had done it a second or third time – and were looking for more in the same genre. The whole approach started to become influential not just as a course for exploring faith but as a way of approaching a number of topics. Short courses quickly emerged for those preparing to baptize a child and those preparing for lifelong relationship. Then it became clear courses on many other subjects could be helpful. Eventually the idea for this volume appeared.

The approach to each course is the same and is explained in detail in *Being With: The Core Course* (Norwich: Canterbury, 2025). Because the method is new to most leaders, we strongly encourage leaders, in addition to reading that book, to do the training, which can be accessed through the Being With website, before leading a course. We imagine most participants will join one of these courses having previously completed the original Being With course – and certainly familiarity with the approach, culture, etiquette and theological vision are helpful; but any of these courses could be joined by someone without previous exposure to Being With. Indeed, that's the assumption for Being With Baptism and Being With Your Significant Other.

While this volume is largely made up of talks for each of the courses, the testimony of those who've completed the course seldom focuses on the talks. People's experience is most often about the quality of relation-

PREFACE

ship, trust and understanding that grows up between the participants and the space given for people to make their own journeys and articulate their deepest sentiments. The wonderings are crucial in this. The *Core Courses* book explains the psychology and method behind the wonderings. It is enough here to say they are not questions, but invitations to reflect, recall, imagine and ponder. They are not to be rushed. People's silence is not a problem: when people don't share it's seldom because they have nothing to say, more often because they're assessing whether they trust the group enough to hear what they deeply want to say, or because they're finding words to say it precisely, or because they're absorbed in what others are saying.

As to the talks, they don't pursue a 'how to' approach, nor do they try to convey information in a 'five things you should know about …' way. They seek to offer angles and perspectives not commonly available elsewhere and, in the case of more familiar material, to give new life to well-worn subjects. Almost all the talks are adapted and abbreviated from material found in my publications. I haven't pointed to the source of each talk, but among the publications I've drawn on are *How to Preach: The Moment of Truth*; *Act Justly*; *Humbler Faith, Bigger God*; *A Cross in the Heart of God*; *With*; *Walk Humbly*; *Incarnational Ministry*; *How Then Shall We Live?*; *A Nazareth Manifesto*; *Learning to Dream Again*; *God's Companions*; and *Improvisation*.

I am glad for all those who've enjoyed Being With courses, for those who've been part of leading, organizing and promoting this movement, and for those whose feedback has improved the courses. I hope and trust these courses will prove a blessing in countless settings in the way the original course has.

1

Being With Church

Ten Wonderings and Addresses

One: Communion

- *I wonder where and when you have ever felt close to God.*
- *Tell about a book or song that changed your life or made you see the world differently.*
- *Tell about a time you shook hands with or hugged someone and it was difficult but important to do so.*
- *Tell about a meal you were part of that expressed something really important.*

Church means two things: communion and community. Communion means the way we are with God. Community means the way we are with one another. Today we're talking about communion. The principal way we find communion is through the service called the Eucharist.

The Eucharist happens in five stages. The first is called gathering. When we gather, we become aware of three things. First, the presence of God. We remember how Jacob recognized God in the one with whom he wrestled all night, and how the disciples recognized God when Jesus broke bread on the road to Emmaus. Second, the company of one another. When the presider says the greeting the congregation changes from an assortment of individuals into the body of Christ. But, third, we become aware of who is absent. We realize if we stand alone before God, God will ask, 'Where are the others?'

BEING WITH

The second stage of the Eucharist is hearing. Here we learn to listen, not just to find our place in the story but to discern God's word in every conversation. We practise the virtue of hope – the conviction that God has acted before to save and will act again to liberate. In the sermon we learn to identify the role in the story we are called to play, and discover anew the sense of God meeting us for the first time.

The third stage is responding. When we say the creed, intercede and share peace, we embody faith, hope and love. As they intercede together, thus putting themselves in the place of others before God, Christians develop the skill of distinguishing pain from sin, suffering from evil, need from want. They practise the virtues of patience and persistence – prayers are seldom answered straightaway – and of prudence, for they learn only to request what they can cope with receiving. By having to share the peace before sharing the bread, Christians learn that reconciliation is as necessary to their lives as their daily bread. They practise the virtues of mercy and forbearance, of humility and honesty, of patience and courage.

The fourth stage is eating together. By sharing bread with one another around the Lord's table, Christians learn to live in peace with those with whom they share other tables – breakfast, shop-floor, office, checkout. They develop the skills of distribution, of ensuring all have enough. They develop the skills of equality, of the valued place of differently abled, differently gendered and oriented people, those of assorted races and classes and medical, criminal and social histories. They develop the practices of giving and receiving, of handing over the first fruits of labour and receiving back the first fruits of the resurrection. They realize their simple actions anticipate God's eternal destiny. They practise the virtues of justice, generosity and hope.

The last stage is being sent. When Christians are sent back out into the world, they learn what it means to be salt and light, to be distinct yet among. They develop the practices of service and partnership, of seeking out the ways of God in the most troubled corners of the world. They learn the habits of cooperating with people of very different principles and stories, of resolving conflict without violence, and of standing beside the weak and afflicted.

There's a folk tale that offers a parable of worship. Once a rich man fell in love with a young maiden. She was lovely in form and lovelier in character. He grieved because he knew his face was hideous and his heart was cruel. He considered how he could win her hand.

He went to see a mask maker. He said, 'Make me a mask that I shall become handsome. Then perhaps I may win the love of this noble young woman.' The man was transformed into a handsome figure. He tried hard to summon a character to match. It was sufficient to win the heart and hand of the fair maiden. Ten years of happiness followed. But the man had to know if his wife really loved the man behind the mask. So he knocked a second time on the mask maker's door. 'It's time to remove the mask,' he said. He walked anxiously home. He greeted his wife. To his astonishment, she made no comment. There was no scream, no horror, no revulsion. He searched for a mirror – and saw a face as handsome as the mask. He was overjoyed – but confused. He ran back to the mask maker. The mask maker said, 'You have changed. You loved a beautiful person. You have become beautiful through loving her. You become like the face of the one whom you love.' That is what Christians seek to do in worship.

Two: Prayer

- *I wonder what part of prayer you find the hardest.*
- *I wonder what part of prayer comes most easily to you.*
- *I wonder what part of prayer is the most important part.*
- *Tell about a time when you prayed when it felt really special.*

Prayer is when we allow the wonder of eternal essence to saturate our earthly existence. It's when we self-consciously listen to God, seek mercy, call out and open our hearts, celebrate and meditate on God's wonders and place ourselves in the company of God's creatures and servants. Prayer is when we stop closing our ears and eyes, and let ourselves become part of the conversation the members of the Trinity are having with one another.

We conventionally think of five kinds of prayer. Prayer certainly, perhaps centrally, means:

1. Adoration, or wonder. It means being taken out of the mundane and routine and being astonished and dazzled by the breadth and detail of creation and the depth and passion of redemption. This often doesn't need any words.
2. Confession, or recognition of our error. It means painful admission of purposeful sin and participation in widespread evil, and resolve to be done with such ways of thinking and saying and doing and begin again the new life made possible in Christ. This often only needs one word: sorry.
3. Thanksgiving. This means receiving all the contours of life as the gifts of a gracious God. It means renarrating the events of each day as a letter of love from God to oneself. It means expressing love and joyful thanks in return. This only needs two words, carefully spoken: thank you.
4. Petition. This means explicitly looking to God to transform all in life that does not reflect divine glory and specifically requesting God to meet needs, heal bodies and change hearts. Unlike the other kinds of prayer, this often involves a lot of words.
5. Silence. This means humble meditation, the simple offering of time, the stillness that attests to the fundamental priority of God's activity, the simple opening of the ears of the heart. This recognizes that prayer is fundamentally about God speaking to us, not vice versa.

We're all different and we all take more easily to some kinds of prayer than to others. I suggest changing the conventional order and putting petition first. Good manners always says, 'Put your own needs last.' But prayer isn't about good manners. I say put your own needs in God's hands straightaway, and then your heart is ready to be filled with the needs of others. In a monastery at dinnertime the monks who serve the food have a light meal before they serve everyone else. So when the dinner comes round, their mind is fully on the job of attending to the needs of others, and their tongues aren't hanging out. Petition works the same way.

Let's reflect briefly on how you become a person who can pray. If we start this time with petition, petition teaches you the meaning of solidarity. If you're going to pray for a person or a people regularly it's going to push you to discover more about them. Petition also teaches you how to watch the news. When you follow a news story, you don't join the hasty scramble for blame. You simply ask yourself, 'Who or what might I pray for in this story?' And petition teaches you to make a list of colleagues, old friends, family members, godchildren, congregational members, neighbourhood residents, missionary partners and other congregations.

Moving to wonder, you need to keep the company of those for whom exultation in the sheer joy of life is a simple habit, like a puppy or a child. You begin to find purpose in rain showers that replenish and challenge in every journey. You discover a new reason for learning to amplify the wonder of your heart, to stretch your imagination with the glory of God.

As to confessing sin, it means keeping your imagination open to how a story can look from a perspective other than your own. It's a reason to read fiction, poetry and biography, because they train you to see the patterns of human self-deception reflected in your own life. It's also a reason to keep up friendships with people very different from you – people who remind you that not everybody takes the things for granted that you do.

Moving to thanksgiving, it means spending time in the company of those less fortunate than yourself. This is not for their benefit but for yours. Because it's hard to value a gift – even to realize that something *is* a gift – unless you know what it means not to have such a thing. And the rhythm of thankfulness peaks appropriately at moments of sharing food: for then we recall the progression of planting, growing, harvesting, transporting, selling, storing, preparing, eating, digesting and clearing that constitutes a genuine process of being fed; and thankfulness is a reassertion of understanding all the labour and relationships and the gift of life and growth involved in bringing food to a table.

Finally, silence is a time to discover the intimacy and vulnerability of resting for both our urgent present as well as our eternal future in nothing other than the grace of God.

So after a while we realize there are just two parts to our life: praying, and becoming a person who can pray.

Three: Bible

- *Tell about a passage in the Bible that meant a lot to you at a certain time in your life.*
- *I wonder if there's a story in the Bible that is in some ways like your story.*
- *Tell about a person in the Bible you feel you can relate to.*
- *I wonder if there's something about the Bible you've never understood.*

In the third chapter of the book of Daniel, in the Old Testament, we're given a story of a furious king of Babylon, Nebuchadnezzar, who sets up a great statue and, when he hears that three Jews refuse to bow down to it, throws them into a fiery furnace. It turns out that the furnace doesn't burn up the three men, Shadrach, Meshach and Abednego, but that a fourth figure appears alongside them. This story explains why we have the Bible.

Israel was in exile in Babylon, represented by the fire in this story. Israel had lost all the things that made it great – the Promised Land, the kingship and the glorious temple. In exile Israel sought to understand what had happened. It compiled the stories of how God had made the earth and called Abraham to inaugurate a holy people; of how Abraham's grandson Jacob had gone down to Egypt with his family, and their descendants had become Pharaoh's slaves; of how Moses had led the people to freedom across the Red Sea and had received the Ten Commandments on Mount Sinai and died before entering the Promised Land; of how Joshua had conquered the land, and how life had been fragile until Samuel anointed Saul as Israel's first king; of how under David and then Solomon Israel had reached the zenith of its power, before splitting into two kingdoms and declining until the northern kingdom was obliterated and the southern kingdom carried off to Babylonian exile. The paradox was that Israel in exile discovered a new face of God: a God who wasn't there to fulfil some kind of a contract and act for Israel to bring plenty and safety, but was committed to be with Israel through good times and bad, in a covenant of companionship.

The Old Testament has three parts – the Law, the Prophets and the Writings. The Law refers to the first five books, which aren't just a collection of laws but are better understood as the foundation stone of Israel's relationship with God. The Prophets tell the history of how Israel both was and was not faithful to the Law, and record the message of a series of prophets to call Israel back to faithfulness. The Writings are a collection of poems, songs, epigrams and stories that reflect in different ways on both Israel's and more general human experience of standing before God.

The 27 books of the New Testament are in total much shorter than the 39 books of the Old Testament. They tell a story in three stages and an epilogue. The first stage is the birth, life, death, resurrection and ascension of Jesus. The first three Gospels, Matthew, Mark and Luke, follow a broadly similar pattern, and often have different versions of the same stories. The fourth Gospel, John, is in many ways different, but still keeps the same shape of Jesus ministering in Galilee, coming to Jerusalem, dying and rising. The second stage is the life of the very early church, told in the Acts of the Apostles, in which the Holy Spirit comes down at Pentecost and from there the apostles take the gospel around the Mediterranean. The third stage is mostly composed of letters to early churches founded by the apostles: many of the letters are written by or attributed to Paul, once a leading Jew who became the best-known leader of the early church. This stage is about the way the church encountered and resolved the problems it faced in understanding its identity and message. The epilogue is the book of Revelation. Revelation is a bewildering book unless you understand it as written in a context where the beleaguered early church needed reassurance that God's will would ultimately prevail and that all would indeed be made new. While the Gospels and Acts are to be read at face value, Revelation is best read not as a factual prediction but more like a parable.

The crucial point to notice is that just as the Old Testament was put together at a time of adversity – the exile in Babylon – so the New Testament emerged in response to an apparently devastating setback –

Jesus' crucifixion. In both cases what seemed a total disaster became the beginning of transformation and discovery.

There has always been controversy in the church about the authority of scripture. That controversy is found in the Bible itself, for example where Peter and Paul dispute whether the Holy Spirit is calling Gentiles to become part of God's chosen people. For most of the church's history, most people couldn't read, and (in the West) the Bible was only available in Latin, so people depended on the interpretation of the clergy. During the Reformation the Bible was translated into everyday languages, and people questioned a lot of things the church did that could not be justified from the Bible. Later, people started to criticize internal inconsistencies, and tensions with scientific accounts.

Anglicanism traditionally balances scripture with two other authorities – tradition and reason. Tradition means there's a place for what the Holy Spirit has shown the church over the centuries. Reason means there's a place for discernment, questioning and new understanding.

Above all the Bible is a gift to the church to understand God's character and purpose. It shows us a God who longs to be with us, in the way God is with us in Jesus, now and forever.

Four: Baptism

- *Tell about a turning point in your life.*
- *I wonder how much your sense of identity is given to you and how much you find it.*
- *Tell about a person who believed in you.*
- *Tell about a time you realized you couldn't do it on your own.*

Baptism is the establishment of a new identity – a new creation. The candidate comes to the water of baptism as the Israelites came to the Red Sea. To come to the Red Sea they had to admit, first of all, that *their lives were chained by slavery*. They had to admit, second, that there was no hope in going on as they were and thus they had to *resolve to leave* Egypt and slavery. They had to recognize, third, that God had a destiny for them that would constitute their flourishing as never before, and that *their only future lay in God's hands*. And then, finally, confronted by the daunting water in front of them and the raging chariots of slavery and death behind them, but strengthened by the events of the Passover in which God's plan had begun to be revealed, they had to believe that *God alone had the power to take them across the sea*, to transform their situation from slavery and death to liberation and rebirth – from fate to destiny.

The second part of baptism is washing. Fundamentally baptism is an enactment of death and resurrection. Just as we believe the Holy Spirit is especially present when we re-enact Jesus' last meal with his disciples, so we believe the Holy Spirit is especially present when we re-enact Christ's baptism in the Jordan. What happens at baptism is that God places a song in your heart. But it is very important that there are other people present – because it is very easy to forget the tune. So you have godparents. It is up to the godparents to learn the song in your heart so well that they can sing it back to you when you forget how it goes. And what is the song? Well, the story of Jesus' baptism shows us what the song is. Three things happen in this story: the heavens open; the Spirit descends like a dove; and a voice says, 'This is my beloved child.' Each of these events has great significance.

The beginning of the song goes like this: *heaven is open to you*. The gospel begins with the tearing of the heavens and ends with the tearing of the Temple curtain. The veil between you and God has been torn apart. Heaven is open to you. There is no limit to God's purpose for your life: it is an eternal purpose. The second line of the song goes like this: *God's Spirit is in you*. Remember the end of the flood, when the dove brought the twig of new life back to Noah? Well, here is the dove descending on Jesus, bringing the gift of the Holy Spirit. You are now the temple of God's Holy Spirit. You are the place where others will encounter God. God's Spirit is in you. The third line of the song is: *you mean everything to God*. God's words are, 'This is my beloved Son.' These words mean, 'Jesus means everything to God, and everything God gives to Jesus God gives to us.' You mean everything to God. And what does the song mean? It means, 'You are the song in God's heart and God will never forget how you go.'

After the stripping and the washing comes the clothing. In one congregation a baby was brought for baptism – a child who had been cherished and prayed for by the whole community from long before conception. The reading for the day was a passage from Colossians, which speaks of being clothed in Christ. After the reading, the assembly divided into groups of seven people, children and adults together. Even the tearaways intent on disrupting the service joined in. Each group was given a strip of coloured towel, and wrote on it the virtue that they believed was the one they were asking God to bestow upon this new young Christian. There was then an opportunity for each group to tell the others what they had chosen. The towels were then whisked away, and during the 'stripping' – the decisions and promises – they were sewn together. The baby was baptized naked in a large punch bowl and, when he emerged from the water for the third time, he was clothed in a huge towel made up of all the virtues for which the congregation had prayed.

Baptism affirms God's eternal decision to be with us. It is about God's decision far more than it is about ours. The candidate may think that he or she is like a merchant who went and sold all he had to buy the pearl of great price, but the candidate is wrong, for the candidate is the pearl – the merchant is God.

Five: Church

- Tell about a good experience of being church.
- Tell about a not-so-good experience of church.
- I wonder what would make church better.
- Tell about a community of any kind that changed for the better and what made that change come about.

Imagine being utterly one with God, completely reconciled with your neighbour, truly at peace with yourself and wholly in harmony with creation. There's a word for those who seek such perfection: that word is church. How and why church has come to mean a host of other things, many of them controlling, judgemental, posturing and pretentious, is a long and complex story, much of it sad; but for all its missteps and misperceptions, church is the principal and definitive way essence takes form in existence, from the moment Jesus departed till the moment essence pervades existence and Jesus is all in all.

Church means broadly three things. It refers initially to the body of Christ – the fully human, fully divine place where divinity and humanity meet, most explicitly in Jesus, but also in God's people, shaped by baptism, renewed by the Eucharist, empowered by the Holy Spirit, the place of reconciliation between heaven and earth, between essence and existence. Church is not the full embodiment of Jesus Christ, nor is it the complete fulfilment on the Last Day – but in the meantime it is the physical and spiritual bearer of who Christ is and what it means and entails to be in full communion with him. Church means, second, the local embodiment of those seeking to inhabit this vision. It's a group of people doing their best to live with each other under God. Third, and less straightforwardly, church means those wider structures, institutions, relationships and practicalities that enable the first two to flourish. Part of the paradox is that the attention of the world (and, to be fair, much of the church) tends to be drawn to the third dimension, thus often missing the most vital, vibrant and thrilling facets of what church really entails.

To be the body of Christ means to dwell in the freedom Christ brings – freedom from the prison of the past and from the fear of the future. It is to recognize that, through baptism, you have given up the claim that your individual body is the unit of creation, and allowed that body to be grafted in by the Holy Spirit to the true body, Christ's body, through which you participate in the life of God. You have given up your distinct identity and you have yielded the final say on your own worth, purpose and flourishing. So to participate in the body of Christ is to discover and re-encounter your nature and destiny. It is hard to acknowledge that you no longer belong to yourself: it is to break the habits of a lifetime. Thus it's vital to be among a community in which such a recognition is universally held and assumed. In such a community you may learn to take the right things for granted. One of those things is that your life is set on a much greater canvas than your daily strivings, mundane desires and perpetual squabbles might suggest. The way we discover that broader canvas is worship.

The pitfalls of the church are two: people expect church to be an encounter with divinity and are impatient when that divinity is everywhere clothed in humanity, sometimes humanity of the most obstinate, unimaginative and unattractive sort; or people are overwhelmed by the desires of their own imperfect humanity, and attempt to use the capacity and potential of church to assert their personal needs for affirmation, security or control – or, worse, exploit the opportunities of church to manipulate, take advantage of or seriously harm those to whom they have privileged and trusted access. The first mistake is to forget how weak you are and to expect others to be made of stronger fibre than you are yourself; the second mistake is to forget how good and beautiful and true is the enterprise in which you are engaged, and to reduce it to the most unworthy devices or desires of your own heart.

To belong to the wider structures, institutions, relationships and practicalities of church is to recognize that communion means not just intimacy with God, not just a local congregation gathered as one, but also something less intense and less tangible: a body of people united around a faith, a person, a set of practices or a form of words, unlikely to know one another well if at all, always likely to oppose unity to truth and pragmatism to hope, perpetually struggling to balance competing goods and to find understanding for one another's different stories and setbacks, opportunities and challenges. To exalt the body of Christ as intimate communion alone is to risk self-deception and self-indulgence. To exalt church as local congregation alone is to hazard an exclusive and narrow convergence of the likeminded. To seek the welfare of the whole is to experience the highs and lows of politics: sometimes it can be noble, visionary and far-sighted; other times it can feel tawdry, cheap and hollow.

To be church means to be willing to make your life transparent to others, be prepared to do humble and simple tasks, accept that your control, insistence on your own way and right to be offended will all be in jeopardy; but at the same time to be part of a movement following in Christ's footsteps, have your eyes opened to miracles of healing and transformation, and be ready to meet Christ face to face.

Six: Discipleship

- *Tell about a time you had to admit you were wrong.*
- *Tell about a time you felt you were really sure of something.*
- *Tell about a time you felt confident enough about someone to go with them to a place you had not been before.*
- *I wonder what it's like to sense you've been given something you feel you must share with others.*

In 1961 a bunch of engineers in Burbank, California, were trying to make a jet plane that was clever enough to spy on the Russians but was, at the same time, simple enough that an ordinary mechanic could repair it in emergency conditions on the ground. The lead engineer at Lockheed, Kelly Johnson, tossed a bunch of tools to his design team, with a single word, 'Kiss: Keep it simple, stupid.'

At the start of Jesus' ministry, Mark describes what Jesus is about. He gives us four verbs, all single-word imperatives. Number one, *repent*. It's an unfashionable word. On any list of winning friends and influencing people, starting with a smile always comes top. 'Repent' isn't on that list anywhere. So why does Jesus say it? For the same reason Alcoholics Anonymous starts its 12-step programme with, 'Admit that you are powerless and your life has become unmanageable.' Jesus is saying to Israel, to humanity, to you and me: 'Admit that you are powerless and your life is unmanageable.' We are all addicts. Because sin is addiction. It's giving something power over us that ought never to have power over us. It is making something less than God our god. And we all do that. All of us. All the time. And into that meticulously constructed but ultimately false world comes Jesus, and, like a toddler with a pin or a child seeing the king has no clothes, he simply says, 'Repent.' And we have a straight choice: the dung-heap of lies or the fresh but chilly air of the truth. He keeps it simple. Very simple.

But what he doesn't do is leave us alone. He has another word. He says, '*Believe*.' Believe is the other half of repent. Repent means 'I have failed to save myself.' Believe means, 'But there is someone who can repair me, indeed longs to repair me and already has repaired me, if I would only accept and receive it.' As a child my favourite game was sardines. One person goes and hides and everyone else goes looking for them. When they find them they don't shout and scream, they quietly fold themselves into the background and wait for others to come and do the same. If you're one of the last to find everybody you walk into a dark place and quickly become aware of a host of pairs of eyes and smiling faces glad to see you. It's like a silent surprise birthday party. That's what we call coming to believe. You thought you were alone, but you find companions who struggle like you do, a place in a drama that's full of people like you, and a God who in the power of the Spirit is always at your side. Believe. It's not grabbing a tight hold of a difficult idea; it's allowing yourself to be cradled by the glory of God. Simple.

But it doesn't stop there. There's a third word: *follow*. Whether you've got family responsibilities or staff liabilities, whether you've got delicate contracts or longstanding commitments, Jesus calls you regardless: 'Follow.' For Jesus, there's no believing without following. We've created this extraordinary notion that believing is an internal matter, about thoughts, feelings, ideas and experiences – and hence people say belief is a very personal thing. But Mark's Gospel knows nothing about such a novel idea. It's simple: believing means following, and it has a huge economic impact on a person's livelihood and an enormous social effect on a person's family. There's a great emphasis on leadership these days, but the simple truth is, you're a leader if you have followers. Most of leadership is choosing the right person to follow.

And the final word is *fish*. 'Fish' was a code word in the early church. The Greek word icthus, which means fish, was an acronym for 'Jesus Christ, son of God and saviour'. It's said that in dangerous times, on meeting a stranger a Christian would draw an upper arc. If the stranger added a lower arc, making a fish, then it would reveal they were a Christian too. But the meaning of this fourth word, fish, is much simpler. The difference between believe and follow is that Jesus is going to make a difference not just to your heart and soul but to your life and circumstances. The difference between follow and fish is that following Jesus isn't going to affect just your life but the life of everyone you meet. You want everyone you know to follow too. That doesn't mean if they don't follow you force them, manipulate them, impose yourself on them or show any less respect for them. It doesn't mean you ever imagine the way to follow Jesus has to be by following you. But it means you never call Jesus 'my' God, as if there were a bunch of divinities out there and you can take your pick. You never assume this is just a private matter. The meaning of fish is simple: you want to bring others into the company of Jesus.

Remember Kelly Johnson tossing his aeronautical engineers a bunch of tools in California in 1961. Think about his one-word motto: KISS. Keep it simple, stupid. Repent. Believe. Follow. Fish. Because Christ, in the power of the Spirit, is among us to kiss humankind. And Christ the mechanic has to find a way to repair the world that can be adapted to conditions on the ground. And all he has to repair the world is a bunch of tools. And that bunch of tools is you.

Seven: Ministry

- *Tell about a time you just showed up for a group, event or movement and got a pleasant surprise.*
- *Tell about a skill you have that you sense has never been fully put to use.*
- *Tell about a time you found something in you you never knew you had.*
- *I wonder what it's like to speak of God to people and speak of people to God.*

For all, some of the time, and for some, most of the time, church means not just to participate but to initiate, promote and lead. This is the difference between discipleship and ministry. In some traditions particular individuals are set apart to conduct roles that are considered integral to the church's life and indispensable to its flourishing. But such roles by no means exhaust the activities of ministry. Ministry means taking the initiative on any aspect that builds up the life of the body.

There are three kinds of ministry: self, skills and Spirit. The ministry of the self relies on no particular qualities, only the willingness to show up and join in. For this reason it's perhaps the most important ministry, because everyone can offer it. It's also the most vulnerable ministry, because one cannot fall back on one's talents or hide behind one's specialization. A person volunteering for a lunch club for otherwise-isolated elderly people may bring culinary skills, but those could become an excuse to hide in the kitchen and avoid genuine encounter with the people the programme seeks to be with. If instead the person simply offers to wait at tables, or even simply sits and eats alongside the elderly people, they are much more at the mercy of conversation and need to fit in more adeptly to the pace and expectations of lunchtime culture. Anyone can do it – but many would choose to be in the kitchen, which more nearly resembles the bustle and purposefulness of a working environment.

The ministry of skills is often regarded as the goal of a healthy community, but it risks devolving into a pattern where disciples simply replicate their professional or technical aptitudes in a congregational setting. It's marvellous to have a qualified accountant as a church treasurer, so long as the person doesn't assume the professional status of accountancy acquires the same seniority in a congregation as often it would in a commercial setting, so long as the identity of accountant doesn't trump the identity of disciple, and so long as the ethos of the secular workplace informs but doesn't dominate the ethos of church. It's wonderful to have a trained teacher to do Christian education, so long as corresponding transitions are made. The danger remains that everyone simply does at church what they do elsewhere, and church feels rather more like elsewhere as a consequence. Expressed differently, the ministry of skills seems to depend less on prayer, less on grace, less on miracle, and rather more on sufficiency, competence and adequacy.

The ministry of the Spirit is described rather more in the New Testament than the other ministries. Some have or develop skills in public speaking; but preaching is a gift rather than a skill – in other words, it's bestowed by the Holy Spirit for the building-up of the body, rather than simply transferred from being honed in another context. The brilliant speaker who has nothing of the gospel to say is not a preacher. The gift of healing is not the same as the skill of physician or surgeon; healing is configured in relation to repentance, forgiveness and reconciliation, rather than in relation to diagnosis, medication and cure. Prophecy is not the same as prediction: it's about being so soaked in the tradition of the scriptures and the imagination of the church and the contours of the kingdom that one can name a truth that others cannot yet perceive. These are spiritual gifts. What marks them out is that they're shaped by and useless without prayer. They are spoken, embodied and shared prayers.

Some things are so central to church, so crucial to understanding who God is and who we are, that some people are set aside to ensure they are done well. Such people are known as priests, or sometimes by other similar names. The church is not the only way the Holy Spirit makes Christ present in the world. But the church is the most reliable way we find our collective bodies shaped into the body of Christ. The most time-honoured ways this happens are through prayer, the Eucharist, baptism, scripture reading, pastoral care and preaching. This is why the church sets aside specific people to become so proficient at those things, and so adept at enabling others to make those things the framework of their lives, that the rest of the church can relax and know those things are in safe hands.

I remember sitting down with a close friend at university and telling her I was hoping to be a priest. I've never forgotten what she said. 'If you're not a priest now, ordination won't make you one.' What she meant was, being a priest isn't being taken up into a cloudy netherworld of vestments, prayer books and angels. It's being practised in the presence of God and being a reconciling presence in the life of others. In that sense, all of us can be priests. I didn't say all of us *are* priests, but all of us *can* be priests. Because all of us can grow in the practice of the presence of God – all of us can become people who develop the awe and tenderness and humility and wonder and gentleness that come from knowing that God is at work in us and in others the same way God was at work in the life of Jesus Christ. And all of us can be a reconciling presence in the life of those around us. Those are perhaps the most wonderful things in the world to be – a person in whom and by whom our reconciliation with God and our reconciliation with one another are discovered and mediated and experienced. This is the sense in which we're all called to ministry.

BEING WITH

Eight: Mission

- *Tell about a time you were hungry.*
- *I wonder what it's like to feel you still haven't found what you're looking for.*
- *Tell about someone who gave you something you didn't want but it turned out you needed.*
- *Tell about a person you know who's deeply hungry and what you think they're hungry for.*

There are two kinds of hunger. There's a hunger that has a name. It's a hunger where you know what you want but you haven't got it or can't have it. Such hunger can become all-consuming, transforming your temper, your relationships, your whole character.

But there's another kind of hunger. It's a hunger that lingers deep, disturbingly, in the bottom of your soul, but it doesn't have a name. There's no simple solution to it, no hot meal or job title or box ticked that will satisfy it.

For 50 years in Babylonian exile, Israel was focused on the first kind of hunger – quite simply, 'I want to go home.' Everything that was wrong was crystallized in one simple fact – Israel was 500 miles from the Promised Land. But Israel did go home. Jerusalem was restored, the Temple rebuilt, the walls raised again. But when all that was done, Israel was still hungry. It turned out going home wasn't all that Israel was hungry for.

The 2004 film *The Chorus* is set in south-east France in 1949. A tyrannical headmaster, M Rachin, presides over a reform school for out-of-control boys, set in an old castle known as Fond de l'Étang (which translates as 'Bottom of the Pond' or 'Rock Bottom'). An out-of-work music teacher, Clément Mathieu, arrives to replace a teacher who's leaving because his arm has been savaged by a pupil. The new teacher faces a high level of hostility and studied aggravation, and his more lenient policy on punishment brings him into conflict with the censorious head.

But the story really begins when M Mathieu decides to teach the children to sing. All but one have some kind of serviceable voice, and most of the boys play along because it's less demanding than the regu-

BEING WITH CHURCH

lar curriculum. The one boy, Pierre, who keeps aloof, is the wildest of them all, but M Mathieu begins to realize that the wild and suspicious Pierre has an astounding treble voice. Gradually the chorus of boys grows in skill and confidence, performing to the local countess. But it cannot last. Part of the school burns down due to arson; M Mathieu is held responsible and fired, and he's forced to leave without saying goodbye. But then you see two men, 50 years later, leafing through the scrapbook M Mathieu wrote up about his time at the school. And you remember the film started with a 62-year-old orchestral conductor at the height of his powers performing a Strauss waltz. And you realize this is that same man, and that same man is called Pierre, and he was the tearaway delinquent who became the treble soloist and is now the living embodiment that M Mathieu's work was not in vain but brought forth a hundredfold.

The film is about the distinction between the hunger that has a name and the hunger that has no name. The boys know all about the first kind of hunger. They want food, they want some control over their lives, they want exercise, they want to make misery for anyone who tries to pin them down. But the real drama of the story is about the second kind of hunger. The boys are very, very angry. But most of them aren't exactly sure what they're angry about or who they're angry with. They're hungry, but food and exercise go little or no distance to meeting their hunger. M Mathieu doesn't give the boys what they think they want. He doesn't meet the first kind of hunger in any significant way. He takes a huge gamble on reaching them in the hunger that they don't have a name for.

We often think of practical Christianity as striving to meet people's hunger – the hunger that has a name, for the starving food, for the thirsty water, for the naked clothing, for the sick medicine. All of which is good and right and true. But people want and need more than that. Almost always, what they want is something no one can give them. Christianity isn't simply about satisfying people's hunger. It's a huge gamble on the hunch that what people are really hungry for is something they don't know the name of, and wouldn't initially recognize even when they found it.

And what is that mysterious discovery, that extraordinary food? It's the wondrous truth that there's something even deeper, even more long-lasting and even more insatiable than our hunger. And that's God's hunger for us. Discovering that is for us like discovering choral music was for the boys in that reform school. For some of us, like Pierre, it unearths a gift that was longing to get out. For others, it's a realization that together we can make something beautiful we could never make alone, that there's a place for all shapes and sizes and voices and energies in a song that takes all our energies to make but comes from a force much bigger than us.

Are you hungry? Does your hunger have a name, like a yearning for a job or a partner or a home or new start? Or is your hunger deeper and more insatiable than that, something that even gaining those precious things won't assuage? If you're hungry – deeply, deeply hungry – hear the good news, the news that you've been waiting all this time for: God's hungry. Hungry for you.

Nine: Death

- *Tell about the first time you became aware that you were going to die.*
- *Tell about a death that was really hard.*
- *Tell about a death that was beautiful.*
- *I wonder what part of death is the most difficult to think about.*

I wonder when you lie on your bed how long it takes you to get to sleep. This can be the most terrifying moment of the day. All the deepest anxieties of our lives are crystallized in this instant: however dynamic, accomplished or abundant our life has been, it's as if at this moment, poised between waking and sleeping, we have to renounce it all and feel naked, weak and empty. It's an experience of standing on the brink of death.

This makes it ironic that the very thing we long for with every fibre of our body is to go to sleep, to dive deep into the darkness of oblivion and be replenished to face the next day. It's ironic because our deepest fears are to be utterly alone and to cease to have meaning. Yet every day we urge each of these conditions on ourselves and become extremely anxious if we can't achieve them. It's as if sleep is teaching us one of the most important lessons of life.

BEING WITH CHURCH

When we step back a little and place things on a larger canvas, we confront a larger paradox. We exist in a world of myriad complexity, subtlety, intricacy and wonder. Meanwhile we have an acute or dim recognition that behind, beyond and within all this life and existence, there is some logic, purpose or intention. Even if you have very little notion of a discernible purpose or intention, you're inevitably searching for some kind of logic: all of us are, all the time, every time we check the weather forecast or try to work out whether that tumour we're worried about is malignant or benign. Then there's the realization that this logic is more than just a cold or mechanical chain reaction, but has purpose, intention and (and this is the crucial step) personality. This personality is by its nature shaped for relationship. For Christians, being shaped for relationship means God is not just always looking to enter into and sustain relationship with us but is also inherently made up of relationship – what we call the Trinity of Father, Son and Holy Spirit. Thus relationship isn't an afterthought for God – relationship is the very essence of what God is, and thus what eternity is. Jesus is proof of these two things – proof that God is shaped to be in relationship with us and proof that God's inner life consists of relationship.

But here's the contradiction. We die. Apparently our breathing stops, our organs shut down, our consciousness ceases, our body begins to decay and we are finished: no feeling, no awareness, no life, no future, no anything. No one can explain how a world and a universe that has such complexity and intricacy can collapse into the still, silent, inert form of a dead body. No one can identify the logic behind why all the processes that create the miracle of life are finally thwarted by the absurdity of death. No one can understand why the God who looks in every moment to establish or sustain relationship is content to see that relationship come to such a sudden, overwhelming and permanent end. It seems totally illogical, uncharacteristic, unjust and incomprehensible.

Here we have to confront something uncomfortable about most versions of the Christian faith. Faith is often based on an assumption that if there is a God, the job of that God is to fix human problems, enhance existence and arrange benefits. In other words, that God is a piece of technology whose role is to improve our life. It's an utterly human-centred arrangement. Not really faith at all: more the demand to honour a contract we never actually made – a contract by which we agreed to be born and God agreed to do the rest. We treat God like a government we voted for but that then reneged on its election promises. When was that election again? Who among us chose to be born? At what point did we enter into a deal with God? On what grounds do we expect better of life than we find it gives us? What gives us the presumption to treat God like this?

Let's go back to the idea that the heart of all things is relationship. If there's hardship and yet there's still relationship, it is well with our soul. By contrast, if there's prosperity but no relationship, there's no reason to rejoice. Thus God is fundamentally not a means to secure comforts but the one in whom we find everlasting and inexpressible relationship. An ancient prayer puts it succinctly:

> God of time and eternity, if I love thee for hope of heaven, then deny me heaven; if I love thee for fear of hell, then give me hell; but if I love thee for thyself alone, then give me thyself alone.

The so-called 'problem of suffering' assumes that God's role is to bring health and flourishing – and if God fails to do that, God is bad or weak. But what if God's role is to be with us always, in person in Jesus, in myriad ways through the Holy Spirit, and forever in heaven? God is not an instrument we discard if it malfunctions. God is the essence of all things who astonishingly chooses to be with us, even in desperate hardship – and even, in the crucified Christ, in indescribable agony. That doesn't make suffering go away. But it turns God's engagement with suffering from a pretext for rejection into a reason for worship.

When we lie on our beds at night, or on our deathbed facing eternity, we do indeed face the loss of everything. We lose everything – but God. The one thing we don't lose is communion with God. The one and only thing that in the end really matters. The source from which all blessings flow. So, and only so, may we rest in peace.

Ten: Money

- *Tell about a time you spent a lot of money on something.*
- *Tell about a time someone else spent a lot of money on you.*
- *I wonder what kinds of things make the best investments.*
- *I wonder if you really had way more money than you needed what you'd do with it.*

Many people ask, 'Why should I spend my money on the church?' That question is based on a misunderstanding. For a start, it's not our money. Things don't belong to us. They belong to God. Like everything else, money's something we look after for a while but can't ultimately keep. The choice is not whether to hang on to it or give it away, it's who to give it to.

That's why the word 'spend' is also wrong. 'Spend' is a verb that gives us a sense of power, a sense that we can make things happen by dispensing money. But we don't ever really do that. What we actually do is invest money. Every act that we call spending is in fact taking a risk – that this bar of chocolate will make us happy, that this newspaper will keep us informed and entertained. If we use the word 'spend', we hide the reality of that risk. If we replace 'spend' with 'invest', then we recognize we can't control the outcomes of our risky ventures, and we broaden our imaginations to consider what really lasts forever. Christians believe in a personal God but the most basic understanding of God would be 'that which lasts forever'. If we're in the investment business, which we all are, why wouldn't we invest in that which lasts forever? It makes all other investment look absurdly short-term.

John Wesley has the best advice. He says, 'Consider yourself the first among the poor you are called to serve.' Wesley recognizes that we have deep, pressing and real needs and only when those needs are met can we really relax and live for others. The economy of gift believes that generosity is the best investment. Hoarding goods and living in constant anxiety is, in the end, idolatry, because it's investing too much worth in something less than God. It's not so much wrong as foolish and sad.

The word 'church' is wrong if it's taken to mean something that's separate from ourselves and separate from God. If you believe in the economy of gift – if you're in the business of investing in forever – then you want to be part of the body of Christ, the embodiment of eternal grace. So all your money should lie with the church, minus the part you hold back as you consider yourself first among the poor you're called to serve. I'm not saying don't pay taxes, because taxes provide the ordered government that makes freedom possible and the basic services that make life liveable. I'm not saying don't give to charities, because charities provide the concrete acts of mercy for which a majority in a democracy would not vote. I'm not saying live a life of begging and destitution, because Jesus instructs us to love not only God and our neighbour but also ourselves, and loving ourselves is part of the way we show our gratitude to God. But I am saying as Christians our whole lives are oriented to the economy of gift and investing in forever, and the word for the place where gift and forever meet is church. God isn't a distant and arbitrary landlord whom we call up twice a year and summon to fix the plumbing. God is the one who has invested everything in us and who invites us to invest everything in return. If your faith isn't alive, maybe it's because you haven't invested much in it.

Few members of most congregations are rich. Most have followed a path in life that brought no great financial reward, or have faced obstacles in life that depleted what resources they might otherwise have accrued. But most congregations believe in greater income equality, in environmental sustainability, in fair trade. To bring such things about in our nation requires huge political will, which we can hope and pray and strive to foster. The way to change the world is to join a community that believes in these things. Everyone knows the words of the anthropologist Margaret Mead: 'Never doubt that a small group of thoughtful, committed citizens can change the world; indeed, it's the only thing that ever has.' But not everyone hears those words and then joins such a community. Christians have a word for a community of prophetic action: we call it church. And what it strives for is called kingdom. Joining a church is the most political thing we ever do. If we want to change the world, we have to practise what we preach. We can't go on calling for government, business and civil society to live our values unless we're prepared to face the cost of living them ourselves. It's called living God's future now. It's called the realm of God.

Commentary

This course is intended as an immediate follow-on course for those who've enjoyed the Being With course and would like either to discover more about how the ideas connect to being part of the church, or more specifically to recognize publicly that they are or have become a Christian and accordingly to be prepared for baptism and/or confirmation. Like any such course, the ceremony itself may come after or part-way through the course.

The sequence of subjects is not intended as definitive and the host and storyteller may choose to arrange them in a different order as suits the context – for example if one member is due to miss a session when the subject is prayer but is sad to do so, that session could be relocated to later or earlier in the series. That said, experience of leading such courses has taught me that the two things for which people are most eager on beginning to attend church are how to understand the service and how to pray; so these are the first two sessions. As ever, the talk about worship isn't designed to 'tell' in the manner of a guidebook that says 'You'll find this follows this'; instead, it offers a frame in which participants can infuse their own meanings. Likewise the session on prayer offers a simple fourfold structure into which participants can insert their own experience. It's often the case that an introductory session on prayer is largely moving participants on from an assumption that intercessory petition is the only kind.

There's a whole course on the Bible later in the book, and many newcomers to church are acutely aware of their lack of scriptural knowledge, so this session is more instructional than most. But the course does not give in to the assumption that being a Christian is essentially about knowing the Bible well. It keeps the approach of all the Being With courses that no scriptural knowledge is necessary for doing the course, and it remains vital for the host to close down any attempt by a participant to show off their extensive (real or imagined) familiarity with the Bible.

The baptism session isn't just there for those preparing for baptism: it's significant for what it means to be church. There's some overlap here with the content of the Being With Baptism course: participants who do both may find that connection reassuring. The church immediately follows baptism: the emphasis is consistently that being a Christian is not a solo quest or pursuit but a collective endeavour and commitment. There's a profound cultural assumption that Jesus is intriguing but church is dull or corrupt; this assumption needs to be faced head on rather than circumvented. But discipleship, understood as an individual commitment, follows church, to balance the collective with the personal. This course follows an understanding of the threefold distinction between discipleship (being with God), ministry (being with the church) and mission (being with the world). Thus after sessions on baptism and discipleship there follows a session on mission, which strives to embrace both reactive and proactive understandings – where you give a person what they ask for, and where you offer a person something you value yet they don't necessarily know they want or need.

Finally, there are two sessions that don't logically fit into a pattern but seem vital before closing. One is on death. Again, this ground is covered more fully in Being With the End of Life later in this book. But it's important here because more than any of the other sessions it's obviously not just about head knowledge. The last session is on money. This is an indication of maturity: if a person is to belong to the church, they need from the outset to do so as an adult who shares in the responsibilities of the community – and money is a good route into the other responsibilities church entails.

2

Being With the Bible

Ten Wonderings and Addresses

One: Genesis

Genesis 4.8–10

- *Tell about the brother or sister you have, had or imagined having.*
- *I wonder who you get into an argument with almost every time you see them.*
- *Tell about someone whom you don't get on with but would be the first to defend if they were in trouble.*
- *I wonder who comes into mind when you hear the words 'your brother or sister'.*

What *is* it about siblings? We can't live with them; we can't live without them. If someone attacks them, we're first to step in; if they're sick, we can't sleep for worry; but leave us alone in a room with them and in no time we find ourselves turning from wallflowers into fireworks. One man invited his 93-year-old and 91-year-old great aunts and his 89-year-old great uncle to join him for Christmas dinner. The great uncle said, 'Pass the roast potatoes, would you', and proceeded to help himself to a generous portion. 'Stop it – put those back,' snapped his older sister. 'Don't be so greedy.' The younger sister pleaded, 'But surely, it's Christmas Day!' The older aunt was not to be deterred. Looking imperiously at her 89-year-old brother, she said, 'He *has* to learn!'

BEING WITH

This is the soil out of which the story of Cain and Abel becomes the story of everybody. The book of Genesis isn't the slightest bit sentimental when it comes to the realities of growing up with a brother. Here are Cain and Abel; both bring their gift to the altar. Abel's is received; Cain's is not. In no time Abel's blood is crying out from the ground.

A few chapters later we have Abraham and Lot, who were cousins but in one place are called brothers. We have this resonant sentence, 'Their possessions were so great that they could not live together.' Ouch. Feel the quality of that for a moment. And then there's Isaac and Ishmael. Anyone got a half-brother? You're the older one and you're constantly told you should be nice to your little brother even though every time you look at him you think, 'It was your mother that ruined my parents' marriage. How can I not hate you? Why should I love someone who's taken away my dad's attention that used to be all mine?' Or you're the younger one and you think, 'I didn't choose this domestic arrangement so why do I get blamed for it? What do I have to do to be taken seriously in this house and not be treated as a toy?'

And we haven't even spoken yet about Jacob and Esau, and what happens when one parent starts using a child in her manoeuvrings against the other. That makes it yet more complicated, when you're piggy in the middle between your parents! And finally there's Joseph and his brothers. It's as if in that story every element in all the previous stories comes together in a volcano of fratricide and parental favouritism and an overinflated ego – and yet profound love. If your life is a chaos of thinly veiled warfare, and a desperate struggle for recognition, and love you long for but daren't ask for, and long-festering resentment, and freshly minted fury – welcome to Genesis. You'll be quite at home.

Remember, what immediately precedes this story in Genesis is that of Adam and Eve. And in the Adam and Eve story God calls to Adam and says, 'Where are you?' '*Where are you?*' And here in the next chapter God calls to Cain and says, 'Where is your brother?'

'Where *are* you?' 'Where is your *brother*?' Those might be the two most important questions you'll ever be asked. And the order's important. When God comes to you 'walking in the garden at the time of the evening breeze' and says 'Where are you?', do you make an eager answer, or are you skulking in the bushes hoping not to be seen? Can we answer that question right at this moment: 'Where *are* you?' Are we answering eagerly, or are you shrinking into the shadows?

Only when we've faced up to that first question are we ready for the second question, 'Where is your brother?' Imagine you're standing before the Lord Jesus at his judgement seat in heaven, and he's looking at you with eyes of compassion and mercy and love like you've never seen or known before. And imagine he's saying to you the words God said to Cain: 'Where is your brother?' And suddenly you realize you've got this whole salvation thing wrong. You thought it was about keeping your nose clean and hoping God overlooks your foolishness and pride. But Jesus is saying, 'What about the others? Did you leave them behind? Where are they? Where is your brother?' Do you have an answer? Is your life drenched in ifs and buts and excuses and explanations? Where is your brother? What's your answer? There's only one answer Jesus wants: 'Right here beside me.'

We can live 100 years, we can be decorated by royalty, we can win a string of Olympic gold medals, we can be awarded an Oscar, we can find a cure to the ten most dangerous diseases on the planet. But in the end, all that matters is our answer to these two questions. 'Where are you?' 'Where is your brother?'

Maybe the way to start to be with the Bible is, every single day for a month, at the same time each day, to sit still and let God ask us these two questions: 'Where are you?' 'Where is your brother?' Two questions that bring us face to face with ourselves, and face to face with God.

Two: Exodus

Exodus 14.21–41

- *Tell about a story that you're not sure is true in one way but is certainly true in another.*
- *If you could ask God one question, I wonder what it would be.*
- *Tell a story that was like a foundation narrative of your family.*
- *I wonder if anyone has ever given up something important so that you could have a better life.*

One day a teacher gathered a class of 25 8-year-olds in a circle. He poured out a large quantity of sand, saying, 'This is the desert.' He took some little wooden figures out of a box and said, 'These are the children. The children were so hungry that their parents took them a long way to find food.' He moved the figures to the far corner of the sand to represent the children crossing the desert and reaching Egypt. He told how the people found food, and how the children grew to be a great number of people; but these people came to be the slaves of the Pharaohs who gave them food. He told how one night they escaped and rushed to the Red Sea. He unfolded a piece of deep blue felt to represent the sea. He told how their leader Moses raised his arm and prayed to God and how God made a way for them through the sea, and he moved the wooden figures through the sea, one by one. Then he showed them how Miriam led the dancing on the dry shore. (You can do a lot with wooden figures.) Then he said, 'I wonder where you are in this story.' They each placed one of the figures and later explained where they had chosen to put them. Some were dancing; some were just about to cross the sea; some were halfway; some were still in slavery. But one said, 'I know this isn't true because I saw it on the TV.'

The crossing of the Red Sea is the most important event in the Old Testament. What might it mean to say the story is true? That class of 8-year-olds discovered two contrasting notions of truth. They were discovering the way a scriptural story can come alive in your experience, when suddenly one of them introduced the question of historical fact.

BEING WITH THE BIBLE

For many people the problem with miracles like the crossing of the Red Sea is not a historical one. They assume that the God who had what it took to create the world presumably had the capacity to suspend conventional laws for a few minutes now and again. More significant for these people are the moral questions miracles leave unanswered. Why did the God who intervened to save the Israelites not step in to stop the Holocaust?

The moral problem with miracles is compounded on the occasions when they don't suit everybody. Pushing back the waves is quite a stunt and doesn't seem to hurt anyone. But crashing those waves back down on the pursuing Egyptians isn't much fun for the Egyptians. It seems legitimate to ask whether a God who could deliver the Israelites from slavery could not have done so in a less bloodthirsty manner.

Here are two guidelines to bear in mind when reading a story like this.

The first is that these stories really matter. Working out where we are in them, as the 8-year-olds discovered in the classroom, isn't just an intellectual exercise. It is about the social, economic, emotional, political and cultural heart of our lives. This is a story about people in slavery, and it's bound to be hard to read if nothing in your life remotely corresponds to slavery. We should read the crossing of the Red Sea as a story that exposes the truth about our lives.

The second guideline is to remember the Bible is about Jesus. It wasn't that Jesus was God's last resort when things had got to a pretty pass: Jesus was God's plan all along. And the central event that focuses all God's plans for Jesus and all his plans for us is Jesus' resurrection. A miracle. *The* miracle. And the reason the crossing of the Red Sea matters so much is that when the early Christians came to terms with the enormity of what had happened in Christ, they looked back to this story. They saw sin and death and evil as slavery, they saw the cross as the raging waters of the Red Sea, and they saw the dry land as Jesus' resurrection. They understood the whole event as a story about Jesus. And because it was a story about Jesus, they realized it was *the kind of thing God would do*.

So just like the earliest Christians, when we read stories of miracles in the Bible, or when we hear stories of miracles today, we ask ourselves, 'Is this a story about Jesus? Is it about God; life being laid down out of longing to set us free and restore us to everlasting relationship?' In other words, 'Is it the kind of thing God would do?'

Three: Law

Exodus 20.1–17

- *I wonder if you've ever felt you just needed a bit more of something and what that something was.*
- *Tell about a time when you had too much of something.*
- *Tell about a time you had a lot of something but didn't realize it.*
- *I wonder what things never run out.*

Do you think you have enough? If there's one anxiety most people can share, it's an anxiety about not having enough. The Ten Commandments dismantle this nagging assumption that there is not enough. Think about the psychology of stealing. Stealing is saying there isn't enough in the world and if I'm going to have what I need then someone else is bound to suffer. But God said, 'You shall not steal.'

Look at the fourth commandment, remember the Sabbath day. Think about the psychology of working every day. Breaking the command to rest is saying there's only one saviour in this universe and it's me. There isn't enough time but I might just pull it off. I have to save my career, I have to save the world. I can't stop. But God said, 'You shall rest.'

Look at the seventh commandment, you shall not commit adultery. Adultery is more often a symptom than a cause. But the mindset of adultery is simply that one is not enough. By contrast, marriage is the great proclamation that one is plenty. All is focused on a single other – another mind, another imagination, another myriad of experiences and energies and enthusiasms and enjoyments. Could one ever exhaust that person? One other person is always more than enough when you believe that that person will listen to you until you run out of things to say, when you trust that that person will wait for as long as it takes for you to understand why you are the way you are, when you realize that that person will always impute the best of motives to your actions however clumsy you feel inside.

Look at the third commandment, you shall not make wrong use of the name of God. Think about what is in our minds when we do so. It's when the language at our disposal doesn't seem to convey the strength or depth of feeling in our hearts. It's inadequate to express the depth of our distress on these occasions. So we invoke the name of God. We make the holy into the trivial and thus impoverish the language. Whenever we exaggerate we do the same thing. We say the truth is somehow not enough.

And then there's the second commandment, you shall not make yourself an idol. Surely the psychology of this is that God is not enough – not big enough, or at least not near enough. So I shall make a god I can relate to, a god my size – a car perhaps, a career maybe, even the scales that tell me how much I weigh. And now we're getting nearer the heart of the problem. There's an anxiety that we don't have enough – not enough property, time, love, language. But the heart of the matter is that we feel we don't have enough God. God is not enough.

And that's why the moment in which God speaks these words is so significant. Israel has come out of Egypt, but is already beginning to wonder if it wouldn't have been better off staying. This is the moment when God says,

'*I have set you free.* The problem is not that I am not enough for you – it is that I am *too much for you.* Your imaginations are simply too small to comprehend me. I love every creature I have made, but I treasure each one of you as if you were the only one. Can you imagine?

'No, you can't, can you. I can see you can't. If only you could let your imaginations go and enter the land I am promising you, and let me set you free. So here are some rules to remind you of what matters most, that I am more than enough, that my abundance is always greater than your scarcity. Have no other gods: more of them means less of me. Have no idols: they will never be remotely enough, and will lead you to forget that I am plenty. Keep the Sabbath: I will give you all the time you need. Look after your ageing parents and don't steal – I will give you everything you need. Don't kill people – they are part of the everything I am giving you. Don't misuse language – yes and no will be enough for you.'

Really it comes down to the first commandment and the last. Here are you, anxious, covetous, feeling more and more sorry for yourself, trapped in your stunted imagination, more and more a slave. And here, says God, am I, creating you in all your intricacy and beauty, forgiving you time and again even when your greatest hatred is for yourself, and coming among you to be your companion in Jesus.

Just you, and just God. Face to face. And that's the moment when God stretches out two hands and gives you the Ten Commandments, just as if you were Moses. God says,

> 'Here are some gifts. They will help you remember your freedom. They will challenge your imagination to realize that I am a God of abundance, who gives you more than enough, far more than you could ever want or need, who created galaxies no one may ever see, who has depths of forgiveness no sinner may ever require, who gives you in Jesus more love than you could ever realize.'

And we take the gift from God's hands, and we look into God's face, and we say, 'May these commandments be to me always a gift and never a burden. Write these words on my heart so I never forget that you are always more than enough. For now I realize that, with you, one is plenty.'

BEING WITH THE BIBLE

Four: The Kingdom
1 Samuel 8.4–20

- *Tell about something you discovered in a time of adversity that makes you the person you are today.*
- *Tell about someone who stood by you through a difficult time.*
- *Tell about someone you struggle to understand because they're great in some ways and difficult in others.*
- *Tell about a time someone told you a story you knew but now from a very different perspective.*

If you read the book of Judges you find the refrain, 'There was no king in Israel, and each did what was right in their own eyes.' After Moses crossed the Red Sea and the Israelites wandered in the wilderness, Joshua led them into the Promised Land and defeated many of the peoples who lived there. What followed was the period of the judges, where the 12 tribes settled the land and from time to time faced an external threat, whereupon God raised up a leader, known as a judge, whose strength or leadership or wisdom saved the people. Finally the elders come and say to Samuel, the last of the judges, 'We can't go on like this. Raising up leaders is too fragile and a hereditary system isn't working. We need a king.'

Samuel prays. He receives a fascinating answer from God. God says, 'The elders aren't rejecting you. They're rejecting me. Listen to them. Don't refuse them. But make sure they know exactly what they're letting themselves in for.' So that's what Samuel does. He says, 'This is what a king will do. He'll take your sons to be warriors, he'll take your daughters to be housekeepers, he'll take your property for his entourage, he'll take a tenth of your produce in tax, he'll take your slaves, cows and donkeys, he'll take your sheep: take, take, take, take, take, take.' But then Samuel reaches the climax of his warning, five sonorous words you'd expect to shake the elders to their bones: 'You shall be his slaves.' Everything in Israel's memory – leaving Egypt, crossing the Red Sea, being given the Ten Commandments, entering the Promised Land – *every single thing* has been about freedom, about being delivered from slavery. And now here are the elders proposing a course of action that will erase that whole history and take Israel back into bondage. They had escaped Pharaoh – and now they're creating a Pharaoh of their own. Samuel's saying, 'You must be out of your mind.'

But the elders aren't deterred. They insist on a king. Why? Because they demand to be 'like other nations'. Here's the decisive parting of the ways. Samuel's saying, 'This is the whole point: you're not supposed to *be* like other nations.' God has said to Samuel, 'This desire to be like other nations is a denial of Israel's identity; a wish to live outside relationship to me.' But having exposed the real issue, Samuel doesn't insist on his own way. He has listened to the elders and warned them, as God instructed; now he gives them their heads. He goes ahead and anoints Saul king.

This story demonstrates the two guidelines that help us understand what's going on in almost every Old Testament story. Here's guideline one: the Old Testament was written to answer the question, 'If we are God's chosen people, why are we in exile?' Israel found itself deported to Babylon in the sixth century before Jesus. It wrote the majority of the Old Testament as it came to terms with its catastrophic loss of identity, shorn of land, king and Temple. So the central question the Old Testament's asking is, 'What went wrong?' The debate over having a king is part of Israel's heart-searching about whether it was walking in God's ways or straying from them.

And so to guideline two: how is God still faithful to us? Somehow in Babylon Israel discovered who God was like never before. We could call it a God of *with* rather than a God of *for*. Rather than assuming God's job was to fix all Israel's problems, Israel started to see God as sharing its life, good and bad. The Old Testament is a constant debate – a constellation of arguments about all the unresolved issues in Israel's identity, story, faith, worship, discernment and hope. The Old Testament isn't a linear story with a single message. It wasn't written straight through, from Genesis to Malachi: it's a collection of perspectives from different eras and a constant process of editing as each new compiler adds a new spin on events. It's not a simple account of a vengeful judgemental God superseded by the loving God of the New Testament; it's a lively debate about God and humankind, and almost every view expressed in the New Testament can be found in some form in the Old.

Don't write off the Old Testament as a backward book about a provincial people looking to a two-dimensional God that's been somehow replaced by the New Testament. It's a profound wrestling with who God is, what God wants, how we respond and what happens when we get it wrong.

Five: Exile

Daniel 3.1–30

- *I wonder what it feels like to be in exile.*
- *Tell about a time you really hoped to avoid care, anxiety, fear, pain or threat.*
- *I wonder what it's like to do something you know will bring hurt or criticism or hostility your way.*
- *Tell about something you thought was worth doing even if it didn't achieve the desired outcome.*

The book of Daniel is a story about a people who lost their home, lost their hope, lost their security, lost their families, lost their heritage, lost their land, lost their story … and found God.

Nebuchadnezzar is God. He's got so many staff he's oozing them. He makes an enormous golden statue and everyone has to bow down and worship it. Anyone who doesn't is thrown into the blazing fire. Shadrach, Meshach and Abednego are having none of it. Their story shows us what faith means.

What faith *doesn't* mean is freedom from care, anxiety, fear, pain or threat. Shadrach, Meshach and Abednego don't avoid the fiery furnace. Christians don't believe they're immune from suffering, sealed off from worry, aloof from conflict, inoculated against panic, exempt from grief. Quite the opposite. As this story makes clear, Shadrach, Meshach and

BEING WITH

Abednego face suffering, worry, conflict, panic and grief precisely *because* they're people of faith and *because* they uphold God's name.

What faith *does* mean is one of two things. This story shows us both of them. When Shadrach, Meshach and Abednego are thrown, bound, into the fire, *God is with them*. There aren't *three* figures walking in the flames; there are *four*. What Christians call faith is what we see in this story. Jesus is with us in the fire. The destiny of Shadrach, Meshach and Abednego is settled not before they reach the fire by some stunt that makes them avoid the flames; nor is there any dramatic rescue from the flames. Their salvation takes place *in* the flames, as they discover God is with them *in* the flames. Here's the bad news: God isn't going to spare you from the fire. God isn't going to rescue you from the fire. Here's the good news: *God is going to be with you in the fire*. That's the gospel.

In this story the fire represents Babylon. Shadrach, Meshach and Abednego aren't spared from the fire, nor rescued from the fire; they find they're *with God* in the fire. Somehow the fire is a fire not just for them but for God too. The same is true for Israel in Babylon. Israel isn't spared exile. Israel isn't rescued from exile. Israel finds in exile that God's there too. The appearance of the fourth figure in the fire sums up the experience of exile for Israel. God is *with* us. That's faith. And we see the same in Jesus. Jesus has his own fire, which we call the cross. Jesus isn't spared the cross. Jesus isn't rescued from the cross. Jesus is *with* God on the cross. When we see the cross, we see that God is with us, however, whatever, wherever ... forever. This is our faith.

But of course that's not all that faith means. Shadrach, Meshach and Abednego *do* emerge from the fire. But look how it happens. They're called out by Nebuchadnezzar! Nebuchadnezzar was the agent of imprisonment, punishment and trauma, and he becomes the agent of deliverance, transformation and restoration. Nebuchadnezzar sees Shadrach, Meshach and Abednego and sees that God is with them; and because God is with them they feel the force of the flames but the fire has no final power to damage them, distort them, destroy them.

I wonder if you know who Nebuchadnezzar really is. I wonder if there's been such a person or power in your life, dominating, oppressing, threatening, hurting. I wonder what it's like to go into the flames. I wonder what it's like to feel that whatever that Nebuchadnezzar has done to you, in Jesus, God is with you, and nothing Nebuchadnezzar can do can damage, distort or destroy you. I wonder what it means to imagine Nebuchadnezzar's transformation and the hope that all your grief and suffering and exile will one day be redeemed and become part of what we call the gospel.

The centre of the story is what Shadrach, Meshach and Abednego say to Nebuchadnezzar. We hear these words with trembling. 'If our God whom we serve is able to deliver us from the furnace of blazing fire and out of your hand, O king, let him deliver us. But if not, be it known to you, O king, that we will not serve your gods and we will not worship the golden statue that you have set up.'

What Shadrach, Meshach and Abednego say to Nebuchadnezzar is finally what the members of the Trinity say to one another. When Jesus goes to the fire, when Jesus hangs on the cross, what does he say to the Father? Is it so different from the words of Shadrach, Meshach and Abednego? 'If you will to deliver me from the cross, O Father, then take this cup away from me. *But even if not*, be it known to you, O Father, that my love for you will hang on forever, and that those who somehow find that they have lost you can hang on to me.' That's what makes Jesus' final words so wondrous. Jesus loves us so much that he goes to the cross even if there's no certainty of resurrection. Jesus isn't just keeping his side of the bargain. Jesus is loving *'even if not'*. That's the definition of love.

We've come face to face with God. We've come to the foot of the cross, the heart of Jesus. We've come to the definition of love. It lies in those four little words: *'But even if not.'*

Six: Incarnation

Luke 2.1–7

- Tell about a good Christmas.
- Tell about a difficult Christmas.
- I wonder why God bothers with us.
- Tell about something that's not well known but you think is really important or impressive.

Christmas is a cosmic thriller of four mysteries and a truth. The first mystery is this. Why did God bother to create the universe? Think of it. 100 billion stars in every galaxy, 2,000 billion galaxies in the universe. Why? Why this astonishing, colossal project which defies description or comprehension? And why did God create life on this planet, tucked away in an obscure corner of that vast universe? Why did God bother? That is the first mystery: why did God bother?

And the second mystery is why, given the mess we made of things, did God continue to bother? Why did God not give up on us when humans turned out the way they did? The Old Testament is a passionate story of love and hate, delirious joy and crushing disappointment. For reasons that are a mystery, God sent a rainbow to Noah and promised never to destroy the earth again. But why God made that promise, and whether it became a matter of regret, who can say? Why did God continue to bother? Imagine God's Christmas letter. Venus has grown up a lovely girl, Mars is a real sweetie, Mercury has his ups and downs, but Earth ... Earth still seems unable to help herself and struggles with the simplest practices of peace – but, well, who knows what next year will bring? Fancy writing the same letter for thousands of years. That's the second mystery. The first mystery is: why does God bother? The second is: why does God continue to bother?

The third mystery seems to be the greatest mystery of all. It is the most baffling part of the whole story. Given that God bothered to make the universe and the world within it, given that God continued to bother with the world despite the way things turned out, the unfathomable mystery is this: why do we not bother – why can we not be bothered? I don't know if even God has the answer to this one. It defies all logic. We have been given this whole world, a playground of delight. We have been given time and space to grow and learn and experiment and discover. We have been given taste to relish, sight to dazzle, touch to treasure, hearing to enthral. We have been given beauty beyond value, music of the heavens, hearts to love and minds to ponder. Most of all we have been given a story that makes sense of the whole mystery, an invitation that shows us where we fit in to this great cosmic drama, a promise of companionship with God and a place at his table forever. And yet we can't be bothered. What a startling mystery: why do we not bother?

And it is in the context of these three mysteries that we approach the mystery of Christmas. Given that God had bothered to make the universe and place us in it, given that God had continued to bother over it, given that we couldn't be bothered, why at backward Bethlehem, why to a child-mother in an obscure cattle-shed – why, when God chose to enter the story, to be bothered so much as to set aside all the trappings of majesty – why did God come with so little bother? Why was Jesus wrapped in humble rags, not robes of gold? Why was Jesus laid in a dirty feeding trough, not a jewel-encrusted four-poster bed? Why didn't God trumpet the whole world and make them notice, make them be bothered? Why was there no broadcast to the whole universe that the saviour of the world was coming to town? Why did Jesus come as a baby at all, and not a mighty warrior for justice and truth? Where was the anger? Where was the fury? Where was the righteous resentment that said, 'You have rejected my openhearted love, ignored my bountiful promises, scorned my kingdom of peace'? This is the fourth mystery: why did God come with such little bother?

Four mysteries that go together to make up the drama of Christmas. But surrounded by a great mystery is an even greater truth. The truth is simply put. God did bother. And, just as significantly, still does.

BEING WITH

Seven: Jesus' Ministry
Luke 4.14–21

- *Tell about a time you felt left out.*
- *Tell about a time you felt isolated.*
- *I wonder what it's like to experience discrimination.*
- *I wonder what it's like to feel you're in constant danger.*

Each of the Gospels has a moment near the beginning that sets out the whole gospel. Mark has the parable of the sower. John has the wedding at Cana. Matthew has the Beatitudes. Luke has this moment – the 'Nazareth Manifesto'. He portrays Jesus on the Sabbath in the synagogue, being given the opportunity to choose his signal text for his whole ministry. You can see him working his way through the great scroll of Isaiah, all the way to chapter 61. And what he gives is the four things we mustn't forget when it comes to remembering whom the gospel is for. He's giving us the whole gospel, in a way we can't forget or wriggle out of or ignore.

So here are the four categories. Number one, the gospel is good news for the poor. Poor means, in any room where the decisions are made, the people who aren't in that room. Poor means any who have to go without so those they love and care for can have a little. Poor means all who, whenever they get paid, find someone creams off a big percentage and they're left with not enough. Poor means those who, when Jesus calls, have nothing to leave behind, so they can come straightaway. Poor means all who have nothing but each other. Poor means those from whom the most evocative words in our language – home, belonging, dignity, respect, safety, trust, love – have been taken away. Good news means *you're going to get those words back*.

Number two, the gospel means release for the captives. Captivity is prison. Prison means loss of control. Prison means shut in by a door that only opens from the outside. Prison means not knowing how long till that door opens, if it ever will. Prison means shame, it means exclusion, it means punishment, it means being hidden out of sight, it means not being allowed to move very far, it means violence, it means fear, it means isolation, it means powerlessness. Prison means your life is in someone else's hands and they get to choose when you eat, if you sleep, if you exercise. Prison means your life is not your own. Release means *you get your life back.*

Number three, the gospel means recovery of sight to the blind. Today we don't read this as suggesting disability is a deficit. We don't define ourselves by the one thing we're perceived to lack. But what we still experience today is social exclusion by discriminatory judgement. Exclusion means overlooked for resources or opportunities for which you're perfectly well qualified. Exclusion means humiliated because you're perceived to be different. Exclusion means not seen when you're in the room, not counted because you don't matter, not wanted because you don't belong, not trusted because you're not understood. Recovery means *being heard, seen, cherished, wanted.*

Number four, the gospel means letting the oppressed go free. Being oppressed means living every day under threat of someone's anger, tip-toeing around someone's violence, vulnerable to someone's exploitation, constantly at risk of being attacked, robbed, hurt, used, tormented. The first category meant at risk because of what you lack; the second meant impoverished because of constraint; the third meant vilified because of what you are: this category means subject to the whim of somebody else, manipulated by someone more powerful, at risk from those who could destroy you at any moment. Oppressed means facing cruelty, danger and injustice at every turn. Going free means *having the devil taken off your back.*

Notice how in the gospel Jesus goes on to become each of the groups he's talking about. Homeless in Bethlehem, Egypt and around Galilee, he's poor. Arrested in Gethsemane, he's in prison. Cast out of Jerusalem, he's excluded. Nailed to a cross, he's oppressed. Jesus isn't just talking about liberation; he's living it.

And the most radical and powerful word Jesus says in Nazareth is one we haven't yet mentioned: 'today'. 'Today' shakes us out of our desire to park this for another time, our tendency to intellectualize and theorize and prevaricate and never get to the moment of truth. No one's much bothered about what Jesus is saying until he says, 'Today'.

You may be familiar with the Ignatian practice of the Examen. The Examen is where you sit down quietly at the end of the day and review all its events, recalling your feelings about each one, noting what hurt, if you got it wrong, when God has been present to you, and where the Holy Spirit was drawing you towards life. I'd like you to think of Jesus' words in Nazareth as a morning version of the Examen. Imagine praying, each morning, like this:

- Show me where your children are poor. Awaken me to where I impoverish others. Visit me in the place of my own poverty.
- Show me where your children are imprisoned. Awaken me to how I incarcerate others. Visit me in the ways I am in prison.
- Show me where your children suffer discrimination. Awaken me to when I exclude others. Visit me in my own experience of rejection.
- Show me where your children are oppressed. Awaken me to how I dominate others. Visit me in my own place of fear.

And then at the end, instead of saying Amen, you say, 'Today'. That's your agenda for today. For every day. Because the good news is that Jesus hasn't left us out – so we must leave no one else out either.

Eight: The Cross

Mark 15.25–32

- *I wonder what it feels like to keep someone else's secret.*
- *I wonder what it's like for someone to be very angry with you for something that's not your fault.*
- *Tell about a time it was easier for you to help others than to help yourself.*
- *Tell about someone who saw you when no one else did.*

The 1994 film *Priest* introduces us to Fr Greg, a young and earnest Catholic priest. He's gay. He begins a secret relationship with a man he meets in a bar. Meanwhile he hears the confession of a teenage girl called

BEING WITH THE BIBLE

Lisa. He learns that she is regularly being abused by her father. Later Lisa's father comes to confession and Fr Greg is horrified to realize this man bears no remorse for what he is doing.

The two traumas of his life come to a crisis. He's arrested for public indecency. He's forced to leave the parish. Meanwhile Lisa's domestic ordeal comes to light. Lisa's mother emerges from an angry crowd and says to him, 'You knew.' She repeats, witheringly and vengefully, 'You knew.'

Of all the ironic statements at the foot of the cross, the most poignant are the words of the Temple authorities, who say, 'He saved others; he cannot save himself.' This perfectly sums up the story the Gospels tell. It's a double irony because the authorities think the joke's on Jesus and that they're identifying the irony that Jesus can't do for himself what he can do for others. But meanwhile what they *can't* see is that the joke is finally on them, because first of all they've been drawn into identifying that Jesus has *indeed* saved others, a major acknowledgement for them to make, and secondly that there's something unique about Jesus that makes both him and his suffering different from others. And that pretty much sums up the gospel. Jesus saves us but at terrible cost to himself.

Christ's Passion contains two great miracles. One is obvious, the one that God did – the miracle of resurrection. The other is subtler. It's the miracle of what Jesus *didn't* do. He didn't come down from the cross. He stayed there. He outlasted our hatred and cruelty and enmity. After everything we could throw at him, physically and verbally, he was still there. His endurance demonstrated the love that will never let us go. His perseverance showed that nothing can separate us from the love of God. For ever after we can connect to God, not through our striving but through Jesus' suffering; not through our longing but through his lingering; not through our achieving but through his abiding.

It's not the Jesus we want. We want the Jesus who comes down from the cross, the Jesus that rights wrong, ends pain, corrects injustice, sends the wicked away empty, sets the record straight and makes all well with the world. We want answers, we want solutions, we want a technological Jesus who fixes the problems. And we want those problems fixed now. We want the Jesus who comes down from the cross. This Jesus will not come down from the cross. This Jesus bears all things, endures all things and never ends ... This is not the God we want.

But it's the God we *need*. Oh, how badly we need that God! Answers, explanations, solutions – they don't give us what we fundamentally need in the face of suffering and sin. What we need is love. What we need is a wondrous love through all eternity. What we *need* is a love that sticks around, a love that stays put, a love that hangs on. That's what the cross is. A love that hangs on.

At the end of the film *Priest*, Fr Greg returns after his time of humiliation and exile. The anger and hatred still smoulder in the neighbourhood and in the parish. Lisa's mother's incandescent words, '*You knew*', are still ringing in his and our ears. Lisa hasn't been seen in the church since the truth about her household came to light. The senior priest, Fr Matthew, implores the congregation to receive Fr Greg back as their father in God. When it comes to receiving communion there are two stations for taking the bread, one from Fr Matthew, the other from Fr Greg. Every single worshipper at the service lines up to receive from Fr Matthew. Fr Greg stands alone, the body of Christ in his hands, totally shunned and visibly humiliated by the whole congregation. Seconds tick by and his isolation is ... crucifying. Somehow he finds the courage and defiance to continue to stand alone – to hang in there. And then slowly but purposefully one solitary figure shuffles forward and stands before him to receive communion. It's Lisa.

Their eyes meet as she receives the communion bread. Her eyes say, 'I know that you knew about my dad. But I know that you couldn't do anything about it. I understand your present powerlessness. I know it's because you believe in a greater power. You show me that by your courage in being present here right now. You're being crucified, but you're showing us a love that will not let us go.'

That's the irony of the cross. If Jesus had saved himself, he couldn't have saved us. His powerlessness shows us the endurance of God. Jesus hangs on the cross to show us the love that hangs on. Hang on to that love. It will never let you go.

Nine: Resurrection
John 20.11–18

- *Tell about a time you realized you'd never see someone precious again.*
- *I wonder what it's like suddenly to realize something you've wondered about is actually happening now.*
- *Tell about a time you felt the force of the word 'new'.*
- *I wonder what the words 'forever' mean to you.*

I want to show you resurrection in nine words.

The first three words are all terrifying words. This is the first: gone. Mary Magdalene comes to the tomb on the first day of the week. And what does she find? The body of Jesus is gone. If ever insult was added to injury. That's the first sensation of bereavement, loss, grief: he's gone. Gone. Gone where? Who knows. Gone away? It's so final, ultimate, irrevocable. So unyielding, uncompromising, ruthless. You don't get any choice in it, it happens by some outside force. Gone. Mary Magdalene feels that outside force. Jesus is gone. What an unforgiving word.

And then comes the second word: over. You start to look back on all the things that once were but are no more. Mary recalls the tenderness of Jesus' voice. The way she felt when she was with him, like she didn't want the day to ever end, like this was a conversation that went to the heart of her soul. It's over. She thought about the people whose lives he touched, the children he healed, the song he put in people's hearts. She remembered the times with the Twelve, when they all felt as close as a group of people can ever feel to one another, honest and faithful and courageous and true. Over. Over and gone. Lost and gone. Mary stares into the darkness of the tomb. It's over. Jesus, and that whole Jesus thing, that turning the world upside down together. Over.

But there's a third word that's even worse. Gone is about the present – he's not here. Over is about the past. It's finished. But there's an even more terrifying word that's about the future: never. If gone takes the life out of a body, and over snatches the memories away, never robs us of all hope. Never. It's like a boxing match where gone knocks the stuffing out of you, over brings you down to the canvas, and never goes beyond all mercy and kicks you out of the ring. 'It's not going to happen,' says never. 'Whatever silver lining or small consolation you're holding on to, it's a fantasy.' Never. Brutal, cruel, final.

Those three words tell us where Mary Magdalene is at the beginning of our story. But here is the fourth word. Here. It doesn't add up: Jesus is here. He's in front of her. It's like a scene from a pantomime. Her body's facing the tomb but her head turns behind her to Jesus. Then her body turns to Jesus but her head turns to the tomb. And her words are spoken in both directions, as if her head and body are going in opposite directions. It's supposed to be funny. Because how else to communicate the wonder of this moment? Here. Jesus is here. I though he was gone. But he's here.

And quickly there's another word: now. It's the central word of the nine words of resurrection. Now. Not something you can postpone till you've thought about it. Not something you can tuck away and re-examine when you've recalled all your scepticism and misgivings. Now. What in the world could possibly be more important or take your gaze away from this moment: now. This is it. Creation gave us life on earth. But that's a long time ago. On the last day we'll be given eternal life with God. But that's a long time away. This is now. This is time collapsed into one moment, one man, one woman, in a garden, God in Christ, Israel in Mary, here, now. This is the whole Bible, the whole of eternity in one face-to-face encounter: now.

And here's the word that goes with here and now: new. Is anything really new? Mary discovers, yes there is. A person who died in agony two days previously, standing utterly alive and thrillingly real, in front of her, with hands she can grasp and a face she can kiss. That's new. A world made new. A life made new. A dream made new. Oh yes. This is new. For sure this is new.

But there's more. Look at the last words in the story. Mary turns her own experience into a message to tell to the disciples. And this is the first word of what happens as she tells her story: again. Feel the tremor that goes through your body when you recognize the force of that word: again. You thought it was gone, over, never. But it's again. That's the resurrection: it's both new and again. It's creation repeated and the Last Day anticipated: new and again. Like a hug with your best friend, like your favourite holiday destination, like the most exquisite dessert you know how to cook: new and again. The best two words in the language: and even better together.

But there's another word: always. It ends up being the last thing Jesus says to the disciples: always. 'I'll be with you always.' It seemed each hope was blocked; now every single one is open – always. It seemed the truth was gone, over, never, but it's turned into always. Always and again. Death will no longer be the perpetual curse in every hope. Regret need no longer be the lingering poison in every memory. Always.

There's only one word left: forever. Mary's agony, of gone, over, never is our insight into the grief of God at our indifference and inertia in the face of eternal love. Mary's agony, deep and crucifying as it is, lasts two nights: God's agony lasts as long as time. But there's something longer, wider and bigger than time: and that's forever. Mary sees the risen Jesus, and she passes from time to forever. She discovers what is longer than everlasting, truer than always, beyond permanent. She's looking straight into the heart of forever.

Faith is the astonishing change, the wondrous hope, the indescribable peace that begins in your gut and spreads, perhaps slowly, to your head and your heart and your hands when you realize the three terrible words – gone, over, never – have been engulfed by the six tremendous words, here, now, new, again, always, forever. We have a word for the moment that happens. We call it resurrection.

Ten: Pentecost
Acts 2.1–13

- *I wonder what you like to cook.*
- *Tell about a community where everyone's gifts were accepted.*
- *Tell about a time you felt powerful.*
- *I wonder what Jesus looks like today.*

The TV show *Ready Steady Cook* challenged chefs to make a meal out of an assortment of inexpensive ingredients. The day of Pentecost, the birthday of the church, is an invitation to do the same with the church. You start with people. We're not alone. If we've been battered or bruised by church, rejected because of what we believe or who we are, chewed up and spat out because we trespassed into a power game, antagonized or alienated by something too clumsy or superficial to commit to, then we might well want to take our ball home and say faith is just a private thing. But if we actually want to do something in the world, we need to do it together.

Then the next ingredient is diversity. Making a meal is about getting the best out of a variety of ingredients – not reducing everything to one ingredient. In a healthy community everyone finds the things about them that had elsewhere been seen as deficits are here discovered as assets. Elsewhere you were dismissed as shy: here you become a person who pays attention to detail and enjoys keeping records. There is no church other than the one made up of ordinary people.

We live amid an argument raging about identity. Race, sexuality, gender, nationality – these identities, often taken as a threat and thus as the pretext for persecution and exclusion, are all about going back to find a true self, distinct from other people and other ways of being. There's an important conversation about where we're each coming from, not least to understand and address how frequently people can be ostracized and diminished. But the real conversation is about where we're together *going* – a society that lasts forever has a place for everybody, is shaped by truth and justice and peace, is about the flourishing of every living being, where suffering is no more.

BEING WITH THE BIBLE

The next ingredient is to get organized. Once you look around the room and say, 'It's just us – we'd better get busy', you begin to realize the power of organization. An organization is a group of people who've called in some favours, used their contacts, drawn on their experience, sought extra training, pooled their skills, raised awareness, advertised widely, raised funds, experimented with their programme, started to envision the future and planned a critical path to getting there. It's an extraordinary moment when it dawns on you that you've got something, you've started something, there's a spirit in the air and people have hope in their hearts, and you've brought together strands of individuals and constituencies that wouldn't previously have met, known, understood or cared much about each other. That's what organizing can do.

Every church needs a healthy dose of humility. Just remember people have been at this for 2,000 years. The chances that everyone before us got this totally wrong and we're going to get it totally right are quite small. Yes, plenty of those people were manipulative, cruel and small-minded. But I'm guessing the large majority were well intentioned, kind and generous. Any church that says, 'This is the way we've always done it' is really saying, 'We're going to go on doing it the same way regardless of whether it's working or not.' That's complacency and laziness masquerading as faithfulness.

We've almost got the full recipe. We just need the most important part. And that is to live in no power but the Spirit's power. It's the Spirit that decides what kind of a meal this is going to be. It's the Spirit that decides if this is going to be a sandwich under the bridge with those sleeping outside or a High Mass in a crowded cathedral with the great and the good clustered around. It's the Spirit that decides if it's all the colours of the rainbow gathering round to proclaim joy or if it's a pensioner in a flat clinging on in bereavement and too stretched to fill the gas meter.

That's ready, steady church. That's all the ingredients. We've all been there when it didn't taste right, when it actually tasted terrible, when it tasted so bad we didn't want to taste it ever again. But we all know how it's supposed to taste. It's not about quantity. It's not about expense. It's not about how many are eating or how stylish is the table. It tastes of humble bread, bread of trust, bread of truth, bread of toil. And it tastes of wine – wine of sacrifice, wine of suffering, wine of beauty, wine of glory. Because there's only one church that matters, and it's not wealth, it's not size, it's not power, it's not numbers, it's not grandeur, it's not acclaim. It's a church that looks like Jesus. Jesus the tiny baby dependent on others for life. Jesus the young child longing to discuss truth in the Temple. Jesus in the desert resisting temptation. Jesus in the synagogue proclaiming jubilee. Jesus saying blessed are the poor. Jesus embracing the outcast and the unloved. Jesus betrayed by his own, scorned by the powerful, forgiving his persecutors, raised from the dead.

God sends the Holy Spirit to give us everything we need to look like Jesus. Nothing more. And nothing less. Now. And forever.

Commentary

This course differs from all the other courses in one specific respect: in this course a passage from the Bible is read between the wonderings and the talk. It does change the dynamic significantly, because it's the only thing that intrudes on the group and doesn't come from the group itself – unless you count the talk, but the talk is customized by the insertion of references to what the participants have shared, which to a great degree modifies the sense of its being alien or imposed. The best way to ameliorate this potentially jarring element is to invite a member of the group to read the passage in question. This will involve printing it out (if in the room) or pasting it in the chat (if online). Not all participants may feel comfortable reading, so find a way to make it easy for people to offer or decline, for example by emailing ahead of each session seeking a volunteer.

While the ten sessions in the course are inevitably episodic, they are intended to follow a sequence, and the whole is designed to be comprehensive, albeit in a way that inevitably leaves out a great deal. The sessions go beyond telling a story, although some kind of a story is assumed: they also communicate a way of reading the Bible critically yet devotionally – as a historical document yet also as a text through which the Holy Spirit can speak to us today. The talks dovetail with the theological outlook described in the original Being With course: that is, that being with us in Christ was the reason for creation, and that the cross demonstrates this utter and eternal commitment rather than working as a mechanism for alleviating our human predicament of guilt and mortality.

By starting with Cain and Abel the course gets away from a common fixation with the Genesis creation stories, which, while important, can be misleading as an introduction to the Bible, not least because they zero in on the question of historical accuracy, which is unhelpful as a first discussion point. It's no good talking about the wider purposes of the Bible and its extraordinary and unfathomable gifts if you then plunge straight into a part that exemplifies a lot of the obvious problems. But the Cain and Abel story is profoundly relatable, and thus subtly affirms the point that we trust what the Bible says about God because it so accurately tells the truth about us.

The two sessions from the book of Exodus, the crossing of the Red Sea and the giving of the Ten Commandments, constitute the two most important events in the Old Testament. In the first, the historicity question is vital and unavoidable. In the second, the key is to reconfigure the familiarity of the commandments into a different way of understanding what law is really about. Such a reframing can be especially liberating for those who have been shaped by an understanding of religion as rule-keeping.

The next two sessions address less well-known parts of the Old Testament. Both have a twin role of introducing those elements in the narrative and broadening participants' understanding of what the Bible (especially the Old Testament) is. Many Christians – and this could include the host and the storyteller of this course – are embarrassed about the Old Testament, both because they fear they don't know it very well and because they don't know what to say when people complain there's a lot of wrath and smiting in it. Painful events in the Holy Land only exacerbate these anxieties. This course is deliberately half Old and half New Testament precisely to address those concerns. It's crucial to understand that the Old Testament was largely written or at least compiled during the exile and that it includes rival accounts of how things went badly wrong for Israel. Among those accounts is the notion that Israel should

BEING WITH

have been more ruthless towards its enemies – which accounts for the bloodthirsty passages. But this is by no means the only theory, and many other passages tell a very different story.

It's fashionable in some circles to use the term 'Hebrew Bible' in place of Old Testament. This sounds scholarly and is intended to be respectful to Jews. But it plays into an idea that Judaism is 'less than' Christianity, having a shorter Bible, and ignores the revered Talmud and other sacred writings. It also suggests the Old Testament 'belongs' to Jews, whereas the New Testament assumes it's part of a tradition that includes the Old. So it's a well-intentioned but in some ways misleading way of speaking that 'others' the Old Testament without necessarily meaning to do so, and this course doesn't adopt it.

The New Testament passages select themselves more easily. A more vigorously theological structure might have started with incarnation, but that could be confusing to a beginner. Jesus' ministry is too broad to be contained in one session, but the sermon in Nazareth addresses much of the teaching, engagement with poverty, and controversy, if not the miracles. The cross and resurrection are obviously vital. And Pentecost is a way of talking about the rest of the New Testament; no attempt is made to cover Paul.

Those looking for further material on the Bible to explore in this genre may wish to look at my book *The Heart of it All: The Bible's Big Picture*, which attempts to summarize the whole Bible and includes suggested wonderings in an appendix.

3

Being With Baptism

Four Wonderings and Addresses

One: Godparents

- *Tell about a really important moment in your life.*
- *Tell about a time someone reminded you of something vital you'd forgotten.*
- *I wonder what is one thing a godparent can give a growing child.*
- *Tell about something special an older person once gave you.*

Baptism is a precious and holy moment. It re-enacts the first public event of Jesus' ministry. And just as we believe God is especially present when we re-enact Jesus' last meal with his disciples, so we believe he is especially present when we re-enact his baptism in the Jordan. At baptism, God places a song in your heart. But it's very important that there are other people present – because it's very easy, especially when you are only a few months old, to forget the tune. So you have godparents. It is up to the godparent to learn the song so well that they can sing it back to you when you forget how it goes.

And what is the song? Well, the story of Jesus' baptism shows us what the song is. Three things happen in the story: the heavens open; the Spirit descends like a dove; and a voice says, 'This is my beloved child.' Each of these events has great significance.

BEING WITH

The beginning of the song goes like this: heaven is open to you. Look at what happens in the story of Jesus: the gospel begins with the tearing of the heavens and ends with the tearing of the Temple curtain. The veil between you and God has been torn apart. Heaven is open to you. There is no limit to God's purpose for your life: it is an eternal purpose.

Now, you may find that your godparents sidle up to you when you are making a choice of career: they may say, 'Don't dive for cover, don't just do what your parents did or want: heaven is open to you. The sky isn't the limit: there is no limit.' Or if a time comes when you are facing serious illness, even death, your godparents, knowing the song in your heart, may say, 'The angels are waiting for you, they know you by name: heaven is open to you. Death is the gate to the open heaven.'

And the second line of the song goes like this: God's Spirit is in you. Remember the end of the flood, when the dove brought the twig of new life back to Noah? Well, here is the dove descending on Jesus, bringing the gift of the Holy Spirit. You are now the temple of God's Holy Spirit. You are the place where others will encounter God. God's Spirit is in you.

If a time comes in your life when you feel alone and surrounded by hostility, you may hear a godparent gently whispering a tune: 'You may feel evil is all around you, but you can still worship, for God's Spirit is in you.' Or if a time comes when you are wildly successful, you may hear a sterner song: 'God's Spirit is in you – everyone may worship you, but don't forget whom you worship.' You may be cross with your godparent at the time, but they may be singing the song in your heart and reminding you of your baptism.

So, heaven is open to you; God's Spirit is in you: and finally, the third line of the song of baptism: you mean everything to God. God's words are 'This is my beloved Son.' These words mean, 'Jesus means everything to God, and everything God gives to Jesus he gives to us.' You mean everything to God.

There may come a time in your life when you feel a deep sense of your own sin. Then you should hear your godparent say, 'You are everything to God. You still are, whatever you have done, however unworthy you feel.' Or you may wander away from the church because God seems so distantly cosmic and ethereally vague, when you long for intimacy and passion. Then you may hear your godparents sing, through their tears, 'You are everything to God.' Remember your song.

So, this is what baptism is: God places a song in your heart. And so your godparents' role is to learn that song so well that they can sing it back to you when you forget how it goes. And this is the song: 'Heaven is open to you; God's Spirit is in you; you are everything to God.' This is the song that makes your heart sing. And what does the song mean? I'll tell you. You are the song in God's heart, and God will never forget how you go.

Two: Safety

- *Tell about a precious possession as a child.*
- *I wonder what it feels like to have something you cherish snatched out of your hand.*
- *Tell about a time you found it hard to let go.*
- *Tell about a time you felt safe.*

The baptism of a child has many poignant moments. The parents and godparents are asked to make a public declaration of faith that's unusual in our culture. The pouring of water on the baby's head evokes the daily bathtime of a parent's care and the liberative parting of the Red Sea to free the Hebrews from slavery. The anointing of oil commissions this tiny tot for a unique future, affirming that God creates each one of us for a purpose, and we eventually find that purpose in God. The candle displays the conviction that God lights a fire in each of us at baptism that may burst into flame as we find an adult faith later in life. But for all these resonant moments, the most poignant of all is when the priest asks the parent to hand over their precious child, their child that in some cases they've waited years for, made sacrifices for, prayed for, longed for, who is to them more precious than the rest of the world combined.

In John's Gospel Jesus contrasts three kinds of characters: the wolf who comes in and steals, perhaps the Roman occupying army; the bad shepherd who fails to protect and guide the sheep; and himself, the good shepherd, who knows each of his sheep by name, whose sheep recognize his voice, and who lays down his life for his sheep. He says, 'I give my sheep eternal life. No one will snatch them out of my hand.'

Think about that word, 'snatch'. It's a childish word. It's what we say to young children who are arguing. But the word connects with our deepest fears about a child: that something, someone, some disease, some stranger, some disaster will snatch that child from our hands. A parent can never say to a child, 'No one will ever snatch you out of my hand.' The parent does have to let go eventually, however foolish the child's choice of lifestyle, however ghastly their friends, however dangerous their career, however unspeakable their choice of life partner. Suffocating with self-serving love is just as dangerous as letting go too early, and invariably counterproductive.

But Jesus *can* say, 'No one will ever snatch you out of my hand.' Jesus does know your child by name. Jesus does lay down his life for your child. Jesus will embrace and walk with your child forever. 'Ah, but', we understandably say, 'who is this Jesus who claims to be and to do all these things?' Jesus says, 'I and the Father are one.' In other words, Jesus says, 'I am inseparably bonded to the essence that is before and beyond this present existence. When I say, "Nothing can snatch you out of my hand," that means not just the conviction of now, but the embrace of forever. Your child's destiny is as secure as being held and cherished by the eternal loving hands of God.'

In infant baptism the parent hands the baby to the priest; one of the most difficult and trusting things a parent can do. But it's not handing over from security to danger. It's handing over from the love and care of a parent, which for all its passion, sacrifice, commitment and attention can never be permanent, impermeable or total, to the love and care of God, which can be and is all of those things, now and always. The parent is handing over their child from now to forever. It's perhaps the most significant moment of our lives, besides the moment of our death. Because death is the other moment when we transfer from now to forever. The parents, in handing their child over to be baptized, are saying, 'This is a rehearsal for a final goodbye, the separation of death. It's a statement that if we can face the truth of this handing over from now to forever, we can face the final one too.'

Because in the end the Christian faith is simply this. God chooses not to suffocate us with love but to hand us over to existence. That means God lets us go into a world of danger, temptation, distress and challenge: all of which lie inside that little word 'snatch'. But when we turn to the risen Christ, we see one whose hands bear the nail marks of love, nail marks that say, despite everything it costs, 'I will never let you go.' That could be a tragic gesture. What turns it into the entry into eternal life is the discovery that Jesus and the Father are one. Baptism is the moment we recognize our mortality and Christ's divinity.

If we are safe in Christ's hands, we are safe with the essence of all things forever. Nothing can snatch us out of those hands. Nothing, never; whatever, forever.

Three: Sign

- *Tell about a time you saw a person do something incredible.*
- *Tell about a time someone wasted a huge sum of money.*
- *I wonder what it's like to use freedom badly.*
- *I wonder what it means to use freedom well.*

John's Gospel is made up of signs. Jesus makes his way around Galilee and back and forth to Jerusalem, and in every place, he performs signs – turning water into wine, giving sight to the man born blind, raising Lazarus from the dead. The most significant sign of all is the sign of the cross. Each of these signs is a depiction of who Jesus is, and what kind of life he's inviting us into. But there's one sign that's different from all the others. The difference is that, whereas Jesus performs one sign after another, this sign isn't performed by Jesus. It's performed by Mary, the sister of Martha and of Lazarus, whom Jesus has just raised from the dead. Mary's sign transcended its setting in a meal, maybe a meal to celebrate Lazarus' return: no one remembers what they ate that night; but what Mary did has never been forgotten.

So what did Mary do? She did three things, all of which in different ways were both extraordinarily beautiful and utterly outrageous. First, she wasted a huge sum, £30,000 in today's money. That's a lot to spend on perfume, and it's even more money if what you're going to do is pour the whole lot over someone's feet. You can see the open mouths. It's shocking, but mesmerizing. Unbelievable. Yet unforgettable.

The second thing she did was to break social taboos on a grand scale. Feet more or less correspond to the nether regions in the first-century imagination. They need washing, because this is not a culture that has a fully developed appreciation for woollen socks. But that washing was generally the job of a non-Jewish slave. Feet weren't used to receiving the touch of an equal; the touch of a woman, horror of horrors – this is intimacy to a spectacular degree – and not just touching by hands, but rubbing and caressing and surrounding by hair. You can hear the cartoon eyes popping out on stalks. Everyone's horrified: but they can't look away. It's erotic – but it's something more powerful even than that: it's a sign of utter devotion. Unbelievable. Yet unforgettable.

The third thing Mary did was to prepare Jesus' body for burial. This kind of perfume was what you put on a dead body to stop it rotting before you put it in a tomb. Presumably she'd put a cheaper version on Lazarus not long before. But if pouring away a huge amount of money was reckless, and washing the oil off with her hair was salacious, this was either morbid or inexplicable. Here's a man in the prime of life, with a host of followers and doing miracles for toffee, and you start preparing his body for the grave. What on earth does she think she's doing? Unbelievable. Yet unforgettable.

Why does it matter? Because this is about God. This is about a God who crossed a thousand boundaries to kneel at our feet. This is about a God who was so devoted to us as to face death for us. This is, fundamentally, about a God whose life is so poured out in love for us that the odour of devotion doesn't just fill the whole room – it fills the whole universe. The reason this sign is so important is that a disregarded woman portrays for us the truth at the heart of all things: God's reckless, transgressive, death-defying pouring-out of all the wealth and glory of the universe into the embodiment of love for us in Jesus. And Mary, pondering the wonder and the mystery of her brother's being raised to life, is the first person in John's Gospel not just to realize who Jesus is, not just to appreciate the enormity of what he represents, but to set about imitating him in all his overflowing and superabundant extravagance. Mary realizes Jesus doesn't just want our worship, he wants us to follow his path. The best form of worship is to do just as he does. Imitation is the sincerest form of flattery. Mary turns her life into an icon of God's love. It's ridiculous, embarrassing, criminal, dangerous, wasteful. But she doesn't care. *Because so is God.*

Baptism re-enacts the Hebrews' crossing-over from slavery to freedom, and our own crossing-over from death to life. It asks us: how are we going to use that freedom; how are we going to live that life? Is our life fundamentally a shrewd calculation of how to squeeze the most out of scarce resources, a sober estimate of days to be lived, materials to be consumed, impact to be measured, mark to be left? Or is our life to be like Mary's: an icon of God's desire for and devotion to us? Imagine your whole life crystallized into one portrait: wouldn't you want it to be a portrait that embodied God's extravagant love? There comes a moment for each of us where all our striving, studying, searching, surviving is stilled into one iconic gesture. Mary shows us a gesture that fills a whole room, a gesture of a love whose fragrance pervades the whole universe. Mary was no one special – someone's sister. But we're still talking about her, because she made a gesture that embodied a thousand prayers, a sign that pointed to the heart of God.

May those to be baptized have parents who love them with the extravagant love of God. May they grow up in a community of faith that embodies divine abundance and isn't caught up in parcelling out and managing human scarcity. May they be people of whom others say, 'That's taking it a bit far!' or 'Watch it! You're wasting all those resources on something as useless as devotion and passion and beauty.' May they be people of whom others are embarrassed because they're uncomfortably like Jesus, people whose gestures are remembered in 2,000 years' time because they depict heaven, people whose lives are an icon of God's wondrous love. And may they grow to be people who, like Mary, do something unbelievable. Yet unforgettable. As unbelievable and unforgettable as the revelation of God's extravagant desire for us.

Four: Three Words

- *Tell about a time when after a lot of confusion something suddenly made sense.*
- *Tell about a person who is or has been really precious to you.*
- *I wonder what it truly means to honour someone.*
- *I wonder what it's like when someone loves you, but not in the way you want.*

I want you to think of the Old Testament like this. Israel settles in the Promised Land, having been rescued from slavery and given a covenant. The problem is, Israel can't stay faithful to the covenant. The obstacle is, Israel finds itself in exile in Babylon, 500 miles to the east. The surface question is, how on earth is Israel going to get back home? The deeper question is, how are Israel and God to be reconciled?

One of the most crucial passages in the Old Testament comes in the first seven verses of Isaiah 43. The very centre of these verses – the centre of the message of the Old Testament – is the moment everything in the Bible, for the first time, makes sense. Here are the most revealing and perhaps the most important words in scripture: 'You are precious in my sight, and honoured, and I love you.' God's whole life is shaped to be with Israel.

When we baptize someone today, we hear God saying these very same words to her that God says to Israel in exile. 'You are precious, honoured and loved.' Words at the heart of the Old Testament. Words at the heart of the Bible. Words at the heart of the universe. Let's look at those three words to see what they are truly telling us, and truly saying to this child.

We'll start with 'precious'. Precious means something of infinite value. It means I don't know whether to put it on the mantelpiece in the centre of the room where everyone can see it and admire it, or whether to hide it in many layers of velvet cladding so it can never get broken and lodge it in the deepest vault of the safest bank so no one could ever steal it. That's how precious you are. Precious means intricate, deftly and finely woven or crafted, with a design that would need a microscope fully to

BEING WITH BAPTISM

enjoy, with a subtlety and delicacy beyond the skill or imagination of any but the most accomplished artisan. Precious means unique, inimitable, astonishing; it means I would give up everything else just for this.

Honoured means respected, cherished, even revered. More subtly it means, 'I understand you are not me; you have your own rhythm, identity, metabolism, style, history. The point of our relationship is not to make you a pawn of my ambitions, a clone of me, an agent of my desires. It is for you to become all that you are called to be, as I become all that I am called to be.' Honoured means, 'I cherish you. I don't seek to change you, use you, become you. I enjoy you for the wonder that you are. I treasure the privilege of being in relationship with you.'

Loved means a movement of the heart and an act of the will. It means something is moving in me, beyond my thought, decision or resolve, which draws me to you, regardless of your virtue, or even reciprocation. I interpret your actions in the best light, I light up with life in your presence, I'm overjoyed at the very thought of you. But love also means sheer determination and selfless resilience. I change your nappy however smelly it is; I stay in touch with you however little you seem to value it; I stretch out my hand to pull you out of the swirling torrent even though we've never previously met.

And here's the thing. We need all three words. You might think the third word contains the other two, but the truth is … it doesn't. Think of a domestic argument where one party says, 'But I love you.' The other party says, 'If you love me but don't honour me, it's not the love I want.' Think of the minority-ethnic employee who's told, 'You're a precious part of this organization', but privately thinks, 'You don't honour my traditions, you don't love me, you just need my skills and glad my being here helps you tick some boxes.' Think about the war veteran who comes back from the Remembrance Day parade and thinks, 'Yes, you honoured me today, but the rest of the year you're ashamed of the war I fought in. I'm not precious, I'm an embarrassment; I'm not loved, I'm kept out of sight, because my life-altering injuries don't support the victorious story you want to tell.'

Precious, honoured and loved. We need all three words. Not loved without being honoured. Not honoured without being precious. Not precious without being loved. These three words are at the epicentre of the Old Testament.

Now look what happens when the adult Jesus makes his appearance in Luke's Gospel at the start of his ministry. Heaven is opened: in other words, we're about to discover who God really is. A voice from the cloud speaks. 'You are my Son, the Beloved; with you I am well pleased.' In other words: you are precious, honoured and loved. The love God has for Israel – the key to the whole Old Testament – is now fulfilled in Jesus.

And that's reflected in what happens when we baptize people today. Baptism is God saying to them, 'You are precious, honoured and loved.' All three. It's what parents say to their baby every day. It's the fruit of baptism and the most wonderful gift. You are precious, honoured and loved. It's the secret of everything. God created the world and came among us in Christ and will be with us forever, because God's whole being is devoted to saying, 'You are precious, honoured and loved.' It's what we want to say to each other. It's what we long to hear a community say to us. It's the gospel of Jesus Christ. And it's revealed in Jesus' baptism. And ours.

Commentary

This course is written to prepare parents (and potentially godparents, something well worth trying online) for the baptism of their infant child. But it can be easily adapted for adult baptism, even though Being With Church is specifically designed for that purpose.

There are three ways to do the course. One way is to give the materials to the parents, invite them to read the talks and discuss them between themselves, perhaps over four separate conversations – where they do their own wonderings together – and then come back for a session with a leader to debrief on what was discovered, address questions and issues arising, and go through the liturgy of baptism. A second way is to run a four-session course for a number of parents at a time, before or after their child's baptism, partly in order to help the parents make significant connections with one another. This can be difficult to arrange but is perhaps the ideal, out of which enthusiastic parents can join other Being With courses including the original one. A third way is to do a single session with the parents of a single child, choosing just one of the four sessions above, and completing the session with an introduction to the baptism liturgy and an invitation to do a further Being With course.

The first talk says it's for godparents but in fact it's a way of reading the most common passage for a baptism – Matthew 3.13–17. It's a way of grounding aspirations for a child in the gospel narrative. The second talk tunes into a primal reason why a parent may want their child baptized – to give them divine protection – and puts this idea of safety on a wider canvas. It's based on the good shepherd account in John 10. The third talk takes a very different approach and describes the extravagance of God and appeals to a similar response from the parents. The last talk focuses on three words at the heart of one of the most significant passages at what might be called the epicentre of the Bible – Second Isaiah – which identifies the central learnings Israel gleaned during the exile. But it's also a way of talking about love without straying into sentimentality or over-associating it with romance.

The wonderings should generate plenty of material about Christianity, parenthood, raising a child in the faith, and the nature of participating in the church – which should be what any baptism course would hope to cover.

4

Being With Your Significant Other

Ten Wonderings and Addresses

One: Three Faces

- *Tell about something you found really thrilling.*
- *Tell about a team you were part of that worked really well.*
- *I wonder what makes a person trustworthy.*
- *I wonder what's hard about sharing your life with another person.*

I want to explore what I'm going to call the three faces of marriage. The first face of marriage is what we could call face-to-face. It's two people looking at each other, attending to one another, seeing the deep joy and desire and yet fragility and fear in each other's eyes. It's two people tracing the beauty of hair and the curious shape of the nose, the softness of skin and the electricity of touch. It's two people enjoying a whole lot else about each other that we needn't go into right now.

The second face of marriage takes place at a 90-degree angle from the first. We could call it the side-by-side face of marriage. It's two people getting on with life together. One person taking the rubbish out while the other loads the dishwasher. One choosing some music while the other lays the table. One clearing the children's toys away while the other reads bedtime stories. One filling out the tax return while the other goes on

BEING WITH YOUR SIGNIFICANT OTHER

the web and makes travel plans to go and see the family over New Year. When it's good, it's because the couple have discovered how to make these mundane tasks a different way of making love. The ordinary is interrupted by moments of touch and tenderness as vital as the waterfall of passion. When it's bad, of course, and the tenderness a distant memory, each of these necessary but sometimes wearisome tasks gets recorded on a silent roster of resentment.

The third face of marriage happens at a further 90-degree angle from the second. We could call it back-to-back. It's two people who are married but are doing the other things in life they need to do when they're not around one another. It's all the work and effort and relationships and hopes and fears that would almost all be there regardless of the marriage, yet are made new and different and meaningful because they exist within the matrix of marriage. When all is well this is as much a way of showing and feeling and expressing love as the other two faces: storing up stories to share, forging an identity that the spouse can be proud of, grasping in one's pocket the memento she gave you last night, quickly calling his mobile phone right after he's due to have had that difficult meeting. But when all is not well there are lingering suspicions that formulate around the seldom articulated conclusion, 'Work is where you go to get away from me.'

Here's the bad news about marriage. I've never known a single couple who were perfect in all three of these faces. We have euphemisms for the ways people discover their frailties. One is 'They had a passionate marriage.' I suspect this means they were pretty intense about number one, face-to-face, but they never quite worked out how to translate that passionate love into numbers two and three, side-by-side and back-to-back.

Another euphemism is 'They're such a great couple.' This means they've got number two right: they seem to interact seamlessly around the home and amid one another's friendships, so one always feels welcome in their presence but never questions they have a deeper bond with each other that creates the music for the lesser dances they can animate and enjoy with everyone else. They've learnt how to be good companions and form a lifelong friendship. But marriage isn't the same as friendship.

I wonder how often 'They're such a great couple' is a euphemism for saying number one, the face-to-face, has literally gone to sleep.

And a third euphemism is 'They had an old-fashioned marriage.' An old-fashioned marriage it seems to me is a way of saying we keep numbers two and three – the side-by-side and the back-to-back – very separate. We concentrate on getting the back-to-back right, because it puts a roof over our heads and supper on the table. But an old-fashioned marriage is a euphemism for one in which the number three, back-to-back existence, of the couple is allowed to drift off into a sphere so separate from the rest of the relationship, and often in practice so much more important than the rest of the relationship, that the couple are only really married for part of the time.

Here's the good news about marriage. It's not supposed to be perfect. It's supposed to be good. To quote Meat Loaf, two out of three ain't bad.

And the theological news of marriage is that the three faces of marriage correspond to three ways we interact with God. We see God face-to-face, and for a time we may think that's the whole of faith, to have that sense of peace and love and joy in the presence of God. But we also walk side-by-side with God, happy to be sharing in the companionship of the kingdom, alongside others whom God has called into witness and discipleship and service. And we also live back-to-back with God, when for short or long periods we can't feel or know God is there and yet know it is God alone who makes our heart sing, and we have committed ourselves to be among God's children and we know the feeling will come back again because it always has before. The most significant and exasperating thing about marriage is that it's the best analogy for what it means to be face-to-face and side-by-side and back-to-back with God.

Two: Contract and Covenant

- *Tell about an agreement you kept a long time.*
- *Tell about an agreement you weren't able to keep.*
- *I wonder what it's like when someone lets you down.*
- *I wonder what it's like when you've let someone else down.*

I want to reflect on two superficially similar, in fact very different, but ultimately complementary words.

During a wedding the couple sign a document. That document is like a great many other such documents we sign in our lives. It involves the setting aside of certain freedoms in order to receive specific goods. It's helpful for setting expectations and especially significant if one side feels the other isn't sticking to the bargain. It's what we call a contract.

But there's another word that conveys a different set of expectations. It's about a promise that can't be enforced, a commitment where the law has no power, an understanding where there's no third-party court of appeal. It's about trust that develops and overcomes setbacks and failures and abrogations and grows deeper through sunshine and rain. It's what we call a covenant.

Now the question is, is marriage a contract or a covenant? At first sight it's an easy one to answer. You can't enforce a marriage. You can't sign a document that says, 'I will always adore you however irrational your behaviour and irritating your conversation.' A contract reduces to a cold transaction something that should always remain a tender aspiration. By contrast, a covenant is saying, 'I will put the best possible interpretation on everything you do. I will always be mindful of the places of pain you're emerging from, the noble goals you seek, the shy hopes you stutter to articulate. I will never look on you with cynicism or suspicion or act towards you out of exploitation or deceit. I will hold your hand when you die and want you to hold mine.'

So you'd expect me to say, reject all thoughts of contract. What marriage partners are entering into is a covenant, a journey of discovery together bounded by trust, which begins this day when you say to one another, 'It matters not what I do so long as I do it with you.' But I'm not going to say that. Because I've learned that when people think they're in a covenant that has no element of contract they can end up acting in ways far worse than any contract would permit. So I'm saying a marriage needs both words.

A contract says something like this. I am never going to criticize you in front of others. I am never going to avoid talking about a difficult subject out of pretence that I'm protecting you. I am never going to let the sun go down on my anger. I am always going to live as if a difficult day with you is better than a glorious day with anyone else. Such commitments don't make a marriage; but they prevent a marriage becoming a prison.

Building on such commitments you can make a covenant. A covenant says, I want to be the person with whom you share not just the terrible things you've done but, even more scary, the unfulfilled dreams you still have. I want to be a person who hears you without judging, walks with you even when there's nothing to say, believes in you even when no one else does, loves you however difficult you find it to love yourself.

Here's the deal. Respect the value of a contract. Contracts are made by people who know relationships get into misunderstandings and disputes and represent wisdom and experience in resolving such conflicts. Contracts represent the humility of realizing you're two people going through something a lot of people have gone through before, and you may have something to learn from their wisdom. Never let your aspiration for a covenant allow your relationship to fall below the level of a contract. But never assume a contract is enough. Let your love allow the wedding contract to blossom into a beautiful, unique marriage covenant that's entirely, uniquely, yours.

Finally, never let your relationship with God devolve into a contract. Marriage is given for a host of things – for joy, for security, for companionship, for children. But most of all it's given as the single most tangible way we learn how to live our life as a covenant. We practise on each other that we may better understand the wonder that God desires to be in covenant with us. Marriage means signing a contract that indicates your longing for your love to grow into a covenant that shows each of you what it means to be in covenant with God.

Three: What Love Is

- *Tell about a time you ran away from something that was just too difficult.*
- *Tell about a person who helped you do something you couldn't do on your own.*
- *I wonder what it's like to think, 'It wasn't supposed to feel like this.'*
- *I wonder what it's like to say the word 'together'.*

I want to portray for you three pictures of your future. The pictures are ones I'm just imagining. The point is not whether or not they *come* true. The point is whether or not they *are* true. I'm not breaking any secrets by telling you you're going to spend the rest of your lives with each other wrestling with what love means. So here are three pictures to help you find out.

Here's picture one. It's in five years' time. You've saved up enough money to buy a house. You've got the choice between a small tidy place near the station or a fascinating but impractical fixer-upper. So you go for the fixer-upper. You make the discovery so many people in your situation have made before you – you realize you're not the first to try to fix this place up. You're beginning to open up the attic space and you discover a horrendous, ugly, smelly mess just where the loft ladder connects. You're both gasping for clean fresh air. You've got five choices. Option one: you clean it up. Option two: your partner cleans it up. Option three: you both close your eyes for up to 15 years and hope it will go away by itself. Option four: you inveigle a relative or friend or pay a contractor to deal with it. Having rapidly surveyed the options, one of you presses Spotify and starts playing the 1984 Foreigner song. One of you belts out at the top of your voice, 'I wanna know what love is.' The other one replies, just as loud, 'I want you to show me.' And you realize there's option five: you can do it together.

Here's picture two. It's in ten years' time. You have a lovely baby infant. You're mindful of the climate crisis, so you decide to go for washable nappies. The big game is on the TV and you've planned your whole week around watching it and beholding a victory that will never be forgotten. Your little tot starts to get a bit whiffy. You start to add up events of the last couple of days and realize the household is experiencing diarrhoea of biblical proportions. The game is incredibly close and gripping but this tot can't wait. You've got five choices. Option one: you can deal with it. Option two: your partner can deal with it. Option three: you can both close your eyes for 15 years ... actually that's not an option. Option four: you can get someone else ... actually that's not an option either. This won't wait. So what happens? One of you belts out at the top of your voice, 'I wanna know what love is.' The other one replies, just as loud, 'I want you to show me.' And you realize there's option five: you can do it together.

Here's picture three. It's in 60 years' time. You're wrestling with whether one of you needs to go into a full-time care home. This time the smell isn't coming from the attic. This time the smell isn't coming from your baby's backside. This time it's coming from one of you. You run through the options. There aren't many options now. Option three – you ain't got 15 years. Option four – no one's going to sort this out for you. You belt out, 'I wanna know what love is.' But no words come back. Your partner of 60 years isn't on that register any more. Option five isn't an option. You can't do this together.

Or can you? Think about it. You've spent a lifetime laughing as one sang, 'I wanna know what love is', while the other sang back, 'I want you to show me.' You've spent a lifetime discovering that the answer to that question lay in the single word, 'together'. So this is the moment you realize, 'Actually, we're still going to do this together.' At the beginning I tore your trousers off because I adored and desired you. Later we took our baby's trousers off because sometimes a nappy just needs changing. But today I'm going to help you take your trousers off because you can't go and do your business on your own. We'll face this together.'

The Bible is a story of a people who fitfully, fleetingly and faithfully realize that God is constantly saying, whispering, imploring the word 'together'. 'I want to do this with you. I want to be with you.' Over and over, God and humanity say to each other, 'I wanna know what love is', and reply, 'I want you to show me.'

And that's what marriage is. It's two people wrestling with what love is. It's two people, in the passion of youth, in the partnership of parenthood, in the companionship of old age, whispering, singing, hollering, 'I wanna know what love is', and replying, 'I want you to show me' – and then realizing, however smelly the task, however daunting the project, however fearsome the challenge, however humiliating the confession, however sad the news, however overwhelming the endeavour, the answer lies in that single, faithful, enduring, simple word: together.

Four: Three Little Words

- *Tell about a person with whom it seemed everything had to be bargained for.*
- *Tell about a person you did a lot for who never seemed to appreciate it.*
- *I wonder what it's like to feel everything's possible.*
- *I wonder what it's like to feel you have permission to be you.*

I want to suggest three words to which you may return should you ever forget the simplicity of love and marriage. Each word requires the unlearning of another word.

The first word to unlearn is '*if*'. Some arrangements are pervaded by the word 'if'. If you keep your side of the bargain, I'll keep mine. If you weren't so annoying, exasperating, infuriating, I'd be kind, gentle and understanding. Today's the day you dispense with that word 'if' – and replace it with the word 'always'. Your love is no longer conditional: it's permanent. 'If' is the language of contract; 'always' is the language of covenant. 'If' is provisional, 'always' is unconditional. Time to replace if with *Always*.

The second word to unlearn is '*for*'. 'For' is the curse of marriage. Do you know how many hours I've spent making a nice dinner for you? Have you any idea what it costs me to work so hard for you to have a comfortable future? 'For' names the accumulation of unspoken resentment, until like a bursting dam it all cascades down and floods a relationship. 'For' is based on guesswork, assumed benevolence, a private sense of unrecognized moral superiority. Quietly put that word away. Replace it with the word '*with*'. 'For' is about entitlement; 'with' is about sharing. 'With' requires constant relating, regular recalibrating, honest rebalancing. The point is never to do it well or quickly or efficiently – but to do it together. It's not a performance to make the world applaud – it's a mystery to enter together more deeply. It doesn't matter what you do, what matters is to do it with you.

The third word to unlearn is '*ask*'. You've done all the asking already. Did you love someone before me? Did you ever do something you're still ashamed of? Is there anything you haven't told me? Asking is good, but the questioner sets the agenda. It's time to cease asking and begin something deeper – something called *wondering*. To share your memories of the past is an act of trust and tenderness. To share your wonderings about the future is intimacy of an even higher order. I wonder what you're looking forward to. I wonder what you're afraid of. I wonder who you most want to talk to. I wonder what you most need from me. A wondering isn't a question. It doesn't set an agenda, it sets a stage. It says, dream with me, ponder with me, explore with me, discover with me. When you ask, you almost always have an idea of the right or desired answer. When you wonder you're both opening your hearts to something neither of you yet know.

Three little words. 'Always' takes away the fear of the future. 'With' means you'll never be alone. 'Wonder' means the future is an adventure.

These are the three ways we relate to God. With confidence that God is never going to go away. With joy in the word together. With awe at God's glory. Marriage is our way to practise the always, the with and the wonder of being together, that we may better be able to comprehend the always, the with and the wonder of being with God. Three little words, which sum up marriage and our approach to God: always with wonder.

BEING WITH YOUR SIGNIFICANT OTHER

Commentary

This is written as a course that should work equally well as preparation for a conventional marriage, preliminary to a same-sex civil partnership (or marriage where that is appropriate), or 'marriage enrichment' for any couple looking to enhance their relationship or recommit after a setback.

Like Being With Baptism it can be conducted in any of three ways:

1. After an introductory session on the wedding liturgy, including reflection on the declarations and vows but also choosing specific readings and music, the couple can be sent these materials and be invited to read and discuss them together, preferably over four different conversations. Then they may meet with the person preparing them and discuss what's arisen.
2. A more ambitious project would be to meet with a group of couples over four sessions, in more conventional Being With course format, only with the couples gathering for the heart of their week and the talk, but separating into discrete couples for the wonderings and (at least part of) the discussion.
3. A more modest approach would be to do one session, probably the first, as the second meeting of a two-session marriage preparation with an individual couple, the first covering the wedding service as described above.

The first talk is an attempt at a comprehensive overview of the key issues in marriage. By dividing them into three, it seeks a humane approach to recognizing all marriages are stronger in some areas than others. It also offers an opportunity to shift attention from the couple to God. The second talk recognizes that love means not only desire, affection and tenderness, but also commitment, respect and trust. It can be a helpful way of talking about how a relationship can be both flourishing and vulnerable at the same time. The third talk uses humour and playfulness to communicate that marriages need to be reshaped over time, and for them to be sustained requires forbearance and mutual renegotiation as well as kindness and willingness. The fourth talk is particularly suited to

BEING WITH

a relationship that doesn't involve children but is still subject to many of the challenges of one that does. It aims for simplicity but, like the other talks, is grounded in practical life examples.

Again, like Being With Baptism, the wonderings should surface most of the issues that would normally arise in marriage preparation. Marriage preparation seldom now assumes a couple is new to sex, but these wonderings can certainly yield discussion in that territory if deemed appropriate or helpful.

5

Being With Child

Ten Wonderings and Addresses

One: Chance and Love

- *Tell about one curious thing about your father.*
- *Tell about one curious thing about your mother.*
- *I wonder what it feels like to contemplate the chances by which you came into existence.*
- *I wonder how you feel about the circumstances of your conception.*

There could have been no existence. There could have been nothing. Perhaps there was, for an almost infinite period – a period that can't be measured in time, because time is a characteristic of existence. This is where humility begins: with the recognition that it would have been simpler, more plausible, less troublesome, tidier for there to have been no existence; in practice, nothing. Yet here we are. A twinkle in the imagination of essence maybe; but existing nonetheless. Humility is founded on the realization that it would have been much more probable that we would not have existed: it is only some balance between chance and love that has made it otherwise.

To begin to wonder is to settle on what it could possibly have been that induced God to conceive, trigger, initiate or imagine existence. Gratitude is apprehension that this balance of chance and love has brought about every ingredient of the circumstances that brought me into existence, that there is nothing whatsoever for which I can claim the credit, that it is all entirely gift, that I shall never be able to discharge my consequent debt, and that I must therefore remain suspended in dumbfounded astonishment and delirious reverence.

For God to bring about existence requires a constellation of sustained intention that yet refrains from control, of meticulous direction and yet relaxed permission; most of all, of risk – risk that things may unravel, sour, hurt, distort, and need sacrificial attention and utter devotion to be drawn back towards glory. Ponder this: what is the name we give to this constellation, to this foundational yet reckless risk without which there is nothing? The name we give is love. Love isn't the afterthought, a sentimental alternative to the harshness of time and chance, conflict and death; love is the beginning, the cause, the formula for what inspires God to bring about existence, the imagination that translates 'maybe' into 'be'. Love is the pivot around which the circle of life rotates.

Love and chance aren't opposites. The process of love is one in which chance is incorporated into reason. Love is not about control; it is precisely the willingness, the urge, the resolve to wait in attentive patience with that other that tantalizingly fails to fulfil desires and expectations or excruciatingly intends to subvert kindness and benevolence. Evolution tells us that existence is perpetuated through the impulse to survive and the haphazard pattern of mutation; but love is always a constant process of improvisation to incorporate and adaptation to accommodate the unexpected, uncharacteristic and sometimes unwelcome. Sooner or later any kind of love faces the fact that it must renounce control.

More profitable than to sift the ocean of chance for sparkling glints of love is to contemplate the myriad moments when the chain of being could have snapped such that your life would never have been. In perhaps every generation a life could have gone in a different direction, been prematurely foreshortened perhaps; the two lives from which each of your ancestors were conceived might never have crossed paths, been drawn together, been fertile in conceiving you at the moment you began; reaching back to the mists or origin, before humans took shape, the stepladder of your prehistory might at any moment have come loose and in so doing snatched away the possibility of your existence. And so for us all. Reflect on how many of your ancestors clung to life to the point where they could conceive the one whose birth eventually led to yours. Realize by how fragile a thread their existence hung. Behold how the miracle of your birth is made up of a concatenation of other such miracles. Your existence is a thing most wonderful: almost too wonderful to be.

Your parents crystallize the marvel of your existence. You did not choose to exist; you did not even consent. You did not select your parents; you cannot begin to imagine the infinitesimal improbability of their union, and of that union conceiving you. You may discern their uniqueness; you are doubtless familiar with their ordinariness. You are perhaps best placed to perceive their fallibility. You may owe as much to their nourishing and saving you in your upbringing as you do to the careful or clumsy way they engendered you. Regardless of their perfections or fragilities, simply accept that you would not exist without them. They may be to blame for much; but without them you would not be alive to apportion such blame. To honour your parents is to recall daily that your existence was not of your making and its purpose is never simply of your determining.

Be humble. Because you depend. What you depend on is whatever it was that made essence issue in existence. You are part of that 'else' that means there is more than simply something. You are part of that existence that is less plausible than there simply being nothing – that has no necessity. You hang by a fragile thread that traces back through countless generations, each one of which is, in its way, precarious and unlikely and remarkable and miraculous. You remain in unquenchable debt to a balance of love and chance that are not opposites but deeply involve each other. Each of these contingencies is focused in the mystery, mundanity and miracle of your parents. And to navigate this life, you need not the knowledge of necessity, the conviction of certainty or the assumption of entitlement, but the establishment, cultivation and restoration of trust: trust in something beyond.

Two: The Unexpected

- *I wonder what it's like to invest huge emotional energy in someone and then find it all goes wrong.*
- *Tell about an experience where you felt you had one rejection after another.*
- *I wonder what it's like to feel you have no capacity to do something but find you're given the strength to do it anyway.*
- *Tell about a time the story didn't turn out as it was supposed to but it still became beautiful.*

This talk is inspired by two people, each coming to terms with the fact that their lives haven't turned out as they hoped and expected. Somewhere along the way, they'd formed in their imaginations a narrative that had a particular shape and direction in which specific things would happen and their lives would have a clear trajectory as a result. They're each left feeling bewildered and powerless, asking, 'What did I do wrong? What do I do now?' and, 'Where is God in all this?'

One story in the Old Testament is very much about things not turning out as expected. It's about the day the prophet Samuel anointed the man who was to become King David. It comes in three scenes. In Scene One, both God and Samuel are full of grief over the failure of Israel's first king, Saul. We can all relate to this. We've all invested huge amounts of emotional energy, time, sometimes money and, more than anything, love in a person where it all went wrong.

In Scene Two, Samuel starts looking over Jesse's sons. Samuel works his way through all seven sons to no avail. It's dispiriting. Samuel scratches his head. This isn't the way it's supposed to go. Like my two friends, his story's not following the assumed trajectory and it makes him question everything he thought he knew about life, himself and God. The sequence of rejections feels like a catalogue of failure, steering way off the plan. This is a story in which Samuel experiences eight failures or rejections – like a resignation and seven failed interviews, or a series of pregnancies that didn't continue to term, or several relationships that somehow foundered. Amid such experiences, any of us would wonder if our failures and rejections are based on an image we try to project, or on who we truly are. God does not reject who we truly are.

But in Scene Three all becomes clear. It turns out Samuel was learning to wait, to discern, not to despair, despite appearances. Because there's an eighth son. When Samuel stopped presupposing what kingly qualifications looked like, he could start to see other virtues. We've all been taken by surprise when an acquaintance or colleague didn't have the expected qualities of a friend or collaborator, but once we got over their difference and our prejudice we started to see their true worth.

The consistent theme of the story is that God takes the person who's been overlooked, the one who's beleaguered, the figure who's an outsider or a failure; finds in that person a quality neither they nor the world recognized; and in the power of the Spirit, transforms that person into something no one dreamed of or imagined. Which makes us recall where, how and why the Bible was put together. The Old Testament was written by a people in exile who, like my two friends, felt their story had absolutely gone astray from where it was supposed to go and were trying to make sense of who they were and who God was. The New Testament was written by a people coming to terms with the catastrophe of the crucifixion, who were finding that in Jesus' resurrection and in the coming of the Holy Spirit they were in a very different but absolutely more wonderful story than they ever supposed.

Which brings us to what this story means to the two people I spoke of at the beginning. This story is saying, your grief is real. In this story, not just Samuel but also God is bewildered and devastated by what's gone wrong with Saul. The story is saying, there comes a time, not straightaway, but after a period, when beyond your grief you can see possibilities that the expected story didn't have room for. The story is saying, don't just look for an identical replica of the story that failed. Maybe God has a different story for you. The story is saying, there may be many failures and rejections as you discover that new story. The key element in the new story may be someone or something you'd never taken seriously or previously considered. And finally, the story is saying, however weak, obscure, frustrated, dismayed or bewildered you may feel, this isn't a story about your strength, your beauty, your height, your luck or your talents: this is

BEING WITH

about what happens when God's Spirit comes mightily upon you, whereupon everything is possible.

In short: this story is telling my two friends, and each one of us, you may have a broken heart, but it's out of God's broken heart that new, very different and very wonderful stories come, and what matters is that God looks on your heart, and God's Spirit comes mightily upon your heart, and, hard as it may be to believe right now, bereft, beleaguered and bewildered as you are, God has chosen you.

Three: Laughter

- *Tell about a time you laughed when laughter wasn't really the appropriate reaction.*
- *Tell about a moment you used laughter as a kind of protection.*
- *I wonder what it's like to feel you're in a situation and there's no way forward.*
- *Tell about a time when it seemed hopeless but somehow everything changed.*

A crucial story in the first book of the Bible comes when three visitors arrive to see Abraham and Sarah. Abraham and Sarah are in their old age, but the visitors say they will have a child. The name of the child is Isaac, which means laughter.

The story describes how one kind of laughter changes into another. In the first part of the story, when the visitors tell Abraham his wife will bear a son, Sarah laughs. It's a bitter laugh – a laugh of endurance, of self-protection, a laugh that isn't about something being funny, a chuckle that says, with painful irony, 'Don't make me laugh.' But then Sarah denies she laughed. The story explains why: she was afraid. What an insight into the life of a woman in her culture: her body, her fertility, discussed by men while she prepares food, and when she thinks they've said something ridiculous she has to lie to hide her reaction. But some while later, she's transformed from the bitter, ironic laughter of endurance to the effervescent, gregarious laughter of joy. 'Now Sarah said, "God has brought laughter for me; everyone who hears will laugh with me."' She's laughing at her own earlier laughter, for now the story's swept up all her sadness and failure and made everything into a pathway to joy.

The question that sums up the whole story is the one the visitors ask Abraham: 'Is anything too wonderful for the LORD?' This question not only sums up the whole of the Abraham story; it also sums up the whole Bible and the whole experience of faith.

Let's trace a line that connects a series of moments that together constitute the biblical story. Originally there's nothing. God speaks, and creation comes into being. Without God speaking, there would be nothing: no universe, no earth, no people, no you and me. Hold that thought. God comes to Abraham, the three figures of the Trinity visiting the tired and barren Sarah and her husband. God speaks and life comes into her womb. Without God, there would be nothing. A millennium later, Israel is in exile in Babylon: the situation is hopeless. God says, 'Comfort ye my people, I'm preparing in the desert a highway for you to go home.' Without God, Israel would still be in Babylon. There would be nothing. Five hundred years later, Mary's a virgin. Yet Gabriel tells her she will bear the Lord. Without God, there would be nothing. Yet Jesus is here. Thirty-three years later Jesus lies in the tomb. It looks like the end of the story. Yet the Holy Spirit calls him out and there is resurrection. Without God, there would be nothing.

You get the idea? Is anything too wonderful for the Lord? The Bible is a series of stories in which things seem to be utterly hopeless, but right at the very utmost point of despair God gives birth to joy. Is anything too wonderful for the Lord? Over and over, God turns the bitter laughter of defence and endurance into the overflowing laughter of convivial joy. Every single time it comes as a surprise. But see what the Bible is: it's not a concatenation of judgements designed to make us all failures and catch us out as miserable sinners; it's a whisper, a rumour, a meme, a subversive word of resistance that gathers into a crescendo saying, 'There's a story bigger than the story you think you're in. It'll embrace you and lift you up when you are at your moment of despondent despair. It'll surprise you even if you've immersed yourself in its patterns and mysteries. However much you weep and mourn, one day you will laugh. Nothing's too wonderful for the Lord. Not back then with Abraham. Not in the story of Jesus. Not ever.'

Christianity isn't a bleak form of endurance, an extended form of mordant humour designed to keep our spirits distracted in the face of a grief too devastating to face. Christianity is, instead, faith in God's promises, which time and again have brought wonder out of nothing, birth out of barrenness, homecoming out of exile, hope out of despair, resurrection out of death. Sometimes when all seems lost, we laugh subversively in the face of our persecutor, resisting the circumstance that oppresses and depresses us. But that laughter is just the foretaste of a laughter that transcends it, a laughter that creates a community, as Sarah discovers when she says, 'Everyone who hears will laugh with me.' It's not merely a laughter of endurance, and it's not limited to a laugh of resistance. It seems most often to come at the end of a long period of barrenness, exile, isolation, misery, failure or abandonment. But in the end, it's a laughter of never-ending joy.

At some point in our lives, we each have to face a choice about which story we're living in. Well may we say, like Abraham and Sarah at the start of this story, this story's about us: life's too hard, some things will never happen, faith is a bitter, sarcastic form of endurance that finds humour in irony and spots absurdity in pomposity. But we each have an invitation to see things like Abraham and Sarah at the end of this story: it's not a story about us; we're given the grace to play a role in a story that's fundamentally about God – a God who becomes most visible at our times of greatest despair, when we can't imagine a good outcome, but discover nothing is too wonderful for the Lord. Christians are those about whom Sarah spoke when she said, 'God has made laughter for me. Everyone who hears will laugh with me.'

Four: Being with Child

- *I wonder at what age or stage you become a child and at what age or stage you stop being a child.*
- *Tell about an early memory from your childhood.*
- *Tell about a time a child was wiser or more honest than the adult or adults around them.*
- *I wonder what a woman can experience in pregnancy, birth and rearing a child that a man cannot.*

A child is a child whether in relationship to a parent or not; but a parent (as compared to an adult) is defined by their relationship to a child. Hence part of the agony of having your child die before you do, especially if it's your only child: are you then still a parent, if you have no child? Whereas you can still be a child even if you have no parents. Likewise the sadness and complexity of feeling a longing to be a parent yet never oneself having a child. Meanwhile any adopted child knows the complex interweaving of biological, moral and role-shaped qualities involved in the notion of parent: is one a parent by simply fertilizing an egg, whether *in utero* or *in vitro*, intentionally, unintentionally or as a donor; by giving birth; by being a caring, nurturing, loving presence; or by being a regular, at-least-largely responsible adult in the home?

So a parent is a moral designation; but not only or always so. Jesus redefines parenthood and other relations in his words, 'Whoever does the will of God is my brother and sister and mother.' And being a child is elevated to a moral status by Jesus' words in the Gospels: 'It is to such as these that the kingdom of heaven belongs'; 'Whoever becomes humble like this child is the greatest in the kingdom of heaven. Whoever welcomes one such child in my name welcomes me.' Thus the role of parent as all-knowing, totally responsible mediator of the complex world to the innocent child – distiller of wisdom, teacher of habits and morals, protector from storms and evils – such a status is undermined and subverted by Jesus' exaltation of the child and that child's privileged access to and perspective on God's realm. 'The Child is the father of the Man': the poet Wordsworth's words affirm the priority of childhood. In short, children teach their parents – about life, about God, about themselves, about parenting.

So being with child subverts the conventional portrayal of the parent's superiority over the child. But there's a third dimension contained in the mysterious and intriguing expression 'being with child'. For a mother, conceiving, carrying, giving birth and breastfeeding are a unique, and perhaps definitive, experience of being with. These are things a father can enjoy and behold and support; but a father's role, while important, requires a different kind of being with.

The simplest, most earthy, primal and physiological dimension of human existence – procreation, the propagation of the species – is also the most wondrous, tender, intimate, complex, mysterious and fraught aspect of living. Marriage is a social attempt to harness and corral the free spirits of loneliness and desire, neediness and longing, within the established roles of spouse and parent. In its combination of mundane and fragile humanity with creative and loving divinity, marriage is inevitably a source of comparison with the divine and human Christ, and Christ's body, the church. Marriage is a long-term exercise in being with one another.

In a marriage, romantic partnership, undefined relationship or brief encounter can come about the intimacy, sometimes profound, passionate, tender, sometimes exploitative, casual or clumsy (in other words sometimes truly and gloriously with, sometimes scarcely or not at all) from which issues the mystery of conception. And out of this much longed-for or deeply feared, planned and managed or ignored and neglected moment can arise, for a woman, often before she knows it, the state of being with child. This resonant phrase rewards gentle pondering. The three words amplify and clarify one another. Does 'child' add a rich, limitless, perhaps definitive context to being with? 'Child' of course can mean zygote, embryo or foetus; newborn, infant or toddler; pre-teen, adolescent or adult. To call someone a child is to note that they are contingent, hint that they are dependent, suggest that they are loved, imply that they are still growing and learning, perhaps allege that they are immature or irresponsible. Thus to try to love a person who's being cruel to you, one can recall that once they were someone's fragile child;

meanwhile to come to terms with the humanity of an admired person who turns out to have feet of clay, one can recognize that deep inside they are still a child, searching clumsily for love and security. In each case, the word 'child' enriches the outlook of being with.

Likewise 'being child' turns one's attention on oneself: one never stops being a child, for, despite Paul's words, there's more to childhood than foolish things. Here child means that we didn't bring ourselves into the world; we have no right to be here; we have no entitlement, we made no original request, had no choice over the circumstances of our birth and early years; despite our best efforts to make ourselves freely choosing autonomous individuals, we're a child in the face of health, weather and so much besides. And yet, paradoxically, and echoing Jesus' words, maturity lies in realizing, accepting, inhabiting and enjoying these unalterable and ultimately overwhelming aspects of our perpetual childhood. 'Unless you change and become like children,' says Jesus, 'you will never enter the kingdom of heaven.'

Five: Participation and Partnership

- *I wonder what it feels like to realize you grew to term in a process no one could control.*
- *I wonder what you make of the phrase, 'For it was you who ... knit me together in my mother's womb.'*
- *I wonder what the phrase to 'be with child' means to you.*
- *I wonder whether breastfeeding is more significant for the mother or for the child.*

Perhaps most challengingly, the phrase 'being with child' begs the question of whether the default preposition of adults relating to children is truly 'with'. Because with implies participation, and participation implies some kind of parity of esteem – in a way that prepositions like 'for', 'to' or 'from' – let alone 'on behalf of' or 'for the sake of' – do not. Thus what the question provokes is whether adults conventionally regard a child as their equal – as having different perspectives, just as valid; unique insight, at least as, if not more acute; and profound qualities, such as wonder, that an adult might be much the poorer for having neglected or utterly lost. Or whether adults take for granted that not just the power but also the wisdom, experience, knowledge, strength and responsibility lie entirely on their side, and the transfer of information and understanding is entirely one-way. The phrase 'with child' challenges such assumptions. It suggests 'with' is the primary way one should imagine relating to a child, and holds up to examination a myriad of other ways, such as bringing up, rearing or raising. And it suggests 'child' has important, vital, perhaps uniquely significant characteristics to qualify the word 'with'.

This brings us back to the mystery of what it means for a woman to be pregnant and to describe that pregnancy as 'being with child'. Because here the 'with' plays down the woman's agency: she isn't generating, producing, forming or constructing a child – she is 'being with' child. Even the conventional alternative expressions, such as 'expecting a baby', or even the somewhat quaint 'in the family way', carry a similar ambivalence or reserve about agency. And the reticence is absolutely appropriate: the woman gives everything – her energy, appetite and shapeliness, her mobility, strength, steadiness of stomach and quietude of head, let alone the prospect of often agonizing confinement; and yet she literally doesn't know what she's doing. The process by which zygote becomes embryo and embryo becomes foetus happens without her intervention, direction or control. Matthew's account of the birth of Jesus begins with the word 'genesis': 'Now the birth [literally "genesis"] of Jesus the Messiah took place in this way.' It highlights the fact that a woman has no more power to turn a zygote into a foetus than she has to create the world: both are miracles, and mysteries. The annunciation to Mary is sometimes spoken of as an egregious invasion of her body by the Holy Spirit; but every pregnancy is a mysterious series of events, largely, with the exception of the conception itself, beyond the woman's control. Being with child means, for a woman, having little more direction of the formation of the child than the child has itself. Little wonder we have such poignant reflections in Psalm 139: 'For it was you who formed my inward parts; you knit me together in my mother's womb. I praise you, for I am fearfully and wonderfully made.' The father and mother together may have planted; the mother certainly watered; but God gave the growth. Even in cases of assisted conception, where interventions have taken place to bring fertilization about *in vitro* or facilitate it *in utero*, there's little or nothing that assists or explains, once conception and implantation have taken place, what it truly involves to be with child.

A similar, and equally moving, dynamic can take place in the mystery of breastfeeding. Often the production of milk can be challenging, the flow not straightforward, the significant areas prone to soreness, the newborn baby fitful and clumsy in sensing and satisfying hunger. Like pregnancy, much can be distressing, uncomfortable, disorienting and exasperating, and, for some, not possible. But like pregnancy, breastfeeding is something a mother does with, not simply for, her child. The precious and beautiful harmony of mother and child, feeding and being fed, is a mysterious partnership. The effort, and the reward, is not one-way. The roles are different, but each party teaches, trains and enjoys the other. It's a wondrous thing to find oneself deeply, truly and thoroughly able to satisfy another's need; it's a precious thing to have one's needs so utterly, fully and comprehensively satisfied – with just a burp to indicate contentment. Few, if any, partnerships, when successful, are so unambiguously rewarding. Like all the best partnerships, there seems to be at work something beyond the skills and needs and desires of the respective parties: there's an unseen force that binds and teaches, harmonizes and dovetails, trains and completes, entertains and reciprocates. Who is bestowing a privilege upon whom? For which party is this the more defining experience of life? In whose soul will this preverbal, primal activity lodge the more irreplaceably and unmovably? For both parties the activity of transferring milk could probably be done more efficiently and speedily, but, as is the essence of with, that would be to miss the point. The point is that this is something definitively done together; efficiency and haste diminish the with that is the purpose of existence, of relationship – the glory of God.

Six: Attention and Delight

- *I wonder what you learn when you pay close attention to a child growing up.*
- *I wonder what advice you'd give to a person bringing up a child.*
- *I wonder what advice you'd give to a child growing up.*
- *Tell about something a child taught you that you wouldn't have seen for yourself.*

There's a lot of for in parenting – especially parenting a newborn. There are relentless nappies to change, equipment to prepare, clothes to wash, pacifying and soothing techniques to hone and implement with greater or lesser success. For a parent who rises often in the middle of the night the sense of mutuality may seem fantastical or sentimental; sense of humour can be an early casualty. Indeed, for many, parenting seems like the ultimate experience of working for, as life becomes a constant stream of washing, tidying, cleaning, mollifying, feeding, sterilizing, transporting, entertaining. It can seem like a blur of give, give, give. But as in marriage, the sometimes-overwhelming demands of for can become an avoidance of, or at least a distraction from, the deeper invitation to with. Because, as in pregnancy, the real, profound and constant changes – the growth, discovery, learning, exploration – aren't achieved or bestowed by the parent; they just come. Again, God gives the growth. A child's maturing is a thing of wonder – a thoroughbred horse on which the parent is at best an attentive rider. The parent who seeks the credit or claims compensatory acknowledgement for their labours or infant-management is missing the bigger part of the deal: some force is acting in, through and with the growing child – a force with its own momentum, own wisdom, own creativity, pace, dynamic and character, such that any parent that seeks to control, bridle or harness it is a prisoner of their own fears and a fool in their own hubris. Parents don't fundamentally 'bring their child up'; they walk with their children as those children learn through practice, failure, patience, experimentation, persistence, reflection and discovery – qualities required of the parent as much as the child. It's a with story from beginning to end. Being with child doesn't end at birth; it's only just begun.

BEING WITH CHILD

And this is where attention becomes so vital. A problem can be solved by applying a solution learned from and applied elsewhere; a mystery can only be entered, and requires a response that draws on deep experience but is new to this unique situation. Being with child is a mystery and not a problem. Wisdom comes primarily from close attention to this child, with this parent, in this context; advice and childrearing manuals have their place, but only insofar as they encourage close attention to the details and particularities of this narrative. It's not a generic issue to be fixed; it's a unique story to be lived. Parenting is not a calling or ministry you can get right at, say, infancy, after which you keep doing the same thing with predictable, reliable and positive results. The child grows. You are called to be with them. Not to make them, shape them, instruct them, train them; but neither to neglect the respective roles in the partnership, where you have a regard for their ignorance, innocence, ingenuousness, vulnerability, fallibility and impetuousness. Instead, the parental way to be with is to pay attention: to observe, remember, enquire, be curious, encourage, wonder, respond, reflect, remind, acknowledge, thank, appreciate. There's no moment to repose in expertise or recline in having mastered this stage of life: in no time all has changed, and only the one who's truly with will perceive the change as it dawns.

And this is where the parent has to make a very significant choice: will they take the *for* approach of lamenting the burden of bearing the unexpected, unwanted, ungrateful, or the *with* approach of delight towards the challenging, stretching and surprising? The choice isn't always so stark, but attention, so as not to be crushing and suffocating, must, to be truly with, elicit delight. And, just as in infancy, arguably even in the womb, the central feature of delight is the way the child is, as much as the parent, the teacher. It's a commonplace to hear a person say, 'That's why we have grandchildren – to teach us how to use our phones and computers.' But the truth is, even before the days of rapidly upgrading personal communications technology, it has always been so. The child has always been the father of the man in speed, agility, hearing, sight; but the child also has the gift of fresh eyes, unafraid questions, uninhibited enthusiasm, unalloyed adventure, unsullied idealism, unqualified loyalty. To discover that your child is your teacher isn't an occasion for humiliation, humour or accusations of hubris; it's not a crossing of the bar, a time to hand over the reins, or a sign that your number is up: it's an occasion for delight, joy, happiness – and of looking back to see it has always been so. Ever since the cradle, this child has been teaching its parents what it means to be alive, to learn, to grow, to be a child of God.

There's a well-known story about the pastor who was walking home from church and passed a gardener laying out rows of vegetables in an immaculate line. 'That's a beautiful garden you've got there,' said the pastor. 'I'm glad you like it,' replied the gardener, 'I've worked hard on it all these years.' Quickly the pastor chimed in, piously, 'You should give glory to God – for it was God who sent the rain and sun and enriched the soil and gave the growth.' 'Ah yes,' the gardener responded, 'but you should have seen what it looked like when God was working on it alone.' This is a story about delight, attention and partnership. Indeed, there is a role for the parent as this kind of gardener, giving care and nurture while God gives the growth; but a child is not a vegetable, and the real delight comes when the child brings something that wasn't already there – something perhaps not immediately wonderful or even welcome, but nonetheless a thing of wonder. It's easy to be touched by a baby's first smile, an infant's first word, a toddler's first step; but just as significant is when a child says, 'If I'm not supposed to swear, why do you?'; 'If you don't like soggy carrots, why do you always put so much water in the pan?'; 'I go to school with lots of different kinds of people, but why do all the people you invite to our home look like us?'

Part of delight, and part of partnership, is the recognition that, while called to be with your child, your child has needs, aptitudes and joys that require learning, discovery and play with people other than you. Being with child, after birth, doesn't mean being inseparable from child; it doesn't mean making child wholly dependent on you; nor does it mean your becoming incapable of finding identity except in the role of parent. With is not possessive; it's not arrogant or consumed by its own needs; it doesn't insist its way is the only way. It sees being with child as an invitation to wider relationship rather than a stockade against the cruel and duplicitous outside world. Just as a parent needs to learn and grow from other adults, and from other children, so does a child. Delight, in short, is not trying to turn a child into a clone, a client or a creation of oneself, but enjoying their becoming a unique, surprising creation of God, church and God's realm.

Seven: Presence and Enjoyment

- *I wonder how much being a parent is about letting go and how much it's about holding on?*
- *Tell about a time a new person changed the whole dynamic of a family, community or workplace.*
- *Tell about an occasion you or someone else improvised in the face of adversity.*
- *I wonder what part of the story of Mary, mother of Jesus, you relate to.*

Parenthood isn't simply biological procreation but a moral status and a vocational role – and for that latter role presence is clearly required. But parenthood comes to be as much about letting go as about being always there, as much about expressing trust and love by giving space as about offering protection and supervision by remaining in proximity. And this is never more the case than when it comes to giving emotional permission and physical breathing room for a child to make a relationship and start a family of their own. So presence, while foundational to the ministry of being with more generally, and inextricable from being with child in pregnancy and often in immediate infancy, can become more complex, and even problematic, in later years.

But presence takes on a different character when one considers that it takes a church to raise a child. A congregation is an almost-unique environment where people of all ages interact in largely informal ways, and relationships can grow up naturally across family, race and class backgrounds. Of course there are lurking dangers; but a congregation has the potential to be a source of significant relationships that put the intensity of the nuclear family in perspective and offer alternatives for nurture, mentoring and imitation. There are many important relationships beyond parent–child: grandparent, uncle or aunt, and godparent are in many cases salvific, or at least highly salutary; fellow disciple or Sunday school teacher are spheres of great potential.

The best way to summarize the ministry of being with child is to consider it as *enjoyment*. Having children discloses the core of existence and of discipleship. It's not, as 'nature' might suggest, about the survival of the species, let alone the fittest – although in subsistence economies, it may be about life insurance for those anxious about care in their advanced years. Neither is it, as a fearful ethic might suppose, about populating the world with at least an equivalent, perhaps increased, number of Christians – since the church grows through conversion and baptism rather than conception and birth. It's not a selfless act of giving others life, in recognition that one's own life is fragile and failing, or a bland hope that one's children will make a world better than one's own and previous generations have done. And it's not about creating a small empire over which to (aspire to) exercise complete control. Being with child is to allow oneself to be drawn into a process of creation, a narrative whose course one quickly discovers to be outside one's control and beyond one's imagination; to find all one's relationships affected by the new presence, its smallness in inverse proportion to its capacity to move, inspire, infuriate, hold to ransom, transform. It's inevitably to generate countless projections, transferences and soon-to-be-thwarted narratives of dreams fulfilled, failures reversed, ideals realized. It's to revise one's assumptions about the self – initially a part of another's body, then wholly contained within and dependent upon another, then separate but inseparable from another, then tied up with another but relating to others, then forming an independent sense of self, then by turns constantly wishing to be dependent and inseparable or again separate and self-sufficient. It foils all attempts to be used: it can only be enjoyed.

Thus being with child is an intense, complex, conflicted and yet widespread case of the ministry of being with. More than perhaps any other sphere, it highlights the ultimate inextricability of discipleship and ministry: in the traditional English breakfast of bacon and egg, where the chicken is involved by contributing the egg while the pig is committed by providing the bacon, being with child is a poignant reminder that being with may look like the work of a chicken, but may turn out to be closer to that of a pig. Being with is not something that can be done at arm's length, simply be put down to resume another activity, be forgotten entirely and resumed the next morning: in this sense pregnancy is an apt template. If any should see ministry as the exercise of skill, discipline and aptitude, they should reflect on the wonder of being with child – the mystery of gestation, symbiosis, formation, development, all of which are well outside and beyond expertise or honed habit. Being with means being present in awe as God gives the growth. If any should see ministry as following an established curriculum of education, instruction, devotion and empowerment, they should reflect on the more-or-less ordered chaos of being with child. Entering into God's business of creation is seldom tidy, predictable or malleable into an ordered pattern. Instead, the ministry of being with is almost always faithful improvisation. If any should see ministry as something that can be performed with 'one hand', while multitasking elsewhere, being with child is an indication that the most important things in life require two hands, full attention – and only thus yield true delight.

Above all, being with child highlights that being with requires one's whole body, one's whole mind and one's whole soul: it takes one to the deepest recognition of one's earthy physicality, its beauty and clumsiness, its creativity and intractability; it takes one to the furthest reaches of thought, the wonder yet fraughtness of conception, the fears about security of relationship, health and financial well-being, the scrutiny of development, sickness, so-called normality; it takes one to the most profound territory of faith – creation and incarnation, providence and anthropology, fall and redemption. The ministry of being with is always the ministry of Mary – being alongside the Christ-child, both caring in the midst of vulnerability and standing in awe of divinity, anxious that one is unworthy to be so close to, so trusted with, so touched by the mystery, and yet realizing that somehow, in ways beyond one's own desiring, deserving or comprehending, one has brought forth the fruit of the Spirit and beheld its glory.

Eight: Innocence

- *Tell about an occasion that showed you the innocence of a child.*
- *Tell about a time that suggested to you a child was not entirely innocent.*
- *I wonder how it's possible for a child to do something terrible.*
- *Tell about an occasion a child told you something you didn't already know.*

During the 1630s, the French colony of Quebec was evangelized by Jesuit priests and Ursuline nuns. They spent a great deal of time with First Nations people, especially the Huron tribe. The Catholic missionaries were bemused to find a people who didn't speak French, and assumed that because the Huron couldn't speak French they obviously weren't capable of rational thought and should therefore be treated like children. By contrast, the Huron wanted to show hospitality to the French missionaries, and the biggest compliment they knew how to give the priests and nuns was to invite them to instruct, feed and dress their children.

The missionaries responded to the compliment by imposing frequent corporal punishment on Huron children. This seemed to the Huron to be a form of brutality that defied comprehension. But the missionaries were undaunted. The priests and nuns were careful to discourage the Huron from loving their children too much, lest they fail to love God above all. Once again the Huron were dumbfounded. They couldn't comprehend any contradiction between loving God and loving children. The French grew weary of these misunderstandings, so they shipped the Huron children off to boarding schools where they could offer their superior customs behind closed doors.

But this contrasts with a painful story. One Friday afternoon in February 1993, 2-year-old James Bulger was taken by his mother for a shopping trip in a suburb north of Liverpool. He disappeared, and 48 hours later his disfigured body was found on a railway line two and a half miles away. Eight days later two suspects were arrested and charged with his murder. Both of them were ten years old. They were, themselves, children.

Imagine discovering that one's own child had been the perpetrator

BEING WITH CHILD

of such a crime. If James' mother spends her days wondering what she could possibly have done to deserve such grief, surely Jon and Robert's mothers must spend each day wondering what in their nature or nurture produced two sons who could become such brutal killers.

The national revulsion against the two 10-year-old boys who killed James Bulger contains a genuine paradox. It was based on the profound need to affirm and preserve the unique innocence and beauty of children. Belief in God was becoming problematic. By contrast, belief in children had become an absolute article of faith. A child who could stoop to murder another child was not permitted to tarnish the image of children in general. Instead, one of two strategies was adopted to avoid tarnishing the innocence of children. Either the two child-killers must be treated as quasi-adults, having done such a ghastly thing. (This was the criminal justice approach, which put them through an adult trial.) Or, they must be vilified and regarded as egregiously and uniquely evil. (This was the lens adopted by the popular media.) What could not possibly be allowed to happen was any revision of the almost universal insistence that children are innocent, wondrous and pure – a kind of foretaste of heaven dwelling within a complex and sometimes sordid world.

But the truth is, children aren't innocent. In the Middle Ages there were of course people aged between infancy and adulthood. But there weren't children. If you look at paintings from the period, there are babes-in-arms and young adults – but there aren't children. By the time you're seven, you're more or less an adult. Childhood emerged in Europe in the sixteenth and seventeenth centuries at the point where a critical mass of people had sufficient economic security to withdraw their offspring from the workplace for a lengthy period in order to give them a formal education. Gradually there grew an aura around a class of humans who were to be kept pure by being protected from sex and death, and earmarked by being separated from adults in clothing. Once the sociological shift was made, a whole host of psychological and biological realities crowded around to underwrite it.

Jesus says, 'I thank you, Father, because you have hidden these things from the wise and the intelligent and have revealed them to infants.' Why would God reveal the truths of the universe to children? You wouldn't put children in charge of a bank or a city – you'd entrust such institutions to the wise and intelligent. So why, when it comes to the secrets of the universe, does God bestow them on children?

Maybe because children are largely ignored. Does it really occur to the teacher, pastor, parent, pediatrician, nursery supervisor or out-of-school club organizer that a child might actually know something they, the adult, don't already know? One children's book, by David McKee, is called *Not Now, Bernard*. The infant Bernard tries in vain to tell his parents that there's a huge monster in the back yard, all ready to gobble him up. Young Bernard's parents simply respond, 'Not now, Bernard', so the bewildered Bernard goes back in the yard and, sure enough, the monster promptly gobbles him up. Then the monster enters the house and starts nibbling at Bernard's parents. But the parents give the monster the same treatment they'd given their son: 'Not now, Bernard.' The book ends with the monster in Bernard's bed, complaining that he doesn't want milk and a cookie at bedtime. 'But I'm a monster,' he says. 'Not now, Bernard,' says Bernard's mother. The moral of the story is clear: listen to children or they will turn into monsters.

It's a good moral. But Jesus' words go beyond that. Jesus is saying, 'Listen to children, because they know something you don't know, something you need to know, something that lies at the heart of the universe, something that lies at the heart of God.' If you want to know God, you're going to want to stay close to children. And listen to what they say. Not for their sake, but for yours.

Nine: The Changing Family

- *Tell about how your experience of what constitutes a family has changed over time.*
- *I wonder whether you see the nuclear family as normal or unusual.*
- *Tell about a household that had turned the ideal of family into a god.*
- *I wonder what family really means to you.*

The family shows us something about society, about the church and about God.

Let's start with society. The institution of family that so many lament in decline was largely invented in the nineteenth century. Prior to 200 years ago, marriage was learning to love the person you lived with. In the last 200 years, marriage has been learning to live with the person you once decided you loved. For most of human history, the household was an economic unit. Most industries were cottage industries and the primary purpose of the home was as a centre of production – reproduction, certainly, but the production of goods for consumption and sale, almost universally. Spouses, children, grandparents and servants all lived and worked together and there weren't a lot of doors you could close to have space or time to yourself. The reason for having children was to provide more hands to assist in production and to offer care for parents who passed into post-productive old age. Desire, intimacy, tenderness and love were secondary to the primary aim of economic sustainability.

But the Industrial Revolution changed that radically. It created the breadwinner, who left the home each day to go and do arduous and often soul-destroying work in a factory. It created the distinction between the public realm of labour and the private realm of leisure. It invented the notion of the child, as a person too young to enter the public world of work and thus restricted to the innocent sphere of the home. It created the role of housewife, as one whose duties were primarily concerned with household management, the rearing of children, and the giving of succour to her weary and heavy-laden husband. It created the nuclear family, because anyone outside these three defined roles of breadwinner, housewife and child had no place in the new configuration of the home. More subtly it invented the notion of religion as a private, intimate, personal, predominantly female phenomenon, most at home in the household, by contrast with the largely male, non-religious, business-like outside world. It's this relatively recent invention, the industrial household, rather than the family itself, that's under threat, because it no longer reflects the social and economic reality of a critical mass of the population. We're entering a post-industrial era, and the shape of the post-industrial family has not yet fully emerged.

There's no reason to be sentimental about the industrial family. It flourished because it met the economic realities and provided everyone with clear roles. But it didn't work for everybody. When you add up the single, the gay, the child at the mercy of parental demands, anger, or worse, the suffocated or oppressed housewife, the breadwinner who faced unemployment or career failure, and the infantilized teenager with the body of an adult but the social standing of a child, you may be looking at a majority of the population. In the last generation, with the changing economic role of women, longer life expectancy, diversifying employment patterns and looser social taboos around sexual expression and divorce, the always-present anomalies and flaws in the nuclear model have become ever-more evident.

Before we leave the industrial family behind, let's pause to recognize what was good about it. It doesn't take an anthropologist to see how the family comes about. It's pretty much all in the traditional marriage service, which refers to the controlling of natural lusts, the creation of a sphere of companionship and the nurturing of a safe space to bring up children. Without the family the boundary-less lusts would result in endless conflict and instability, the isolated individual might be lonely and vulnerable, and the child would be deprived and defenceless. When it works well, the nuclear family can indeed be a refuge from a challenging, frightening and sometimes damaging world. It can indeed be a place of learning and growth in manners and morals, in creativity and wonder, in faith and courage. It can indeed be solid emotional ground where the priceless qualities of trust, confidence, self-acceptance, tolerance and forgiveness can develop and deepen.

The nuclear family isn't something one can idly discount. It's the scene, for most, of our deepest feelings; it's the context, for many, of the greatest damage; it's the garden, for most, of our profoundest love; it's the source, perhaps more than any other environment, of countless analogies; it's the reason, in the face of loss or betrayal, for our most anguished sadness. These seem to be the ground rules about the family – that it's more or less basic to human existence, that it's a place of profound longing and need and nurture and joy, yet can also be the context of deep hurt and intolerable constraint, and that it's had a number of historical forms among which the industrial model is widespread but not definitive.

Family is never going to be heaven. It's never going to be a constant ecstasy of love, a seamless robe of happiness, a dreamland of intimate and harmonious relationships, bounding from touching kindness to profound grace to constant affection to limitless trust. It's never going to be church. It's never going to have the same diversity, the same global reach, or more than glimpses of the same challenge of mission and repentance and witness and encounter. And it's never going to be God. Many exaltations of the family in Christian circles are a turning of the family into a god. Family becomes idolatry when it becomes an end in itself, a good thing that justifies all kinds of bad things, a form of extended selfishness that simply widens the walls of the self a little but has no goal beyond its own embellishment. Family isn't a god; it's not church; it's not heaven. Sometimes it can be the opposite of all these things. But what it can be, and what it can be equally well without all the industrial characteristics that have long been thought indispensable, is a training and an avenue into all these things.

Ten: Family and Faith

- *I wonder whether you would regard Jesus as family-friendly.*
- *Tell about something that wasn't a conventional family but turned out to be more wonderful than a family.*
- *I wonder what God being a trinity tells us about family.*
- *I wonder what it might mean for members of a family to have a combined vocation.*

The Old Testament affirms that family is basic, but is unsentimental about its flaws. Genesis is a litany of sibling rivalry from Cain and Abel to Jacob and Esau to Joseph and his brothers. The story of Abraham and Isaac hardly paints a rosy picture of household as refuge from the cruel world. Prominent men like Solomon have many wives, and resourceful women like Esther and Bathsheba have to live by their wits to survive. At least the Song of Songs suggests some people were having a good time.

The New Testament is confusing in a different way. Jesus makes few statements about marriage, taking for granted the social code where the command to honour your father and mother is basic, discouraging casual divorce and yet denying there is marriage in heaven. But his itinerant lifestyle, his singleness and his radical reinterpretation of family relationships are, to say the least, a transformation of conventional models. For Paul, singleness is the normal state for disciples and marriage is a particular vocation for particular circumstances. You can't really call the New Testament family-friendly. The very first time Mary appears in the oldest Gospel, Mark, the disciples say, 'Your mother and your brothers and sisters are outside, asking for you.' And Jesus replies, 'Whoever does the will of God is my brother and sister and mother.' Elsewhere he says, 'Whoever comes to me and does not hate father and mother, wife and children, brothers and sisters, yes, and even life itself, cannot be my disciple.' And at the foot of the cross, the central moment in history, Jesus both affirms and transforms the family. 'Woman, here is your son,' says Jesus to Mary. And to the beloved disciple he says, 'Here is your mother.'

Now there are many interpretations of this scene. One of the most helpful is that Mary represents Israel and the beloved disciple represents the church, and here, at the foot of the cross, Jesus is saying Israel belongs within the wider purpose of God known as the church. But on a personal level, Jesus is recognizing that the conventional family cannot always provide all the security, stability and endurance we each need, and in the face of tragedy something beautiful can emerge that turns the love of these two people for Jesus into a new kind of love and care for one another.

Family is good. But sometimes there's something more important than the cocooned family that withstands the damage of the threatening world – and that's the redeemed, renewed, resurrected family that emerges out of tragedy. There was once a man who with his wife longed for children. Great was their delight when his wife fell pregnant – but even greater was their horror when one of the scans showed that his wife had developed cancer. Six weeks after the baby son was born, his mother died. After five years in the wilderness, a whole bunch of friends and a complex support team gathered to celebrate a new wedding. At the climax of the service, once the man and his new bride had exchanged vows, the priest ushered forward the young son, now aged five, and said to the bride, 'Do you take this young man to be your son?' Then the priest turned to the boy and said, 'Do you take this woman to be your mother?' No one was pretending this was a pristine idealized nuclear family. But in the midst of tragedy, these people had found something more beautiful than that.

Family can teach us about the nature of God as Trinity. Every time a couple have a first child, they are rightly anxious about how the dynamics of each of them with the child will alter the existing dynamics of each of them together. They're right. It will. It doesn't necessarily make the relationship less; often it makes it much more. But it always makes it different. The same is true when a new child comes into an existing family. The older sibling will always wonder if it's possible to love just as much when there are more people in the game. Likewise the Trinity isn't a self-sufficient solo, or an exclusive mutually obsessed duo: it's three, and yet its love is only enriched, multiplied and deepened by being three rather than one or two. Envy and jealousy are not endemic to family life; insecurity and rivalry, favouritism and cliquiness are not inevitable, however common. Family isn't an ossification of perfection, but a constant improvisation on growing and changing identities, needs and relationships. The Trinity is a constant invitation and inspiration to see how several can still be one without eliding diversity or eroding personality.

While the family can indeed help us understand the nature of God, the best thing a family can be is a centre for mission. The idea of perpetual domestic bliss is at best a fantasy and at worst a doomed attempt to turn a home into a stockade against all enemies, most of all hostility, hardship and death. At best a home is a place from which all parties go out to fulfil the call to be fishers for people, to find Christ in the face of the stranger, to take up their cross and follow Jesus, to love God with all their heart and mind and soul and strength. And at best they each return home with something of what they've found, a new believer, an ex-prisoner, a person who is carrying the cross, a person who's suffused with the love of God, and around the table of fellowship they break bread, meet the crucified and risen Christ, and are renewed in love and service. They live in a triangle of one another, the stranger and God, and come to understand and relate to each in ever-new and deeper ways. Such life doesn't require a nuclear family. It doesn't assume specific gender roles, compliant and submissive children, doting grandparents from afar or even perfect marriages. It may well include configurations of households beyond that imagined by the conventional breakfast cereal advert. But it does require sharing and tenderness, mutual forbearance and intergenerational grace, forgiveness and reconciliation, time and trust, kindness and companionship, loyalty and love, and an understanding of a common goal far beyond the comfort and indulgence of the individuals involved. And when you have that, you might not yet have a church. But you do have a family.

BEING WITH CHILD

Commentary

Neither this course nor the subsequent one on Being With the End of Life focus on a specific life situation, because people's experience and stories are so varied, and their context can change quite suddenly (from wanting to become pregnant to being so, from caring for a dying relative to being bereaved, and many other such transitions). The key insight – and risk – of these two courses is that people have much to learn from others in situations adjacent to their own; in other words, it's not always essential or even beneficial to keep the conversation within strict parameters of similarity. It can be extremely painful for a person longing for a child to have to listen to a person expecting a child speak about the distress of morning sickness, or a new parent complain about many nights of lost sleep; but part of being with is about trusting the process of different personalities, perspectives and contexts and not always sticking to the safety of the similar. The work of the host is even more significant in these two courses than in the others, because the desire to fix or give advice, let alone overshare about one's own particular experience, can be almost irresistible in such tender territory. It's also the case that post-natal depression and the profound grief of bereavement might lead the host to consider signposting a particular participant to support services beyond the group. This should be done privately and not in front of other participants.

Notwithstanding the pitfalls, Being With Child can be especially rewarding if it's made clear it can be a course for anybody, not just those planning or raising a family. Childbirth, yearning for it, preparing for it and managing its aftermath can be so all-consuming that it can be hard for anyone to break into the bubble, even sometimes for those in the wider family. It can be a very healthy thing both to discuss wider assumptions and considerations around having children and to do so in the company of those who might have had children long ago or not at all. (Those who love Being With courses might well join just because they enjoy the format.) But because tears are even more likely than usual, and hurt is never far away, the host needs to be especially alert to keeping the rules about not commenting on one another's responses to wonderings and to linger on issues during the discussion or change the subject as seems most helpful.

The course doesn't seek to replicate parenting courses. It begins with contingency – the realization that each of us might well not have existed and the miracle by which we do. It is intended to begin the course with a sense of awe, wonder and humility. The second talk is about the way vocation can appear out of setback and disappointment, and is by no means always a straight path. It's especially directed at those whose desire to have a child has not been fulfilled but can apply to any context in which things haven't turned out as expected or hoped. The third talk also has a general application but is included in order to speak to the person whose long wait for a pregnancy is finally fulfilled, or a person who finds themselves unexpectedly pregnant and is working out how they feel about it.

The next four talks place being with child in the context of the eight dimensions of being with, as explored in several of my books and explicitly in Chapter 10, 'Being With Being With' below. They aren't aimed at a particular context. The eighth talk might come as a surprise: it doesn't concern infants, and it considers that children might not be entirely and unequivocally innocent. But the overall message is that children might know something their parents don't already know. The last two talks are about the family – questioning assumptions about the nuclear family and reflecting on what family means and could mean today.

6

Being With the End of Life

Ten Wonderings and Addresses

One: Three Whispers

- *Tell about a moment when someone whispered something to you.*
- *Tell about when you first became aware you were alive.*
- *Tell about when you first became aware life comes to an end.*
- *I wonder if there is anything stronger than death.*

We didn't choose to be born, any of us. Yet at some moment in our childhood, each of us realized that we were alive. It struck us one moment, or dawned on us gradually, that we were in the midst of an astonishing, beautiful, exhilarating drama, which careered on, largely without our will or assistance. That drama wasn't just a spectacle: we got to play a role in it. In fact, we had as much chance as anyone to play a part. That drama hadn't always been: once it had not been and, even more pressing, once we had not been; but now we are. That was the moment, that instant in our childhood, when we became aware of life.

But one night we looked into the sky and saw a gazillion stars, many of which burnt out billions of years ago, but whose light we're only now seeing. And we realized all life is just a whisper in the cacophony of the universe. We're a tiny speck in the story of everything. From across the universe, we're even tinier than the most minuscule star is to us. But that whisper is the whisper on which everything we know depends. We're a whisper – a tiny one. It doesn't matter how quiet a whisper is: what matters are the words it says. And the whisper that says the word 'Life' is precious beyond any blast of sound. It's a whisper that communicates indescribable energy, creativity, vigour, joy. The elixir of life. The first whisper.

But a little bit later in our childhood we realize that life isn't the only thing in play. There's something that comes to everyone, to everything, that takes the joy out of life. As you become a teenager, you realize that everyone only deals with it by pretending it isn't there. But it infiltrates every life and every aspect of life with its menace and destruction. Death is what we could call the second whisper. It's a mystery, just as deep and impenetrable as life. Why is there life? We don't usually ask the question, but we're glad there is. We laugh at the question, because everything we can imagine depends on there being life. But if there's life, why is there death? It's unthinkable, intolerable, unjust. Does the second whisper cancel out the first whisper – shout it down, dismantle and discredit it? What's the point of the first whisper if we have to face the second whisper? How do we find our way out of the everlasting wrestle between life and death? Do we fear, deep down, that death eventually wins every time? Is that why we whisper – because we don't want to admit it, try to keep the secret, don't want anyone else to know?

Tucked away near the middle of the Old Testament, half-way through the last chapter of one of its most neglected books, just where no one's going to look for them, are the most important words in the Bible. They're the most important because they break open this perpetual arm-wrestle between life and death. 'Set me as a seal upon your heart, as a seal upon your arm; for love is strong as death.' Those five words are the epicentre of the Bible: *love is strong as death*. There's only one way to say them, and that's to whisper them. Death thinks it's got the better of life – it'll always win in the end. It'll destroy, dismantle and discredit everything, and turn it to dust. But there's something death hasn't bargained for. And that's love. When we discover love, we find the answers to our two greatest questions. Why is there life? Because of love. Love is what life was created for. Will life outlast death? No – but love will. Death can't drown love. Many floods can't quench its fire.

When Mary Magdalen goes to the tomb on the morning of the first Easter Day, she knows more than anyone about the first whisper – because she's seen life like no one's known it before, she's met Jesus, she's watched him heal the leper and raise the dead, she's heard him speak the words of eternal life. But she also knows more than anyone about the second whisper, because she's seen this man who embodied everything life could mean nailed to a cross, tortured, betrayed, denied, rejected. She's seen everything life can be turned into merciless death.

What she finds there is the most important discovery ever made. It's the discovery that makes sense of all the glorious mysteries of life and the desultory mysteries of death. She discovers there's a third mystery. She discovers the central claim of the Christian faith: love is stronger than death. What she discovers is resurrection. This is the mystery that unravels the mystery of life and death. Resurrection is the way, the only way, human beings reach out from the constraints of life and touch forever. And resurrection even more wonderfully is the way forever reaches out from beyond death and touches us with its truth.

We know life is short and fragile; we know death is bleak and cruel. But there's a third whisper, which is the reason life was created and the only thing stronger than death. That whisper is resurrection, and to be a Christian is to whisper it together, in the dawn of the day, in the glow of the evening, in the darkness of the night, every day, so when life is over and death has done its worst, that whisper will still be rustling and will endure beyond any scream or shout. It's a whisper that may mean danger, may require secrecy, but will in the end be the most intimate and joyful truth we share with the one who made life and transcended death. That whisper, which hitherto has always said the one word, 'resurrection', will finally turn into the only word that can match it, the word that makes it irresistible, the word that dismantles death and transcends mortality. That word can't be shouted or screamed, but can only be whispered softly, because it's the secret at the heart of the universe, the secret beyond life and death, the secret of God and us. That word is 'forever'.

BEING WITH

Two: Being with the Dying

- Tell about a time you were with someone who was dying.
- Tell about a time you were not able to be with someone who was dying.
- I wonder what's something helpful you can say or do when a person is nearing the end of life.
- I wonder what you'd want another person to be or to do as you near the end of your life.

We can think of four ways of relating to one another. *Working for* is where I fix things on your behalf. *Working with* is where we partner to solve a problem together. *Being with* is where we spend time together just because it's good to do so – with no specific project to accomplish. *Being for* is where I act in what I judge to be your interests without feeling the need to be in actual relationship with you.

Being with the dying is the defining moment of being with. Why? Because dying is the antithesis of working for. It's everything working for strives to avoid. The central rationale of being with is that it's the only mode of relating in the face of impending mortality – when there's nothing that can be fixed and all anyone can do is try to face what lies ahead. We're all dying, of course: a dying person hasn't, in fact, crossed over to another realm of being – they've just become more acutely conscious of a condition that pervades all existence. But they've become the embodiment of everything humanity most fears: finality, the unknown and the possibility of utter isolation. That doesn't mean there isn't often a lot of working for to be done: in the last stages of life a person may need a great deal of practical care, both with sanitation and with medication, and there are a host of more practical things that can be done in readying the person's possessions and dwelling-place for what will follow their departure. As ever, being with doesn't abolish or remove the need for working for: it simply provides the purpose of working for and highlights ways a retreat into working for can be a distraction from something more important.

Being with the dying comes in two kinds. There's being with those who recognize, as best they can, what's in prospect, have taken stock of what can and cannot be done, and are resolved to use aright the time that is left to them on earth. And there are those who are trying as hard as they can not to name or entertain what lies ahead, who whether by distraction or denial are raging against the dying of the light, whose thoughts are squarely on keeping what they know, rather than anticipating what they don't know. But being with means offering companionship worthy of the courage of the former, while gently but firmly refusing to collude with, and pointing beyond, the despair of the latter.

To be with a person in desperate straits when one has nothing practical to offer them – no solution, no fix, no precious information, no resolution of their predicament – is a vulnerable, exposed place to be. And this is why being with the dying is the definitive form of being with: in almost every other case there's something – however small – that one can imagine offering a person in distress; but in this case there really is nothing, and yet that awareness of one's empty hands is the beginning of being with. When it's clear there's absolutely nothing one can do, one faces a profound parting of the ways: a powerful impulse urges one to go elsewhere, to find another setting, a context where there *is* something one can do, a place where one can again imagine a world where one's skills and gifts and wisdom can make things better, turn things around, achieve results and create energy – an alluring theatre of escape. Death is the ultimate dose of cold water thrown over such magic dust. In such circumstances, presence is a pledge to the person dying that one's own need to be useful and effective is of lesser significance than their need for company, understanding and solidarity. It's also a statement of faith that being with represents a truer reality than working for, both within human existence and within the heart of God.

In this sense the dying person, and the one who's with them, experience a deeper dimension of living than those who are not dying – or who, at least, are not so conscious of the unavoidable imminence of death. The person dying presents their actual and potential companions with the moment of truth: can you be with me when there's no hiding in the realms of working for me? If you say, 'I can't be with the dying, I have to attend to the living', are you not really saying, 'I can only cope with being around those who are not yet aware or willing to name that they are dying'? Presence with the dying is thus a statement, to oneself and to others – not just to the dying person themselves – that we are all dying, and that there's nothing more important than time spent with a person entering the last stage of life.

Every death is different: every person approaching the end has their own particular concerns and fears, doubts and convictions, regrets and expectations. The traditional preparation for death – the confession of and absolution for sin, the handing over of one's life into the hands of God, trusting in the atoning death of Christ – focuses, almost inevitably, on the aspects one can name, address and thus to some degree control: events of the past that can be described, repented of and forgiven, elements of the Christian faith that can be articulated, identified with and responded to. But the very nature of death is precisely a convergence of everything we can't control. The plaintive question, 'What will become of me?' has no straightforward answer. The best answer is, perhaps, 'God created all things to be with you and came among us to reaffirm that relationship. I trust that God will be with you even more tangibly beyond death than now, and my desire to embody that is the reason I'm sitting here with you at this very moment.' But the practice of attention is more about listening to the many layers of the question than about hastening to answer it. The busy offering of readings and prayers and counsel and visits and reassurance may be largely a reluctance to stay in a place of silence and powerlessness and the unknown. If a dying person doesn't articulate the question, 'What will become of me?' it may be less because they don't want to know or don't want to seem frightened than out of fear of exposing the fragility of their companions and provoking a superficial or manifestly inadequate answer.

Being with is both about abiding in the ordinary moments and about not flinching in the sombre and perhaps terrifying moments. There's a place for graveyard humour: death and its proximity turn conventional expectations upside down and relativize so much of the self-importance of habits the world takes for granted: such is the stuff or irony and satire and wry humour. Besides, few people can sustain a level of intensity for very long. Being with means being prepared and willing to talk about news and events, reflections and frustrations one moment, and flip to fears and wonderings, panic and despair the next. A diagnosis that death is impending may initially seem to change everything. But not everything changes, both because ordinary things like cooking meals and engaging with other people's lives carry on, and also because everyone is dying and proximity to death is more about a difference of degree than of kind. Paying attention is the way a companion shows that they are prepared to let this death impact them as existentially as it affects the person going through it. It means entering a level of existence in which one single fact takes precedence over all others. But it also means letting the dying person's perception of that fact shape and colour one's own engagement and response. There is no objective estimation of what's taking place: there's only the dying person's narrative and such complementary or counter-narratives offered by those around them. Attention regards the dying person so closely that their perception of their own narrative becomes clear and, allowing for any confusion brought on by a condition or course of treatment, takes appropriate precedence.

Three: Saying Goodbye

- *Tell about a time you learned wisdom from a person in distress.*
- *Tell about a time it was hard to stay with a person who was in pain or despair.*
- *I wonder to what extent life is a rehearsal.*
- *Tell about a time you felt alone.*

Death involves an overwhelming sense of deficit – of a life that might have been longer and perhaps more fulfilling, relationships that could have endured to the next rite of passage, friendships that never had the chance to flower, projects that will never come to fruition, dreams never to be fulfilled. But mystery names the dimension of *being with* that discloses a truth beyond that immediate shock and wound of deficit – truer living, firmer hope, deeper joy. Rather than see the dying person as drowning in a whirlpool, and companions stretching out their arms from the water's edge to hold on to those arms as tight as they can for as long as they can, mystery turns things round and sees them from the other end: it's the dying person who has insight, wisdom, perspective and discernment, and the companions want to stay close to the dying person not to offer distraction and good cheer but to receive the gold that only the dying person can give.

This is not about maudlin parting words or pious attempts to crystallize life's essence in a pithy epigram. It's about staying still in the place of transition from time to eternity, from now to forever, from the fleeting to the everlasting. This is holy ground, where the mystery of death reflects back on the mystery of birth, where length of days pales into the shadows before realities beyond depth or measurement or conception. The dying person is isolated from the busy world of news headlines and economic swings and urgent emotions and the jostling of opinion and judgement, but they are correspondingly more in touch with the heart of existence, the wonder of fragile breath, the inexplicability of consciousness, the lightness of being. Mystery refers to the way being with a dying person highlights the breadth of such quality in life when the quantity of life seems thin.

It may seem absurd, even thoughtless, to speak of delight. But delight means seeing beyond what can't be to what truly can be – setting aside for a moment the sadness and perceiving the unique potential of this precious moment. Delight is the appropriate name for the cherishing that constitutes the rites of the last hours. It is a beautiful thing to take a person's hand and recall with gratitude the countless things that that hand has touched and held – perhaps the large hand of its own mother, the tiny hand of an infant, the texture of a working implement, the bread of holy communion – and anticipate what it will come to hold: the water of the river of life. It is a tender thing to touch the ear of a dying person and remember with dignity the myriad of sounds that ear has heard – words of love, sounds of the dawn chorus, cries for help, songs of hope – and imagine what it will come to hear: the word of God. It is a profound thing to meet a person's eyes and name with thanksgiving the panoply of sights those eyes have beheld – the fire of a sunset, the birth of a child, the kindness of a stranger, the spectacle of a great work of art – and await what it will still gaze upon: the glory of the Trinity. It is a rare thing to touch a person's nose and speculate with gladness on those smells that nose has known – the fresh-baked dinner, the rose in summer, the perfume of exotic allure, the incense of holiness – and realize what it will perhaps soon inhale: the joy of God's desiring. It is a privilege to come close to a person's lips and reflect with awe on what their tongue has tasted – the soft fruit, the daily bread, the refreshing drink, the wine of the Lord's table – and perceive what it will duly taste: the cup of the kingdom.

All this is delight. Delight sees what is there, not what isn't there. Delight describes a way to be with a dying person that rejoices in their life, both in itself and as a token of all life. There may not be many smiles; there may be no laughter; there may be tears and numbness and dismay; but this cherishing of what has been given, and trust in what it indicates of how much more is yet to come, is a practice of delight that indicates how all life may be cherished, at all times.

Perhaps the most poignant dimension of being with the dying arises in relation to participation. Participation is the epitome of with – the discovery that it doesn't matter what we do, provided we do it together. And dying we do not do together. Even if we were to do it at the same time, we do not do it together. David goes up to the chamber over the gate and cries, 'O my son Absalom, my son, my son Absalom! Would I had died instead of you, O Absalom, my son, my son!': but he can die neither with nor for Absalom. Absalom dies alone. Everyone does. Being with can take the horse to the water of death, but it cannot drink that water together. This is the isolation, the loneliness, the separation that constitutes, for many, the most painful aspect of the whole experience. Living is more than anything about being with God and one another: dying is done alone. Awareness of this casts a shadow but invites humility at every stage of the journey. 'For' may be a pointless, though understandable, distraction; but at the very last, even 'with' has its limits.

Four: What You Can Actually Do

- *Tell about when someone was so truly with you, you felt nothing or no one could be closer.*
- *Tell about when you thought there was nothing you could do to help but it turned out there was something.*
- *I wonder what it's like to feel powerless as someone else is in distress.*
- *Tell about a time a person wanted to help you but you were just glad that they were there.*

Where participation fails, all the more may partnership arise, somewhat in its stead. The principle 'never do for someone what they can perfectly well do for themselves' continues to apply. In many respects normal life goes on. To turn a person's last months or weeks into a continual party in which they are indulged with treats and attended upon like medieval royalty is simply another avoidance – a further instance of the impulse to turn being with into working for.

Partnership may be as simple as a companion doing the grocery run for a dying person yet seeking to involve that person as much as possible in preparing the meal itself. It may be a joint effort in which the dying person explores any revisions to their will while a companion records those alterations, secures signatures and involves lawyers. Perhaps more tellingly, it could involve a companion asking the question, 'Do you think there's anyone with whom you feel a reconciliation is necessary and possible, or for whom a legacy gift might be significant and treasured, with whom I might help you to get in touch or whose whereabouts I might seek out?' In this form, partnership is a kind of working with that assists a dying person to be in the company of those that might be harder to be with. The real work, for example of reconciliation, is something the dying person can only do for themselves: but the facilitative work, of asking the question, perhaps discovering if a conversation on both sides might be welcome, is an act of partnership, a form of working with. Again it requires a change of heart that sees proximity to death as not just a time of loss and calamity, but as a unique opportunity to have long-overdue conversations and offer often-inhibited or overlooked gestures of gratitude or kindness.

But the key dimension of partnership doesn't lie in useful actions and kind interventions. It lies in making a virtue of the tragic limitations of participation. It breaks the heart that a companion cannot ultimately accompany the dying person at their moment of direst need. Participation meets its match. But precisely because the companion is not immediately facing the abyss of oblivion that many fear lies beyond our last breath – precisely because the companion is on the shore while the dying person goes under the waves – the dying person may find they can say certain things and express degrees of feeling that, were the two in exactly the same predicament, would be impossible to share. Just as a child can pummel a parent's chest with the frustrations of life, not yet realizing that the parent shares such inner despair but has found a way to live with it; and just as a person in trouble speaks with a counsellor and puts into words their deepest fears and regrets and hurts, under the understanding that both parties will set aside the fact that the counsellor too knows such pain and loss and anxiety; so being with the dying can mean, for a companion practising this dimension of participation, a willingness to draw a veil over their own bewilderment so that the dying person can let it all spill out, go to the very bottom of the pond, trust that there is nothing that can't be faced, and thus find strength to endure the unendurable. Partnership can involve the wordless and understated sharing of tasks and activities; it can mean provoking one another into acts of courage and hope; but most importantly it means saying, 'Just at the moment I'm stronger than you are, in physique or resilience or faith. Lean on me while you do the things you so desperately need to do.'

The experience of extreme pain constitutes the most troubling circumstance of being with the dying, one that calls, as enjoyment does, upon every previous dimension of being with. It requires presence, a presence that says, 'I am not going to be frightened away by having to watch you in agony and despair.' It needs attention, an attention that says, 'I can see the veins on your forehead, the red flecks in your eyes, the horror of what this is costing you.' It necessitates mystery, mystery that says, 'You are entering a realm of suffering few ever know, and there is

BEING WITH

no answer to why you are being expected to go there.' It involves delight, delight that says, 'I am continually amazed at how you continue to give blessings to me and to those around you even in the midst of this excruciating distress.' It entails participation, even to the extent of saying, 'I will be with you as long as it takes, but I realize the worst of this you have to face alone.' And it calls for partnership, for all that can be done to alleviate the pain must be done. Enjoyment provides no magic dust, no panacea; it's not naive about how miserable such existence can be. But it represents the best that humanity can be – patient witness in the face of terrible suffering.

It may seem absurd to speak of glory. Sometimes the dying person attains a level of peace and acceptance that radiates and blesses those around them. It could be that the willingness of those with the dying person to embody the dimension of delight enables them to articulate wisdom, grace and insight that promises to remain in the memory of their companions for a long time. It may also be that, like the martyr Stephen, the dying person sees the heavens opened and Christ standing at the right hand of the Father. The most heartening reward of being with a dying person is to witness the dignity, courage and faith that they may embody. Not always, of course – medication, injury, pain, fear, doubt or denial may make such experiences rare and precious – but not uncommon.

Glory is perhaps more often discerned in retrospect than as a conscious, live experience. A more sober, yet tender realization may emerge from reflecting on the dimensions of being with the dying person. It concerns the nature and essence of life. Since earthly existence isn't permanent; since it isn't without disappointment, distress and despair; since such wisdom and faith as are to be had come at least as much in adversity as in comfort; and since intimacy, trust, companionship and love are as much to be desired as any gift, the parties close to the dying person may discover that what they have shared is as significant as anything they have ever known. If being with is the purpose of incarnation, creation and heaven; if that purpose is most fully practised in being with one another; and if being with one another finds its apogee in being with the dying, then one may rightly conclude that such an experience, for the companion at least as much as for the dying person themselves, constitutes the defining experience of one's life. If heaven is to offer more tenderness, more solidarity, more passion and more transparency than this, heaven really must be pretty special. This is what it means to speak of glory.

Five: Losing Everything

- *I wonder how easy or difficult you find it to get to sleep, and what keeps you awake.*
- *I wonder if there's ever been a time when you were content for there to be no logic behind the universe.*
- *Tell about a time you felt, if there's this much suffering there can be no God.*
- *I wonder what it's like to lose everything.*

I wonder, when you lie on your bed, how long it takes you to get to sleep. It's ironic that the very thing we long for with every fibre of our body is to go to sleep, to dive deep into the darkness of oblivion, and be replenished to face the next day. It's ironic because, for most of us, what we fear most about death is that very same thing that each night when we lie down on our bed we long for, namely, oblivion.

Let me set out a larger paradox in three dimensions and a contradiction. We exist, first, in a world of myriad complexity, subtlety and intricacy. The world is fearfully and wonderfully made. That's the first dimension. The second dimension is our either acute or dim recognition that behind, beyond and within all this life and existence there is some logic, purpose or intention. The third dimension is the realization, sudden or gradual, common or unique, that this logic is more than just a cold or mechanical chain reaction; it has purpose, intention and (and this is the crucial step) personality. This personality is by its nature shaped for relationship. Relationship isn't an afterthought for God – relationship is the very heart of what God is.

BEING WITH

But here's the contradiction. We die. Apparently our breathing stops, our organs shut down, our consciousness ceases, our body begins to decay and we are finished: no feeling, no awareness, no life, no future, no anything. See how death is a contradiction of all three dimensions of life. When we lie on our deathbed, or perhaps more truthfully when we lie on our bed at night and, for a change, don't seek the oblivion of sleep but search the darkness for meaning and hope, this is the conundrum we wrestle with. How can life end? How can that which brought life into being countenance its obliteration? How can the one who does everything to be in relationship with us tolerate the permanent elimination of that relationship? It seems totally illogical, uncharacteristic, unjust and incomprehensible.

These are the questions that dominate the book of Job. Job is usually thought of as a book about suffering, but suffering is really a subset of the problem of death, and most people could endure almost any amount of suffering if they were sure that restored relationship and abundant life would duly follow. So the real issue for Job and for us is not so much suffering as annihilation. Job's complaint is not about suffering; it's about the way that suffering encapsulates the three dimensions of the paradox we just explored. Annihilation goes against everything else he knows about existence. Job's suffering is unendurable because he has nothing to look forward to. He discerns that God's power is useless if it's not grounded in love.

We and Job have to wait 38 chapters before we get any kind of an answer to Job's question. When God does speak, we and Job don't quite get the answer we long to hear. God's answer is to affirm the mystery of our and the universe's origin and destiny, and to assert that those mysteries lie with God alone. In other words, we're left still clinging on to the three dimensions of our quandary, but now knowing that God endorses that paradox and recognizes our struggle. While not offering a clear-cut answer, God's words restore the relationship with Job and thus affirm that our communion with God transcends death. We aren't given a concrete picture of what our lives will be like in eternity, but we *are* given the one thing we need to know: our communion with God will abide. It's as if we're given a choice: choose the material comforts of life and lose everything forever; choose communion with God and all other things will be added unto you. More starkly, we're shown that the material comforts of life are a false insurance policy in case communion with God isn't available. In Job 38, communion with God feels like shouting at each other through a whirlwind: but both parties are hanging on each other's every word; and that's what intimate communion is.

The reason why the book of Job is harrowing is not just because it's about suffering. Job is deeply troubling because it exposes something uncomfortable about most manifestations of the Christian faith. In most cases our faith is based on an assumption that if there is a God, the job of that God is to fix human problems, upgrade existence and arrange benefits. In other words, that God is a piece of technology whose role is to improve our life. It's an utterly human-centred arrangement. A narcissistic faith. Not really faith at all: more the demand to honour a contract we never actually made – a contract by which we agreed to be born and God agreed to do the rest.

The so-called 'problem of suffering' assumes that God's role is to bring health and flourishing – and if God fails to do that, God is malign or weak. But what if God's role is to be with us always, in person in Jesus, in myriad ways through the Holy Spirit, and forever in heaven? God is not an instrument we discard if it malfunctions. God is the essence of all things who astonishingly chooses to be with us, even in desperate hardship – and even, in the crucified Christ, in indescribable agony. That doesn't make suffering go away. But it turns God's engagement with suffering from a pretext for rejection into a reason for worship.

When we lie on our beds at night, or on our deathbed facing eternity, we do indeed face the loss of everything. But the witness of Job is that we lose everything – but God. The one thing we don't lose is communion with God. The one and only thing that in the end really matters. The source from which all blessings flow. So, and only so, may we rest in peace.

Six: Being a Blessing

- *Tell about a person you didn't know very well but who you admired after they'd died.*
- *I wonder what you would want a stranger to know about you after you'd died.*
- *Tell about something those who know you well would say about you that a stranger would never guess.*
- *I wonder what it would feel like to write your own obituary.*

An illuminating exercise is to go away on your own for a morning and write your own obituary. The point is to look ahead a few years and write the most glowing things you could ever wish someone to say about you. You look at the mundane and unremarkable details of your life to this point and you see them as merely introductory material to the glory that is to come. When you've finished you look back at this marvellous person you've described and wonder, 'Why can't I live like that now? If that's what I admire, why isn't that who I am? What's *stopping* me?' What begins as an exercise in pride and vain glory ends as a humbling act of confession and renewal.

I wonder what it would be like to write an obituary for Abraham. The book of Genesis describes how Abraham's children are to be God's holy people, and through them God will come into relationship with all peoples. This is what the Old Testament is all about.

Let's look a bit more closely at what God says to Abraham in the first three verses of Genesis 12. These verses are so crucial we could call them the manifesto of the Old Testament. Here God makes seven promises to Abraham: I will make of you a great nation; I will bless you; I will make your name great; you will be a blessing; I will bless those who bless you; the one who curses you I will curse; in you all the families of the earth shall be blessed.

The middle one of these seven promises says, 'You will be a blessing.' Not you will *receive* a blessing – but you will *be* a blessing. And if Abraham didn't get it, or needed a little bit more help identifying what this interesting phrase might mean, it's repeated in more detail in God's seventh and climactic promise at the end: *'In you all the families of the earth shall be blessed.'* Here we discover what blessing is really all about. Blessing is not fundamentally about the security that comes through more land, more children, more wives, camels, donkeys, holidays, awards, guns, clothes or body enhancements. Blessing is about others being able to trace their sense of well-being and peace and joy to *you*. God is saying to Abraham, 'I'm going to try to convey all the well-being and peace and joy I have to give the world through one special people, and that people will be the people I give the world through you.'

An obituary is full of events and achievements and births, marriages and deaths. But if you're anything like me, you skip ahead past the ponderous narrative to the final paragraph that says something like, 'Above all, she will be remembered for her ...' – and then it describes what she was really like. And that's not about skill or intelligence or longevity or wealth; it's about character. And when I read an obituary that says, 'Above all, she will be remembered for being a channel of well-being and peace and joy', or, 'God was so transparently at work in his life that you felt, if you stayed close to him, you'd keep close to God', I think, 'I'll have one of those please. I'd like an obituary like that, thank you very much.'

Would your last paragraph say that about you? Would it say, 'She was a channel of well-being and peace and joy'? Would it say, 'God was so transparently at work in his life that you felt, if you stayed close to him, you'd keep close to God.' If not, why not? And with the time God has left for you, what are you going to do about it?

Because, in the end, all the earned or honorary degrees you receive and the money you make or give away and the property you own or bequeath and even the marriages you enter and the children you have aren't going to matter – at least not in the way that this matters. Others will know if you've received a blessing if they can look back and say that you've been a channel of well-being and peace and joy to them – that in you they have found a blessing, that, close to you, they have felt themselves close to God. If you have that kind of blessing, you don't need any other kind of security. Are you a channel of well-being and peace and joy? Do you *want* to be? Do you want to receive God's blessing? Does anything else *matter*?

Seven: Inseparable

- *I wonder in what ways you feel you're different from everyone else.*
- *Tell about a time when hardship taught you something important.*
- *I wonder what it might mean to look like Jesus.*
- *Tell about an occasion you chose a difficult path because it was better than the comfortable path.*

Is faith just a groundless, stubborn and counterintuitive refusal to come to terms with meaninglessness and mortality? What is it really founded on? Paul's words in Romans 8 give us two answers. One redefines what we mean by good. The other redefines what we mean by God. Let's start with good.

Here's how we usually think of God. We know we're not perfect, and life isn't always fair or easy, and we can't have everything we want. But that doesn't stop us wishing that could all change. So God becomes the name for how all that changes. Because of Jesus, we get everything we could possibly want forever. And because of the Holy Spirit, we get a pretty hefty share of that wish-list right now. That's the deal. But Paul is saying, that was never the bargain. When he says, 'All things work together for good', good doesn't mean a decent home, a healthy family, a rewarding job, a wholesome partner and a long life. Paul has a very specific definition of 'good'. His definition is 'looking like Jesus'. He gives us five verbs that describe the way in which the process of coming to look like Jesus takes place. God foreknew, predestined, called, justified and glorified. A lot of the church after the Reformation got hung up on the word 'predestined', but here there's no ambiguity about what it means. Paul says those whom God foreknew 'he also predestined to be conformed to the image of his Son'. In other words, that was what the whole purpose of God among human beings was always all about: making us and remaking us to look like Jesus. Faith means cooperating with the process.

That's what good means. That's what we hope for. That's the bargain. We get to look like Jesus. Nothing about having a healthy family or a long and happy life. Jesus didn't have those things. Nothing about a rewarding job or a wholesome partner. Jesus didn't have those things.

Nothing about a decent home or a loyal set of friends. Jesus didn't have those things. This is the deal: we are conformed to the image of Jesus. If God's doing a poor job at that, even when we're doing everything we can to cooperate, that's when we get cross with God. But bear in mind Jesus was homeless, rejected, betrayed, tortured and executed. We can't be surprised if we get a taste of these things too. In fact, if we don't, we have to wonder if we're still part of the bargain – if we're still cooperating with the process.

Let's turn to Paul's second answer. Paul exhaustively talks us through no less than 17 kinds of exceptions for why we might think we are in an unusually difficult place. He starts with hardship, distress, persecution. You could say these are the predicaments we find ourselves in through our own mistakes, the trouble that comes upon us through bad luck, and the misery we face because of the ill will of others. Then Paul moves to famine and nakedness – in other words, lack of food and lack of clothing, two of our most basic needs. Then there's peril and sword, in other words danger from adverse circumstances and danger from violent attack. Next come death and life, which between them cover pretty much every eventuality for anything we could possibly fear. Then there are angels and rulers, that's to say those who are in charge of this earthly realm and those who hold sway over eternal realities. Then things present and things to come, which again incorporates everything our imagination can comprehend and everything it can't. Then finally there are powers, which seems to be a sweep-up term for everything that's preceded it, and, just in case you were still feeling anything's possibly been left out, Paul finishes off with anything else in all creation.

Notice in this list that these are all things that Jesus himself was exposed to: hardship, distress, persecution, hunger, nakedness, peril, sword, death, life, angels, rulers and all the rest. Paul's giving us a list of everything Jesus went through and saying there's nothing we could go through that Jesus hasn't first gone through. But the list has even more authority because Paul has been through most if not all these things himself. He's not just appealing to Jesus, he's offering personal testimony. By the end of Paul's list we're exhausted but we're also stripped of all our exceptions and get-out clauses.

BEING WITH

Except, perhaps, one. In this long list, there's still one thing missing. There's a lurking suspicion in the hearts and souls of very many people that the problem of suffering, disappointment, sickness and grief isn't about any of these things. It's that God has turned away from you. That God is punishing you, facing away from you, or just doesn't like you any more. That God is cross with you or has lost patience with you. Paul shapes his whole argument to insist that this fear is finally, wholly, utterly groundless. God isn't against us. Any of us. God is *for* us. All of us. Why else would Jesus have gone through hell and high water for us? Jesus' death is proof that God is for us, and Jesus' resurrection is proof that nothing can separate us from God's love.

And so this long list of 17 circumstances tells us two things. It tells us that nothing whatever, nothing we can possibly imagine in heaven or earth, can separate us from God's love in Jesus. But there's a second thing Paul's list tells us. If the point of life isn't to have a designer home, job, family, spouse, leisure time, friendship circle, and the rest; if the point of life is to look like Jesus, then this is the kind of hell and high water you can expect to go through if you're going to end up looking like Jesus – or, to use Paul's language, if you're to be conformed to the image of God's Son.

If you're in distress, and you feel God's broken the bargain that was supposed to make you permanently content, you're wrong: there never was any such bargain. The bargain was that you become like Jesus. If you're facing hardship and you think it's because God's against you, you're wrong: God is for you. Always was and ever shall be. Nothing can separate you from the love of God. Nothing, nothing, nothing, nothing, nothing. Nothing. God is with you at every step, and Jesus has faced everything you're facing. You were with God in the very beginning of all things, you are now and you always will be. Being with God in hardship is always better than being separate from God in comfort ever could be.

Eight: How to Die

- *Tell about something you felt ended well.*
- *I wonder what's the last thing you could give your loved ones before you die.*
- *I wonder what's your biggest fear about death.*
- *Tell about someone who you think died well.*

I once sat by the bedside of a man who knew he had just a few days to live. 'I want to do something for my wife and my children,' he said, 'and maybe for my friends as well. I can't think of anything I can give them now, stuck here in this bed.' I said to him, 'Have you ever thought that you're more than capable of giving them one of the most precious gifts anyone could give, a gift all the more precious because it's so rare?' 'What gift might that be?' he said. I waited to see if he would look at his circumstances and guess for himself, but after some moments of silence, I said, 'A good death.'

What is a good death? The reality of modern medicine is that relatively few of us will be fully conscious, lucid and full of parting wisdom up to the very moment of our deaths. As one person said, 'On the plus side, death is one of the few things that can be done just as easily lying down.' The various tubes and machines will more often than not keep us technically going for some period of time after our last conscious thought or word. So we need to start getting our plans in order now, ahead of time, if we intend to give our families, friends and society the gift of a good death. Preparing us for a good death forces us to live a good life. The less you can do about the length of your life, the more you need to attend to its breadth and depth.

For many, perhaps most, people the unknown that lies beyond the threshold of death is simply the most terrifying thing in all human comprehension, precisely because it defies human comprehension. I'm going to attempt briefly to break that terror down into its constituent elements, to make it easier to talk about.

- For some people the big fear beyond death is judgement. For most of Christian history this has been what Christianity was really all about – preparing you to face the finality of judgement and its separation between heaven and hell. It's amazing how this has become so much less of an issue to people in the last 150 years, and consequently how attention has focused so much more on the conditions and possibilities and desire for justice in this present life. Nonetheless, the fear of hell weighs heavy on many of us as we approach death. While we may not imagine perpetual fire or gnashing of teeth, it's not hard to imagine being alone forever, a very gloomy prospect. And if one adds to that the possibility of everlasting pain, whether due to punishment or some other reason connected to the continuation in some form of our sense experience, it's too much to bear to think about.
- Perhaps the biggest fear for the contemporary imagination, captivated as most of us are by the realization and fulfilment of the individual self, is that beyond death lies simply oblivion. It is rationally hard to square the myriad complexity and texture of human existence before death with total emptiness afterwards. But when we witness the mundane biological process of death in animals and plants, there can seem little observational reason to argue that humans will be significantly different. As Johnny Carson famously said, 'For three days after death, hair and fingernails continue to grow, but phone calls taper off.' We're left with just our bodies and the worms. All the restorative qualities of sleep suddenly go out of the window, and we are faced with a sleep without end, a complete annihilation of the self – for many, perhaps most of us, a horrifying prospect.

Our biggest fears about those we love are that either they will come to hate us or they will forget about us. The Christian conviction is that in our eternal relationship with God neither of these eventualities is possible. God *cannot* turn against us and God *cannot* forget about us. Because of Jesus we will remain perpetually at the forefront of God's heart and mind. This is the gospel. This is the good news about the future that enables us to see our lives through to a good death.

That doesn't mean we don't still have fears about judgement and oblivion. The point about the assurance of Paul's words is that they enable us to face the future *in spite of* our fears about judgement and oblivion. Faith doesn't obliterate fear, but it enables us to live without being paralysed by fear, and thus to take the practical steps that witness to our hope beyond death. The gift of a good death, that last and most precious gift one can give one's family, friends and society, is fundamentally a witness of *patience* and *courage*. Patience to accept one's powerlessness to change the past, and courage to open one's life to the overwhelming unknown of the future. Patience to live with one's humanity, and courage to face God's divinity. That is what it means to make a final offering of a good death.

A genuinely good death is a gift not just to one's friends and family but to society as a whole. A genuinely good death not only requires and inspires patience and courage on the part of the individual; it requires and inspires a matching patience and courage on the part of family, friends and society, because it can be a fearful and paralysing thing to watch a person you love decline, diminish and quite possibly suffer. If the dying person cannot, for good reasons or bad, find the resources to exhibit patience and courage, their family and friends simply have to supply the shortfall. A genuinely good death is a witness from all parties and to all parties that patience and courage are possible, even in the face of profound sadness, even in the face of crippling fear, even in the face of trying and distressing circumstances. A genuinely good death proclaims that God is for us and God is with us and nothing can ever separate us from the love of God. A genuinely good death is a window into the glory of God, a promise that, in Christ, the future is always bigger than the past, a moment of truth that says what lies ahead is not a threat of obliteration but the gift of completion. God has given us the assurance of love and the promise of presence, whatever happens. Let us resolve to present in return the most significant witness we can offer: the gift of a good death.

Nine: Hope

- *I wonder whether you see things half full or half empty – and why you think you're like this.*
- *Tell about a difficult bereavement.*
- *Tell about a person who seemed to live without fear.*
- *I wonder what you think life beyond death might be like.*

The death of Steve Jobs, the man who gave the apple the most attention it's received since the Garden of Eden, and the inventor of sleek devices modelled around the letter 'i', brought renewed attention to a famous commencement address he made about his own illness. The speech at Stanford University in 2005 included these words:

> No one wants to die. Even people who want to go to heaven don't want to die to get there. And yet death is the destination we all share. No one has ever escaped it. And that is as it should be, because Death is very likely the single best invention of Life. It is Life's change agent. It clears out the old to make way for the new.

What makes these words compelling is that here's a man who's found a technological solution to almost everything one can imagine, who's done a corporate resurrection by becoming CEO of a company that ousted him only a few years before, and here he is in the role of dispenser of wisdom, appearing to say that even death can be managed if you go about it the right way. He's so engaging, and he's touching on such a raw nerve, that you desperately want to believe him. And you almost do. This is a man who's found a gadget to fix everything. Maybe, just maybe, he's offering us the greatest gadget of them all. Maybe it's called the iDeath.

But if you've lived through real bereavement and profound loss, I suspect you won't be taken in. Because when you've truly loved someone, and that person is uprooted from existence, and you're left with a gaping hole and an aching soul, there's no wise words or helpful gadgets that can replace the lifeblood you shared or assuage the dizzying dismay of grief. It's like having your lungs taken out so you can't breathe, or your stomach removed so you can't eat. It's as if a bomb blast had created a huge crater in your midriff. In his poem, 'Stop all the clocks, cut off the telephone,' W. H. Auden describes the harrowing emptiness of losing the companion he'd shaped his life around. Auden compares him to the points of the compass, the shape of the week, the time of day and the forms of speech. He concludes with the crestfallen recognition that he'd imagined their relationship would be everlasting. Finally he says, dolefully, 'I was wrong.'

To be a Christian and to contemplate death is to locate yourself somewhere in the yawning gap between Steve Jobs and W. H. Auden. Auden's words are cathartic because they plead that death empties life of all meaning, and they furiously and bitterly throw themselves against the cruel doors of death like a storm wave crashing relentlessly, savagely but fruitlessly against a sea wall. And yet Auden's words are cleansing because he pushes us to restore a sense of balance. It's as if he makes death the only thing he knows, and subjects all other truth to merciless dismemberment in the face of mortality. Sure, death is real, we want to reply, but death isn't all of reality and it doesn't obliterate all that is good and true.

Meanwhile there's something hubristically grating about Steve Jobs' brisk and businesslike approach to death that again makes us look for a sense of balance and yearn for Auden's melancholy. Yet surely Jobs is right at least in this, that maybe death, while sad, is not altogether bad. Maybe most of the things that are truly good about life wouldn't be so good if there were no sense of limitation to make them so rare and precious.

What is our hope in the face of death? Two possible forms of hope present themselves. The first is to conform to the consensus that experiential satisfaction is all there is to long for. Hope becomes the fulfilment of desire – for visible, tangible possession, for deep, evocative feeling, and for abiding, gratifying comfort. The trouble is, death utterly destroys all of these hopes. So the only remedy is to make these desires and their fulfilment so all-consuming that we're able to forget or at least ignore death until the last possible moment. That's why funerals can be so bewildering today. We've evacuated the language of mortality from our shared vocabulary, such that death has become a baffling anomaly.

The second form of hope is to displace a vision for one's own survival and diffuse it into the well-being of all. This is what soldiers do in laying down their lives for their country or for its perception of the greater good. This is what victims' families do when they express an aspiration that the lessons learned from their loved one's death will alleviate suffering or prevent accidents or eliminate malpractice and thus enhance the lives of those to come. Even if most of us live by the privatized experiential satisfaction criteria, when it comes to public statements this is the language we tend to adopt.

Perhaps most of us fuse these two forms of hope, seeking in work and family and a network of friendships some kind of a blend of the experiential satisfaction of the self and the sense of contributing to a greater and one-day-achievable social good. But is this real hope? Is this really much more than an effort of will and imagination and a collective determination to make human endeavour attain a permanence it can never realize?

There is no hope outside God. That's a bleak realization. But flip the coin over and we find that there is limitless hope *in* God. Truly limitless. Literally infinite. How much time and thought and effort and energy we expend trying to find hope elsewhere! But there is none. When you become a Christian, you enter a realm of boundless hope in God. But there's no going back. Leave that realm and you realize how empty and fabricated and sentimental and hubristic and futile all other grounds for hope are. There's nowhere else to go. Nowhere else, that is, to find hope. The cross of Christ tells us that our hope is not without tragedy, not without indescribable cost to God. And many of our lives confirm it. But the resurrection of Christ promises us that out of fear and suffering and tragedy and death arises never-ending, overwhelming, beyond-describing, ever-flowing life in God. The invitation of hope is: are you ready to enter this life at your moment of death? The challenge of hope is: if so, *why not start living it now?*

Ten: Nine Words

- *I wonder what the sense of finality means to you in the context of grief.*
- *Tell about something that was unbearable somehow became bearable.*
- *I wonder what you think resurrection is.*
- *Tell about a moment that changed everything.*

I want to show you resurrection in nine words: nine words that take us from despair to hope, from death to life, from darkness to light.

The first three words are all terrifying words. This is the first: gone. Mary Magdalene comes to the tomb on the first day of the week. And what does she find? The body of Jesus is gone. If ever insult was added to injury. That's the first sensation of bereavement, loss, grief: he's gone. Gone. It's so final, ultimate, irrevocable. So unyielding, uncompromising, ruthless. What an unforgiving word.

And then comes the second word: over. You start to look back on all the things that once were but are no more. The way he walked, with that curious bend at the shoulder. The way his hair parted. The way he laughed. Over. No more laughter. Once it seemed the laughter would never stop, like a joke that kept on getting funnier every time you told it. Do you stay in that place till the reality sinks in? Or do you ever really accept that reality? Over.

But there's a third word that's even worse. Gone is about the present – he's not here. Over is about the past – it's finished. But there's an even more terrifying word that's about the future: never. If gone takes the life out of a body, and over snatches the memories away, never robs us of all hope. Never. It's like a boxing match where gone knocks the stuffing out of you, over brings you down to the canvas, and never goes beyond all mercy and kicks you out of the ring. 'It's not going to happen,' says never. 'Whatever silver lining or small consolation you're holding on to, it's a fantasy.' Never. Brutal, cruel, final.

But here's the fourth word: here. It doesn't add up: Jesus is here. He's in front of her. It's like a scene from a pantomime. Her body's facing the tomb, but her head turns behind her to Jesus. Here. I thought he was gone. But he's here.

And quickly there's another word: now. It's the central word of the nine words of resurrection. Now. This is it. Creation gave us life on earth. But that's a long time ago. On the Last Day we'll be given eternal life with God. But that's a long time away. This is now. This is creation and the Last Day all rolled into one. This is time collapsed into one moment, one man, one woman, in a garden, God in Christ, Israel in Mary, here, now. This is the whole Bible, the whole of eternity in one face-to-face encounter: now.

And here's the word that goes with here and now: new. Is anything really new? Even a tiny baby – surely it's just the recycled DNA of its parents? Well, Mary discovers, yes there is. A person who died in agony two days previously, standing utterly alive and thrillingly real, in front of her, with hands she can grasp and a face she can kiss. That's new. A world made new. A life made new. A dream made new. Oh yes. For sure this is new.

That's what takes place when Mary meets the risen Jesus. 'Gone – over – never' turn into 'here – now – new'. It's the biggest transformation in world history. But there's more. This is the first word of what happens as she tells her story: again. Feel the tremor that goes through your body when you recognize the force of that word: again. You thought it was gone, over, never. But it's again. That's the resurrection: it's both new and again. It's creation repeated and the Last Day anticipated: new and again. Like a hug with your best friend, like your favourite holiday destination, like the most exquisite dessert you know how to cook: new and again. The best two words in the language, and even better together.

But there's another word: always. It ends up being the last thing Jesus says to the disciples: always. 'I'll be with you always.' It seemed each hope was blocked; now every single one is open: always. It seemed the truth was gone, over, never: but it's turned into always. Always and again. A repetition, but a non-identical repetition: everlasting and ever-new. This is now how it will always be. Death will no longer be the perpetual curse in every hope. Regret need no longer be the lingering poison in every memory. Always. Forgiveness isn't going to be withdrawn. Everlasting life isn't going to be curtailed. Read my lips, says Jesus to Mary and Mary to the disciples. Read my lips: always.

And there's only one word left, and maybe we've got so much resurrection we almost don't need it. But it's a crucial word because it takes the tiny episode of Mary meeting Jesus and puts it on a canvas that makes us realize this is the story of eternity, the story of God seeking humanity from before the beginning of time until the end of all things, the story of humanity finally seeking God in return. The word is forever. Mary's agony, of gone, over, never is our insight into the grief of God at our indifference and inertia in the face of eternal love. Mary's agony, deep and crucifying as it is, lasts two nights: God's agony lasts as long as time. But there's something longer, wider and bigger than time: and that's forever. Mary sees the risen Jesus and she passes from time to forever. She discovers what is longer than everlasting, truer than always, beyond permanent. She's looking straight into the heart of forever.

You can't rationally explain grief. We're told it's better to have loved and lost than never to have loved at all. But here's what they don't tell you: only just. You can't rationally explain faith, except to say, it's the astonishing change, the wondrous hope, the indescribable peace that begins in your gut and spreads, perhaps slowly, to your head and your heart and your hands when you realize the three terrible words – gone, over, never – have been engulfed by the six tremendous words – here, now, new, again, always, forever. We have a word for the moment that happens. We call it Easter: here, now, new, again, always, forever.

Commentary

This commentary should be read alongside the commentary for Being With Child. Both courses take risks and in particular consider more than just one context. Issues of bereavement and childbirth are not confined to one episode in our lives: they go so deep they pervade our consciousness for decades afterwards. So it's never the wrong time to do such a course, provided participants have the grace to recognize how tender these issues can be and how easy it is to affect another participant deeply by saying something one never realized could be troubling or hurtful. The important thing to remember is, if another participant is thinking about these things more or less all the time, referring to such things is not a problem; the only problem is closing down the range of legitimate thought or telling someone else what to feel or how to act. It's integral to this and the previous course that differences of background and context are beneficial, rather than inherently problematic.

As with the previous course, the host needs to be clear:

1 tears and other emotions are not a problem to be avoided or suppressed or apologized for;
2 participants are not to comment on each other's contributions except during the discussion time;
3 a participant may say something that makes the host think they need signposting to other services – in which case that should take place outside the session to preserve the participant's privacy and dignity.

Like childbirth, death is a key threshold moment in people's faith journeys. Many are stirred to awaken or reignite faith at such times. So it's an ideal subject for a Being With course. But it's also good to open the course up to people who don't have immediate exposure to or current experience of these issues. We are all dying, after all. The first talk holds side by side the two key words in the course: death and love. It sets the mood for the whole course, that there's a quiet hope of love that transcends death – God's love. But that death is momentous and potentially all-consuming, and even for those who trust and believe, sometimes feels overwhelming in a way that obliterates all other conviction.

Talks two to four cover the territory of the various issues around the end of life, primarily from the point of view of the one caring for or ministering to a dying loved one, all considered within the framework of being with and its eight dimensions. By the end of the fourth session the group should have confidence that all aspects of dying are relevant and worthy of discussion. The fifth talk is similar to the 'Death' talk in Being With Church: it addresses death from the point of view of anyone who foresees their own death with trepidation. Almost no one finds having heard a talk like this before a problem: it becomes a different experience in a new context with different people and at a different moment in one's life.

The next four talks stay with the perspective of the person dying. Talk six is about legacy – what kind of a blessing we might hope to bestow on those who come after us. Talk seven recognizes the true horror of death and considers Paul's words about God's commitment to be with us whatever befall. Talk eight is about dying well: it's an opportunity to reflect on how to prepare for something unthinkable. The ninth talk more specifically addresses what we might anticipate beyond death. In some ways it's the key talk in the course because it should help people confront in a supportive group what it's so difficult to contemplate alone.

The final talk returns to the theme of resurrection touched upon in the opening session. The course earns the right to speak about resurrection because it's been so honest about the depth of anxiety and despair this subject can engender. But by being expressed in elemental, largely monosyllabic language, it retains the intensity of the previous sessions while still ending on a positive note.

7

Being With Yourself

Seven Wonderings and Addresses

One: Be Humble

- *Tell about one of your parents.*
- *Tell about a person you know who doesn't seem to realize how many people it takes to make their life work.*
- *I wonder what you think when you look at a night sky full of stars.*
- *Tell about a time you got cross with someone and then did the same thing yourself.*

Be humble. Remember what it took for you to be here; to think of the imagination of God that brought creation into being – for there could instead have been nothing. Dwell on the many layers of evolution or whatever it took to get from a twinkle in God's eye to the living, breathing being that you are. Reflect on how many of your ancestors clung to life to the point where they could conceive the one whose birth eventually led to yours. Realize by how fragile a thread their existence hung, and how the miracle of your birth is made up of a constellation of other such miracles. And as you contemplate your parents, as you come to terms with both their ordinariness and their fallibility, accept that you would not be here at all without them.

Be grateful. Lord Mountbatten said of Gandhi, 'You would never guess how many people it takes and how much it costs to keep that man in poverty.' But it requires a myriad of angels to keep any single one of us in the life to which we are accustomed. We take for granted that others toil in fields and work in slaughterhouses and travel the earth to bring food to our supermarkets; all we do is produce a card and pay for it. We assume someone will labour night and day to make roads and vehicles and bring oil out of the ground so we can move around. We seldom ask whose sweat produced our shoes, our computer, our shirt (which we boast of having bought so cheaply), and we scarcely pause to consider, when we get a bargain, which link in the supply chain got no reward this time.

Be your own size. There are 100 billion stars in our own galaxy and 2,000 billion galaxies in the universe. Before you tell everyone not to start the party until you arrive, take in the enormity of that reality of which you are the very tiniest ingredient. Before you say to someone, 'Do you know who I am?' ask yourself, in light of the scale of the universe and its venerable age, 'Who exactly am I?' Look at the earth, which you share with so many living beings. Many of the tiny ones scurry and multiply and in hidden ways make it possible for you to breathe, to heal, to digest, to sleep. Realize how you take for granted, when the sun sets, that it will rise again next day. If it wasn't so, what could you do about it? Your life rests in an ecology you will never live long enough to comprehend, still less thank.

Be gentle. Remember the physician's mantra, 'First, do no harm.' In the words of William Blake, 'We are put on earth a little space / That we may learn to bear the beams of love.' There's so much that we've never even paused to imagine. When we look to right and left, we see others who know more or less as little as we do. People tend to do the best they can with what they have and what they know. A little compassion, a little generosity of heart inclines us to look to our fellow creatures with gentleness rather than bitterness, anger or condemnation. How often have you looked upon what another person said or did with horror, fury or scorn, only to find yourself, ten years (or ten minutes) later, saying or doing much the same as them? Be sparing with your horror, fury and scorn, lest they rebound on you and make you lamentable in your own sight.

Be a person of praise and blessing. Recognize that had God not called Abraham there would be no covenant; had God not brought the Hebrews through the Red Sea there would only have been slavery; had God not restored Israel there would have been perpetual exile. Remember that had God not dwelt with us in Christ we would not know we were children of a heavenly Father, made to be God's companions, empowered with the Holy Spirit. If Christ had not died in agony, we would not have discovered we mean everything to God. If Christ were not risen, we would not know our future is in God forever. If the Spirit had not come, we would not know the joy of this good news today. If we had not the gift of baptism, we could not enjoy all these wonders through the church. Like Israel, we were made to be companions to God and a blessing to the creation. No more, and no less.

And when you have taken these steps of humility – the awareness of God, of our neighbour, of the universe, of the weak and of the church – turn over the coin of humility and see that you have been washed in the Jordan, anointed by the Spirit, crowned as one of God's kingdom of priests and clothed with power from on high. Wash one another's feet, be the servant and slave of all, make every act of your life a sacrament of love to others and praise to God: for your existence is a miracle and your redemption is amazing grace. And never cease from singing.

Two: The Challenge

- *Tell about a moment you thought your life might be in danger.*
- *I wonder what you think is uniquely important to your well-being, in contrast to other people's.*
- *Tell about a time in your life when it felt as if you were flourishing.*
- *I wonder what tempts you into pursuing distractions.*

We may reflect on three dimensions of being with oneself:

- First, our basic *survival*, understood as care for the bare essentials of life, such as shelter, income, clothing, food and water; our ability to forge a sustainable existence in reasonable health, comfort and safety; and our imagination or faith about what survival might mean beyond death.

BEING WITH YOURSELF

- Second, our *well-being*, seen as our ability to embody, experience and express the abiding goods of life – such as love, creativity, joy, peace, trust and belonging – in ways that are a blessing to ourself and others.
- third, our *flourishing*, understood as our perceiving, pursuing and, to a significant extent, fulfilling a vocation to a unique trajectory of life in God's realm and/or the church that integrates and employs our personal history – the confused and disturbing elements as well as the proud and satisfying parts – a process perhaps best expressed in the words, 'Strive to be what only you can be; strive to want what everyone else can have as well.'

The strain of being present to ourselves is about withstanding the impulse to divert life into perpetual distraction. This may be because life is too distressing, dull or deathly.

The challenge when life is *distressing* is to resist the temptation to close our eyes (or escape to wonderland) until the crisis goes away. For some, the fervid intensity of danger, of anxiety, of unknown outcome can make life more tangible, more meaningful, more involved than ever before: the adrenaline is running, the emotional barometer is lively, the heartbeat is thudding. Many look back on such episodes as times when they were more deeply aware of what they wanted, needed, loved, craved; moments when senses were sharp and insight was clear. But perhaps more common is the experience that pain, sorrow, anger, injury, regret, disappointment, fear, hurt, loneliness, humiliation or failure are so deep that they are more or less unendurable – and escape into distraction seems the only way to buy time for a while or forever.

It may be that being with oneself at such times truly is unendurable, and that it can only be sustained, for a period, by being with God and being with others. The inability to be with oneself may be somewhat different from the suffering of heartbreak, discomfort or isolation. It may be more about self-rejection. However much one is loved by others, it may seem an insuperable challenge to love oneself. Distraction may seem infinitely preferable to lapsing into self-loathing.

Self-loathing can be a fury at one's own limitations – failures, weaknesses, shortcomings of appearance, intelligence, flair, social graces,

BEING WITH

courage; or it can be mortification for one's sins, betrayals, cruelties, selfishness, envy, meanness. The counsel to 'love oneself' can be profoundly unhelpful if it's heard as advice to accept sin or repent of limitation. To be with oneself means to find ways to separate sin from limitation and embark on a process of forgiving and being reconciled with the former while accepting and coming to terms with the latter. It's vital to avoid accepting what must be repented of or repenting of what must be accepted. Confusing the two constitutes much of the discomfort of being with oneself. By contrast, loving oneself requires a willingness to repent of sin and accept limitation – widely recognized as 'the serenity to accept the things I cannot change and the courage to change the things I can'.

The flipside of life seeming too challenging is life becoming *dull*. If one's need for survival or desire for well-being have not been met then one's life is distressing; if they have been met but our flourishing is elusive, then life may well be dull. If one is missing the drama of a crisis, it becomes tempting to make a drama out of the trivial, just for the thrill of the quickened heartbeat. And a drama often requires an audience, so out of boredom comes not just a crisis but a host of third parties drawn in to gasp or shriek or yell. Such can be the seduction of social media – the impulse to seek in the reactions of others a weathervane or an amplification for our own underwhelming reality, the desire for perpetual 'news' to substitute the novel in the absence of the substantial, and the urge to inflate the ordinary in an effort to stimulate the listless.

Thus the challenges of being with oneself in the face of the distressing and the dull can become avenues into addiction. For a drug is the archetypal form of distraction, one that takes away the acuteness of pain and/ or amplifies the lustre of the flaccid. And addiction is the best analogy for sin: for sin is fundamentally distraction from the reality of being with oneself, God, one another and the creation.

But there is also the challenge of the *deathly*. Being present to oneself is hard because of the inevitability of death. What makes one mortgage the present tense in an effort to preserve it in photograph or indelible memory? Is it not a desperate and yet doomed desire to shore up one's existence against mortality? The deeper human task is to try not to record, retain or embellish one's life, but to live it.

Three: A Child of God

- *Tell about a moment you felt glad to be alive.*
- *Tell about an experience of another culture.*
- *Tell about a friendship that was or is important to you, and what's special about it.*
- *Tell about a time you felt an overwhelming sense of wonder.*

You are a child of God. Think about this in three dimensions. First, the wonder of being alive. We can call that creation. Second, the wonder of being conscious, in relationship, in society. We can call that culture. Third, the wonder of being in relationship with God, now and forever. We can call that Christ. Any of the three would overwhelm us if we allowed them to fill our imagination. But we dwell in all three. Let's take them in turn.

Creation means existence. It means beyond eternal Trinitarian essence, God chose for there to be something else. It's not just our own smallness in the midst of such enormity of galaxies that should engulf us – it's the very fact of existence. The most astonishing of all breathtaking facts is that there is existence – and I'm part of it. There are waves that crash relentlessly on the shore. There's the sun that gives light and warmth. There's blue sky that opens the window on limitless space. There's rain that softens and refreshes. There's wind that rearranges and invisibly presses. Ponder any one of these, or snow, hail, thunder or cloud, and you're lost in depth, texture, newness, replenishment, glory. Then add in earth – soil, vegetation and scales of life – birds that swoop and chirrup, animals that burrow and canter, lizards and insects and micro-organisms. You quickly realize there's a whole drama of existence going on in which humans are ignorant observers or minor characters.

Culture means human existence. It means first of all consciousness, the awareness of being alive, of other people, of the world, of making sense of the world and of formulating plans and acting on them. It means how we interact with one another, how we make meaning, how we find beauty, build trust, discover truth, establish relationship, communicate feeling. It means how we get used to such things, like learning a language, and how we can pick up signals and feel excluded by missing indicators. It means diversity, and rules and preferences and tastes, and skills, talents and gifts. It means how we express ourselves, what we value, what we cherish, seek and avoid. It means how we use things, to cook, to build, to make, to dispose of, to wear. It means art; it means science, engineering, technology. It means the making of micro-existences that can become so absorbing we are unaware of others, unaware of creation, unaware of anything outside a project, obsession, battle or goal. Thus can culture constitute a creation within creation.

Christ means the relationship between divine essence and human existence. There is existence; I am in existence; and yet, astonishingly, the essence that is beyond existence wishes to be in relationship with existence – and to be in relationship with me: to be my companion. The whole of essence is shaped to be in relationship with us, me; and existence – we, I – find no shape unless and until we find relationship with essence. Christ is the point where essence and existence meet. This is our encounter with story. Story is our attempt to make meaning out of disparate events, feelings and experiences – to draw correspondences and resonances between people, things and contexts. Story is the litany of how God encounters us; all story is a shadow, an impression, a ghost, sometimes a parody of the story of God and us. All relationship is an image, practice, preparation, sometimes travesty of God's relationship with us. We have a paradigm of how to meet Christ: be with the hungry, the thirsty, the stranger. We have a pattern of how to conduct such a relationship: eat together, bear one another's burdens, wash feet.

To be a child of God is to dwell in these three relationships in a spirit of wonder. When Jesus says we are to receive the kingdom of God like a child, he's inviting us to retain the balance of awe and simplicity in the face of the glory and complexity of what we are beholding. There is myriad intricacy, in creation, society, God; and yet there is a place for us in all three. There are plenty of occasions when we scratch our heads about the flaws in creation, the woes of society, the mysteries of God. And yet in the end our bafflement is saturated by wonder, the quandary of the question 'Why?' overwhelmed by the quantity of the statement 'is'. We never chose to be alive, we never selected 'society' in a dropdown of possible options, we never identified God as a suitable source of causation, meaning and purpose: these things are all beyond gifts, in the land of grace. Let us wonder – before, and after, we do anything else. Thus we begin to be with ourselves.

Four: Character

- *Tell about something you practised for a long time to be good at.*
- *I wonder what it feels like to realize you should have planned something a long time ago and now it's too late.*
- *I wonder what skill you'd like to develop in the life that lies ahead of you.*
- *Tell about a person who you'd want to be with you in a crisis.*

The predicament of the 12 Thai boys trapped two miles into a cave in the rainy season was as gruesome in its horror as it is gripping in its drama. The two British divers, who discovered the boys, didn't reach them by willpower or luck. It needed relentless attention to detail. It was about years of preparation, careful building of trust and meticulous recognition of reasonable risk.

Looking back on the climax of the Napoleonic wars, the Duke of Wellington reflected, 'The battle of Waterloo was won on the playing fields of Eton.' He wasn't being modest. He was recognizing that the credit belonged to the institutions that had formed people of virtue who thrived in the demanding circumstances of war. The same is true of the Thai cave story. The clue to the discovery of the boys by the divers lay not in Thailand but in the training caves of Wales.

The spiritual writer Donald Nicholl tells the story of two friends discussing the tragic death of a young man on an Edinburgh operating table. One said, starkly, 'I think the surgeon is to blame. He mistook chloroform for ether. I know the man well. He could have become one of the finest surgeons in Europe, but he was more interested in golf. That's how he's lived his life – enough to get through, but no more. That day in theatre a bit of peripheral knowledge was crucial, and he didn't have it.

But it wasn't that day that he failed – it was 39 years ago, when he only gave himself half-heartedly to medicine.'

Jesus told a story of five foolish bridesmaids, whose lamp oil ran out when the bridegroom arrived, and five wise bridesmaids, who took with them enough oil for any eventuality. He's suggesting our character is revealed less by our spontaneous reaction than by our careful preparation.

An athlete trains for months for a marathon race, and no amount of enthusiasm on the day can make up for deficiencies in preparation. A student studies for years for an exam and, again, no amount of thought on the day can make up for deficiencies in preparation. A doctor studies and trains and practises for years to excel in surgery, and no amount of good will on the day can make up for deficiencies in preparation.

News stories focus on dramatic acts of heroism or courage. But such moments rest on long years of training. Those years are about learning to take the right things for granted and developing the skills to do those things when required. A good life isn't primarily about dramatic acts of selflessness, but more about decades of faithful preparation for the moment of truth. The battle of Waterloo was won on the playing fields of Eton. The battle for the young man's life was lost on the golf course. The search for the Thai football team was won deep in the training caves of Wales.

There are two moments: one, the time of moral effort; the other, the time of moral habit. The time for moral effort is the time of formation and training. This is 'Eton'. Training requires commitment, discipline, faithfulness, study, apprenticeship, practice, cooperation, observation, reflection – in short, moral effort. The point of this effort is to form skills and habits – habits that mean people take the right things for granted, and skills that give them the ability to do the things they take for granted. The time for moral habit is the 'moment of decision'. This is 'Waterloo' or 'the operating theatre'. Waterloo and the operating theatre separate those whose instincts have been appropriately formed from those whose character is inadequately prepared. In every crisis, the real decisions are ones that have been taken some time before. To live well requires both effort and habit. There is a place for both. But no amount of effort at the moment of decision will make up for effort neglected in the time of formation.

Learning to live well, or being with oneself, is about cultivating the right habits rather than making the right choices. If one has the right assumptions and habits, many things others might experience as crises of choice will pass without one being aware of them. Meanwhile, if one has not developed such habits, decisions that do arise are likely to be insoluble. It is only moral effort and formation in the past that can offer freedom from impossible moral effort in the present.

Thus being with yourself isn't something you can suddenly choose to do: it takes years of cultivation. It's less like a building and more like a garden: it grows and needs pruning – but it's not something you can snap your fingers and make happen.

Five: Habit

- *I wonder what it feels like to tell someone you've done something really bad.*
- *Tell about a bad habit you have.*
- *Tell about a good habit you've carefully developed.*
- *I wonder what it's like to repair a relationship that went wrong.*

The spiritual life is not like a building, perfect on the day it is opened and gradually decaying every day thereafter. It's more like a garden, sparse to begin with but growing every day and needing regular pruning to prevent healthy growth becoming wild or overbearing. The way to develop a sense of self is to cultivate habits.

It's often said that life is about choices. People who get into trouble are often said to have made 'bad choices'. But a life based on perpetual choice would be a nightmare. Habits deliver us from the tyranny of perpetual decision. The point is to develop good habits. So here are six habits to cultivate a sense of self.

- Habit number one: look inside your heart. Examine yourself. Find inside yourself some things that shouldn't be there. If they're hard to extract, get some help. Name them by sitting or kneeling down with a trusted friend or pastor, and just say, 'These things shouldn't be there. I can't keep confidences. I get very envious. Please help me let God take them away.' In other words, repent. But repent by following or at least looking at Jesus. Because when we're in the presence of Christ, there's no need to pretend or hide. He already knows and he's longing to welcome us back. Self-examination isn't just about finding things that shouldn't be there. It's also about finding things that are there but have been neglected. That's sometimes where vocation begins. Look inside your heart. Make a habit of it.

- Habit number two: pray. Don't get in a pickle about whether to pray with a book or just freestyle, do both. Once a day each. Simple as that. Think about the way you shop. Sometimes I shop with a list; sometimes not. Sometimes it's a pleasure; sometimes it's a necessity; sometimes it's a pain. Sometimes I go with someone else, or even help someone else to go; sometimes I go on my own. Sometimes it's about big things; sometimes it's about little things. Sometimes I really think carefully about it, and check through a kind of recipe list; sometimes I just do it and realize later what I've forgotten. Sometimes I'm overwhelmed by the wonder of the variety of goods and products; sometimes I'm cross about globalization, climate change, treatment of factory workers and materialism. Prayer's just as varied. Just do it: put yourself in the presence of God. Maybe just sitting still for five minutes is the most countercultural thing you can do. Make a habit of it.

- Habit number three: fast. There are three dimensions to fasting. The first is about power. It's about toughening yourself up, so you don't go all pathetic at the first smell or sight of something sweet or tasty. It's about making yourself someone to be reckoned with and not a pushover. Learn how to eat and when to resist eating. Make a pattern of life so you don't just drift to the phone or computer as a transitional object. Get your senses and your self-control in some kind of balance. The kind of thing Jesus did in the wilderness. The second dimension of fasting is to stand in solidarity with those who don't get to choose. If you can't give up a single meal, do you really care about global hunger?

And the third dimension is learning how to be really hungry. Hungry for righteousness. Hungry for justice and peace. Make a habit of it.

- Habit number four: give money away. There will never be a time in your life when you think it's a good time for giving money away. Giving money is like long queues at the checkout and inside lanes on the motorway – they're for other people. Try to tie your money to your prayers. Give money to something you believe in, and pray for the organization you give money to. Start with your church. After all, if it wasn't for the church, none of us would know there was any good news about Jesus, and unless there's a church in a thousand or a billion years' time, no one will know then. Don't make a fuss about it. Make a habit of it.

- Habit number five: read the Bible. Imagine you were going into a crowded airport to meet someone you were longing to see but weren't sure you'd recognize. And imagine you had a photo album of pictures that showed them in a thousand different activities. Wouldn't you study that photo album so you'd almost committed it to memory? That's what the Bible is – a series of portrayals of God. And we study it to get to know God better so we'll have no recognition problems in a crowd. Find a nether region in the Bible and go digging. Buy an accessible commentary and follow a few verses each day. Make a habit of it.

- Habit number six: repair broken relationships. This is the last one, and for many people, the toughest. We've probably, many of us, got one big relationship that's all wrong – and maybe there's not a whole lot we can do about it. Maybe it's just a matter of keeping out of someone's way, if we've done them wrong, or trying to be civil, if they've hurt us. Now may not be the time to make things better. Now may not yet be God's time. But that doesn't mean we let all our other relationships get to that kind of place. Is there someone out there, a sibling, a rival, a long-time friend, a person who always felt inferior to you? Could you write that person a letter to say some things you've always appreciated about them but you've never told them? And what about people whose names you don't know, people from whom you are estranged without ever having done the damage yourself? Could you make a friend on the other side of a cultural or political divide? Make a habit of it.

So those are six habits to develop a sense of self. Examine yourself, the ill that's there and the good that's neglected. Pray, with a formal book and just any old how. Fast, to train yourself and to be in solidarity. Give money away. Read the Bible. Repair broken relationships.
Six ways to cultivate the garden of your soul.

Six: Being Your Own Friend

- *I wonder what it means to be your own friend.*
- *I wonder what it means to live fully in the present tense.*
- *Tell about a person you know who has real physical or intellectual challenges and what they've taught you.*
- *I wonder in what way you'd describe yourself as disabled or differently abled.*

Delight is the finding of hidden and surprising treasures amid the green field of oneself. Sometimes those arise from unearthing previously unknown or unaffirmed talents; more often, it comes from the conversion of aptitudes into skills through education and training, application and regular habit. Delight is about joining a late starters' orchestra, about taking up rock and roll dance classes, about developing green fingers in a newly acquired garden, about discovering still-life painting, about learning cross-stitch or starting to cycle long distances. It's about taking pleasure in being with oneself, not because the activity makes one fit or wins acclaim or produces food or attracts a partner, but because through it one discovers one's limbs, one's fingers, one's eye, and develops one's touch, taste and smell. Delight takes the two-dimensional and makes it three-dimensional, adding texture, depth, quality to what had previously been passing, superficial or ordinary. It turns still waters into a fountain of life.

BEING WITH YOURSELF

Participation and partnership embody the notion of becoming one's own friend. Participation is the essence of with – in this case, the sheer rejoicing in being alive, the consciousness of breathing, eating, awaking, moving, speaking, the ability both to live and to be aware that one lives, the naming, cherishing, relishing and celebrating of physical existence. Most of life isn't experienced like that – but more as a relentless struggle for advantage, pondering of regret, planning for new possibility, enduring of hardship, desire for elusive fulfilment. Participating with oneself means being able to detach past frustration and future fear and simply dwell in the present tense.

Those who live with a severe inherited or acquired physical disability or impairment have much to teach about this sense of participation. When people facing such challenges receive wide public attention, it invariably highlights particular individuals' ability to overcome their physical limitations and achieve great things: it becomes a tale of the triumph of the human will and spirit. But perhaps more important, and more common, is what it means to accept one's physical limitations, even or especially when they are much more considerable than most people's, and learn to love and enjoy the body you have rather than covet the body someone else has. 'We're all disabled – in some people you can't see it' is a helpful slogan; it carries more authority coming from a person in whom you can see it, but who nonetheless has found ways to be with themselves that inspire imitation and provoke emulation. When people become exasperated as they advance into old age, this same ability to be with oneself is often the point at issue. It takes patience, forbearance, gentleness and persistence – qualities valuable at every stage of life, but indispensable in old age.

A related place of learning and understanding concerns those whose disability is intellectual and whose apprehension of the world can sometimes exhibit an engaging naivety and attractive simplicity. Such people can offer an example to those who find it hard to be with themselves. It's not uncommon for people to speak of being transformed by being with a child with profound intellectual and/or physical disability. It may be that such transformation is attributable to the infectious way such a person can take their own existence for granted and evidently be free of the protracted self-doubt, self-criticism and anxiety that pervades so many adult lives. Perhaps this is near the secret of Jesus' mysterious words, 'Unless you change and become like children, you will never enter the kingdom of heaven. Whoever becomes humble like this child is the greatest in the kingdom of heaven.'

Partnership refers to working to best effect by apportioning the tasks to the most suitable people. Partnership with oneself means being aware of one's location across time and among others. Being with oneself across time means recognizing that one may be young and expect one day to be old; or one may be old, having once been young. 'For everything there is a season, and a time for every matter under heaven ... a time to weep, and a time to laugh, a time to mourn, and a time to dance ... a time to embrace, and a time to refrain from embracing ... a time to keep, and a time to throw away ... a time to keep silence, and a time to speak.' To say 'I can't do this' may be a cause of anger, disappointment or impatience; but such feelings may be transformed by the ability to say, 'I can do this – but this is not the season.' Being with oneself among others means wanting to say, 'I would like to have done this', or, 'I feel I should do this', and instead being able to say, 'I'm perhaps not the right person to do this', or, 'It's clear another person would be more suitable to do this than me.' Thus is being with oneself turned from the self-absorbed cultivation of envy, resentment and avarice into a harmonious understanding of the flourishing of oneself alongside the flourishing of others.

Seven: Self-love

- *Tell about a person who asked more of you than you could give.*
- *I wonder what it's like to say no when the other person won't take no.*
- *I wonder what it feels like when someone says, 'Call yourself a Christian ...'*
- *I wonder what it means to love yourself in a good way.*

You're on the phone. The conversation's getting pretty intense. The voice says, 'I need you to come.' You pause. You say, 'I'm sorry, I can't come right now.' The voice says, 'But you said you didn't have plans for this weekend.' You pause a bit longer, on a knife edge between emotional exhaustion and nagging guilt. You say, 'I'm sorry, I need a bit of time to myself.' 'OK,' says the voice, bitterly, 'I get the message.' Ouch. Nagging guilt wins again.

I'm taking a hunch that you've had that phone call. And you know that tussle between nagging guilt and emotional exhaustion. After the words 'OK, I get the message', the trump card, spoken or unspoken, is 'I thought you were supposed to be a Christian.'

Because being a Christian is taken to mean 'permanently open to emotional exhaustion, physical burnout, psychological manipulation and relentless guilt'. Prepared to go to any lengths, in fact, to avoid being called 'selfish'. Two hundred years ago the French philosopher Auguste Comte coined the term 'altruism'. Altruism means living a life for others. Since then, a great many people have assumed altruism was what Christianity was really all about. It may have been Comte that C. S. Lewis was thinking of when he said of a fellow parishioner, 'She spent all her life doing good to others. You could tell the others by their hunted look.' We all know people who seem to say, 'Because I'm worn out being so noble to others, that makes it OK for me to be short-tempered, mean and ungenerous to you.' Altruism assumes that in order to love others more, you need to love yourself less. It takes love to be a zero-sum game, where if you give in one place you have to take away somewhere else. This is a grim view of the world in which someone always has to suffer and love means that that someone should be you.

When you're on the phone to the person who wants more from you than you can give, the assumption is there's only two options – altruism or selfishness. Is there another way?

Selfishness says, 'No one's looking out for me, so I'd better take as much as I can while I can so I have plenty for when things turn bad.' Selfishness says, 'The truth about me is terrible, so I'm going to get all I can and pig out all I can until someone finds out the truth and the game's up.' Selfishness isn't a sign of too much self-love: it's quite the opposite. It's a sign of profound insecurity. It's a moment of panic that says there's no eternal assurance and so I must grab and go.

BEING WITH

For those who've always been told that you should live for others and always put others before yourself or risk being called selfish, here's a suggestion. When you hear the words 'Love your neighbour as yourself', swap the words round and say, 'Love yourself as your neighbour.' In other words, regard yourself as the first among all the neighbours God calls you to love. The God who has a lot to be doing with the whole creation has chosen to start with you. The language of altruism never really grasps this. It makes loving others seem impossibly hard work, because it assumes that you have to choose between loving yourself and loving others. But God loves every one of us while still loving each of us as if we were the only one. We're able to love others because of the way God loves us. And to accept that love, we have to learn to love ourselves.

Let's go back to that phone call. Remember, the best way I can to teach you to love *your*self is to love *my*self, because being a Christian requires me to love myself as I love you. We left the call where you say, 'I'm sorry, I need a bit of time to myself.' 'OK,' says the voice, bitterly, 'I get the message … I thought you were supposed to be a Christian.' Maybe this is what your friend needs to hear:

'If you go on like this, in your insecurity, looking anxiously for appreciation, you're going to make yourself and others miserable. You'll live in the wilderness, wandering unhappily, searching desperately for the affirmation that never sufficiently comes. You'll be a nomad, demanding from everyone, yet belonging nowhere. You're greedily seeking attention for yourself and when you don't get it, you're calling people names for not satisfying your limitless demands. The truth is, I can't give you what you most deeply need. You're asking something from me that only God can give.

'And God is longing to give it to you. You've tried to build yourself up on your own strength and on other people's approval. It's not working. Maybe it's time you learned to accept that God adores you. God knows you inside out and yet he still adores you. If you can only accept that, then you won't be looking for affirmation and approval from me and others like me all the time. You'll begin to see yourself as God sees you, gloriously made, profoundly confused but bursting with gifts and delights. You'll stop looking relentlessly for rewards and recognition. You'll discover that the kingdom of heaven is yours. You'll never be an exile and never be in the wilderness. You'll be everywhere at home. And you'll have nothing that you weren't longing to share with friend and stranger. Most of all, this good news.

'Speak to you after the weekend.'

Commentary

Being with is about four relationships: with God, with oneself, with one another and with the wider creation. The original course works by giving opportunity for the third in such a way that invites reflection on the first. There's a whole course below on the fourth. This course focuses explicitly on the second. Rather like Being With Child earlier and Being With Creation later, this course takes a different tack from what might be a conventional approach. There's nothing about self-esteem, self-care or, for example, the potential harm of social media. Of course there's no reason why such issues shouldn't arise in the responses to wonderings or in the discussion. But this course, like the other two courses mentioned, seeks to offer something not so commonly available elsewhere. That something is a sense of what a healthy relationship with oneself might be.

It's quite possible the course will evoke profound feelings among participants – of self-doubt, guilt, self-rejection, despair, frustration, sadness, grief or anger. Any of the Being With courses can do this. As usual the host's role is not to be frightened of such things, to set an atmosphere of trust and acceptance, to avoid any temptation to comment, compare or fix, and in cases of real concern to signpost to other forms of support.

Like Being With Child, the course begins with placing participants in the biggest possible context: it's about diverting attention away from oneself and decentring participants from the conversation. While there's an important place for addressing our own issues, it's good to begin by recalling we're not the centre of the universe.

The second talk is introductory and framing in a different way: it distinguishes between three understandings of well-being so each may be addressed in its own right without being confused with the others. The third talk builds on the first by expanding on the explicitly theological implications of putting God rather than us at the centre of the story, and thus embarking on a renewed sense of identity.

The next two talks are more constructive. They concern the building blocks of integrity: character and habit. They're not quick fixes, but they point to where true self-love lies. Finally, there's a more playful account of what it means to be one's own friend, based on a relatable scenario.

The course is deliberately shorter than most, seeking to avoid morose self-reflection, and designed instead to stimulate and energize participants in their attempts to make small, positive changes in their lives that come out of a genuine relationship with themselves rather than a series of rapid fixes. It probably works best for those who've done one or two other Being With courses, as unlike the other courses it makes no attempt at any comprehensiveness or profound theological content.

8

Being With Creation

Ten Wonderings and Addresses

One: A Crisis

- *Tell about a time when you were overwhelmed with the glory of nature.*
- *Tell about something about which you've long felt guilty but towards which you've never really changed.*
- *Tell about one thing you've seen change, partly as a result of your own actions.*
- *I wonder what it's like to see someone or something lose their/its soul.*

Have you ever sat still in the early morning and heard the dawn chorus? Have you ever felt your heart rise in a throbbing ovation as the birds of the air form an orchestra of glory and voice creation's praise?

In 1962 the conservationist Rachel Carson published a book entitled *Silent Spring*. Carson pointed out the way pesticides were coming to dominate American agriculture and were damaging not only birds and animals but also humans. Just imagine, she said, a spring in which no birds sang: it would be a silent spring. And if that spring lies in the not-too-distant future for the birds, how long before humanity meets the same fate? First, there will be a silent spring; eventually, there will be no spring at all.

Those who marked the first Earth Day in 1970 credited the publication of *Silent Spring* with the beginnings of the modern environmental

BEING WITH

movement. And Carson's book marks a suitable emblem for ecological concerns, because it synthesizes the four dimensions that have characterized the movement ever since.

The first is the urgent sense of human catastrophe. Ecological concerns, such as those raised by Rachel Carson, have a wide following, but what makes them a focus of universal anxiety is the claim that they threaten to diminish human flourishing in the immediate term and terminate human existence in the medium to long term. 'We're all doomed.' That kind of threat makes the ecological movement unique in its claim on the public imagination. It's a slow-burning version of the threat of nuclear annihilation that mesmerized people's vision at the height of the Cold War.

The second dimension is the profound sense of grief that these environmental threats all have a human cause. This isn't a crisis that's coming from the outside. This is a crisis humans are bringing on themselves. I recall a conversation with an activist friend who was estranged from the church. I asked her what she so disliked about Christianity and she said the biggest thing was that the clergy were always talking about sin and it all seemed so negative and bitter and judgemental and life-destroying. I then asked her why she was so passionate about ecology and without a second thought she launched into a tirade about how people were damaging the air, the earth and the seas, and she wanted to spend her life changing their hearts and minds and reversing the damage they'd done. I said to her, 'Who's the one talking about sin now? You sound more evangelical about the environment than most clergy are about Jesus.' The ecological movement may use different language, but it's generally a lament for human participation in destroying habitats for other creatures and ourselves, and a call to repentance and a new way of living. The earth is like an oppressed and enslaved people, and ecologists are shaking their finger like Moses saying to Pharaoh, 'Let my people go.' For many environmentalists, the question of human survival is just the tip of the iceberg: what's at stake is an economic, social, ideological and sometimes religious transformation.

The third dimension that's found in Carson's book and among the great majority of environmental campaigners is a sincere optimism that

BEING WITH CREATION

the ecological crisis is something that can be significantly addressed through public policy initiatives, through legislative change, regulation and prescription. *Silent Spring* is a great motivator for activists, because the uproar caused by the book led John F. Kennedy to set up a commission to investigate its claims, which in 1972 led to the banning of the insecticide DDT in America, a ban extended globally 30 years later. In 1972 the first United Nations Conference on the Human Environment was held in Stockholm, Sweden, and the public forum on the fate of the earth convened in earnest. Henceforward the great debate in environmental circles has been between idealists, who want to promote a different way of life that's not based on a predatory relationship with the earth, sky and seas, and the pragmatists, who want to focus the movement on achievable legislative regulation. The earth is like the *Titanic* propelling itself towards the iceberg, and the earth's richest nations are like the *Titanic*'s owners saying 'Faster! Faster!' Of course, the problem with the *Titanic* was not that it didn't have a rudder but that the captain didn't use it. In just the same way, say the activists, it's not too late for the earth to change course, once people accept how catastrophic our present navigation is.

But *Silent Spring* also represents a fourth dimension. It imagines a spring with no birdsong: no chirruping, tweeting or crowing. In other words, it imagines the earth without a soul. This is a different kind of concern. Its question is less about the preservation of the planet and its inhabitants, including us, and more about the qualities that can't be measured or assessed. How do you quantify the value of a bird's song? How do you estimate the impoverishment of a sky without the waft of beating wings? Even if the planet can survive humanity's prodigal path of self-destruction, will something precious and beautiful and irreplaceable be lost?

Threat, guilt, change and soul. These are the four dimensions of the ecological challenge. They were all visible in 1962. What will it take for us to respond to them?

BEING WITH

Two: Whose Crisis?

- Tell about a time you felt you were in a lot of trouble and there was no obvious way out.
- Tell about a time when you passed the blame to others that you really should have accepted for yourself.
- I wonder what part of the ecological crisis you feel is the most important part.
- I wonder what part of the crisis feels closest to home.

Briefly put, the ecological crisis is this: the rate of extinction of species is at around 10,000 per annum. Biodiversity has been drastically reduced by deforestation, deep-sea fishing, destruction of coral reefs and use of pesticides. Climate change is accelerating and is especially being caused by the burning of fossil fuels for heating, transportation and electricity production. This is leading to rising sea levels, increasing numbers of cyclones and the melting of the Antarctic ice shelf. Pollution is widespread in oceans, rivers, air and soil. CFC emissions led to a hole in the ozone layer and consequent skin cancers in humans and mammals, especially in countries close to the Antarctic ozone hole. Meanwhile, soil erosion and desertification have been steadily increasing, linked to overgrazing, industrial tillage and the use of inappropriate land (for example, hillsides) for arable production.

The real question is, whose problem is it? There are roughly four answers to this question, and those four answers tell us what we need to know about the whole issue.

The first answer is, the problem is one for governments and corporations. This sees the problem as largely a technological one, caused by the side-effects of technological advance, and to be solved in much the same way. It's sceptical about the potential of sweeping cultural changes: in reality people are not going to abandon their addiction to the car; jet flight is not going to cease; those in developing countries, notably India and China, are not going to desist from desiring the same level of fossil fuel consumption that Americans and Europeans take for granted. It's pragmatic about setting timescales, identifying milestones, establish-

BEING WITH CREATION

ing a critical path towards a broadly similar lifestyle that has far fewer deleterious environmental consequences. The reality of international agreements is that a good outcome largely depends on the US and China acceding to ambitious carbon-emission-capping targets, and in the end only one argument is persuasive: that their own long-term well-being depends upon it. While currently the enforcement mechanisms on high-polluting countries are not sufficiently binding, this approach places its confidence in the market to disinvest in carbon-reliant companies, and governments to introduce policies that have an eye to long-term security. In short, the whole issue is one that can be budgeted for and managed and resolved.

The second answer is, the problem is one for the global poor. From this perspective, global warming is a cerebral and long-term issue for the rich and comfortable: it's a present and tangible issue for the world's poor. Those living in poorer countries, and those on the economic fringe of wealthier countries, are disproportionately affected by climate change. The irony is that these are the people least responsible for causing the ecological crisis. A 2009 report claims that already 300,000 people a year are dying from the effects of climate change – and a further 4 billion are affected by drought, floods, crop failures, reduced agricultural yields, the loss of low-lying lands and islands, and desertification. The danger is that all the efforts of the last two generations in poverty reduction are being undone by climate change, and that bringing more people out of poverty may exacerbate that change. From the perspective of governments and corporations, this may look simply like another management challenge. But from the point of view of the global poor, the disproportionate cost of global warming on those who've done least to bring it about is the height of the injustice that lies at the heart of global trade and economic relationships. Not only have the rich despoiled their lands, but they've caused ecological crisis – and then retreated to leave the poor facing that crisis alone. To see this is to perceive a different kind of ethics, one that prioritizes the poor and believes the rich governments and corporations don't just need to manage the crisis, they need to be held to account and face sanctions and offer concrete reparations. The issue isn't management, it's justice.

The third answer is, the problem is one for the earth itself. I vividly recall a congregation member in my first parish saying, 'You clergy aren't really the church. You'll be here for a while and then you'll move on. We, the congregation, are the real church. We'll be here long after you're forgotten.' The same could be said of humankind's relationship to the planet. We're the priests of creation, fostering and facilitating and enjoying and ordering creation. But the world was here before us and, quite possibly, it'll be here long after we're gone. We've done more damage than any previous species. But arguably the damage has been largely to ourselves. The earth will find a way to recover from the impact we've had on it, even if it takes a billion years or two. But what we do to the planet may make it impossible for our own species to survive. It's important to keep that sense of perspective. Humanity has the ability to do a lot of damage, but the earth will win out over the long term, however much damage humanity does to it. The issue for humanity is less whether there'll be a future for the planet than whether there'll be a future for itself.

And that brings us to the fourth answer, which is, the problem is in the end about God. Not a problem *for* God: if humanity destroys the planet, or makes it uninhabitable, God is perfectly capable of creating a new planet, or a new species to be in special, incarnate relationship with. Instead, a problem arises as an almost inevitable result of seeking a world without God. St Augustine makes a distinction between what we use and what we enjoy. He says that what we use is of limited value and serves mainly to enable us to reach what we enjoy. It quickly runs out and is largely a means to an end. By contrast what we enjoy is an end in itself. It never runs out. It is of value for its own sake. The ecological crisis, in Augustine's terms, is simply expressed: we have used what should be enjoyed. How do we learn to enjoy and not simply to use? That perhaps is the most pressing question of our times.

Three: A Crisis for Christians

- *I wonder whether there's something that seems to bother a lot of people but doesn't really bother you.*
- *Tell about a time you thought you'd ruined everything but it turned out you hadn't after all.*
- *I wonder what's the best way to say thank you.*
- *Tell about when what seemed like a major problem became an opportunity.*

Why is the ecological crisis a problem for Christians? Some would say, it isn't a problem for Christians. Here there's a good argument and a bad argument. The good argument is that God is God. If God has our destiny in hand, then a mere setback like the depredation of the earth isn't an insuperable problem. Surely if we were to ruin the earth, God could just reach into a divine storehouse and bring out another earth that just happened to be lying around for such an eventuality; or even make one specially. This is a good argument because it puts things in perspective. It's true that human sin can never be sufficient to divert the ultimate will and purpose of God. Our sin is never so bad that it can overshadow God's grace. We can destroy the planet, just as we can destroy our lives and the lives of others; but we can't destroy what God will finally make of our lives or the life of the planet. In lamenting the condition of the earth, let's not make humanity too big by exaggerating our ability to ruin everything or make God too small by forgetting that this is always a story about God that we get to play a part in, not the other way round. Christian concern for the environment can't be about self-preservation. It must be based on something else.

Here's the bad argument. If you say Christians hope to be with God forever, and if you say that that life is the union of our soul with the eternal Trinity, then the rest of planet earth, besides human beings, is one of three things. It could be an instrument that can bring us closer to God, through experiences of intimacy, wonder or joy, and thus like a ladder we can kick away when it's got us to the place we need to be. It could be a luxury, like a set of clothes, that make our earthly life more congenial, but aren't fundamentally necessary. Or it could be a limitation that imprisons us, through entanglement, distraction or ensnarement, like a straitjacket, that threatens to keep us from our heavenly home. If the created order is a ladder, a luxury or a limitation, then the environmental crisis isn't a major problem, because the earth isn't something we fundamentally need and depend on.

So the reason Christians care about the environment is not because if we don't we're toast. The reason is that if we're not interested in the home God has made to dwell in with us now, how can we claim to be eager for the home God has made to dwell in with us forever? By the way we enjoy the playground God has given us to enjoy today we show God how deeply we long to dance with the Trinity in eternity. If we don't treasure the earthly theatre of glory God has given us, God can only assume we're not interested in entering the heavenly one. Cherishing creation is the way we show God our gratitude, the way we humbly acknowledge our creatureliness, and an important way in which we worship. Polluting earth, sky and seas, depleting habitats, overfarming land and ocean, eradicating species – such practices tell the rest of creation it's disposable, tell the rest of humanity that its survival is secondary to our comfort, and tell God that we're bent on obscuring eternal grace with temporal consumption. This is sin, in its simplest definition: being so short-sighted that we wilfully shut ourselves out of God's abundance and imprison ourselves in our own scarcity. And we're all a part of it, however often we visit the farmers' market, however many times we sign an email with a pious message about saving paper, however frequently we sprinkle our conversation with words like sustainability and ecojustice.

Those who marked the first Earth Day on 22 April 1970 credited the publication of Rachel Carson's *Silent Spring* with the beginnings of the modern environmental movement. Since then, the ecological cause has gathered pace with each new revelation of the predicament into which humankind has plunged itself. For Christians, the environmental crisis may be a problem. But it's certainly an opportunity. It's an opportunity because Earth Day is perhaps the greatest ever parable of the Christian story. Earth Day celebrates the wonder of creation, in its abundance and diversity. It recalls the day the birds began to sing. Earth Day calls us to repentance when we remember the fall, the human destruction of God's precious gift. It portrays the day the birds fell silent and forgot how the song was supposed to go. But Earth Day does more than that. It reminds us that there was a bird that came to earth and taught us the tune we'd forgotten, making our hearts sing again. And that there will come a day when all creation sings: not just the birds, but the rocks and stones and oceans and mountains themselves will cry 'Alleluia'. And that in the meantime we remember this story by the way we sing and seek to turn our lives and our world into a song. We remember this story by the way we inspire others to sing with us and find in themselves a voice they never knew they had. We remember this story by singing this song back to those who've forgotten it until they remember how it goes.

That's what Christians do in the face of the ecological crisis. They make every day Earth Day. Thus Christians turn Earth Day into what it was always destined to be: Heaven Day.

Four: Enjoying Creation

- *Tell about a time you really enjoyed something.*
- *I wonder if anyone has ever truly enjoyed you.*
- *Tell about a pet that made you or someone else really happy.*
- *Tell about a time you were so absorbed in something you became unaware of anything else.*

Consider a pet dog. Here is presence, constant, abiding, trusting, affectionate presence. Here is attention, devoted, unwavering, perhaps a little self-interested, but nonetheless unblinking attention. Here is mystery, a creature that serves no purpose but companionship, solves no problem but loneliness, brooks no estrangement without immediate reconciliation, holds no grudge, turns to no other master, lives for no joy beyond cherishing and exercise and food. Here is delight, in the simple but abundant moments of satisfied desire, in the gambolling of the meadow and the bounding across the stream, in the diving into the lake and the thrill of chasing a ball, in the utter relish of being alive and releasing energy. Here is participation, for no walk is complete without a dog, and no dog without a walk; it seems churlish to have lunch without sharing some, unthinkable to have breakfast alone, impossible not to spend part of the day together. Here is partnership in some small way, when the guardian character of a barking puppy is welcome in a place of danger, when the warmth of a breathing companion gives succour on a cold mountain. Here is enjoyment, when a bundle of love and loyalty comes into a household with little practical purpose but, when absent or departed, is missed with a scorching wound of echoing grief. Here is glory, for when we see those sad, trusting eyes, the disciple sees the eyes of God – the eyes of the one who adores us, longs for our company, would happily spend eternity with us, forgives our every selfish betrayal and sets aside our every doubting hesitation. We see the eyes of one who never has anything more important than us, who would give and has given anything to be our constant friend, who has little or no thought for the past but can only imagine the glorious things that lie in store for us together.

Such enjoyment in a domestic sphere discloses the nature of enjoyment in relation to God and the creation more generally. The skies, seas and soil offer countless invitations for wonder, fulfilment, recreation, discovery and, increasingly, repentance. In this myriad of ways the creation exists to be enjoyed, and being with God and the creation, amid 'Graces human and Divine, Flowers of earth, and buds of heaven', is a sacrament of praise.

The goal of being with the creation is to enjoy the world as God enjoys it.

An ibex is a large and very rare mountain goat, about 5 feet tall. The male has enormous, ridged horns that curve all the way round to his back. I once climbed a mountain up to 12,000 feet and suddenly caught sight of an ibex 300 feet away. I gently stepped closer and closer. This wasn't a moment I could grab with a quick photograph and move on. If I was going to see the ibex close up, even though I'd already been walking six hours, I had to change my plans for the day. Softly and slowly I went closer and closer, one careful step at a time. I saw its proud chin, its huge curving horns stretching back behind its head. Finally I was 20 feet away from this prince of the mountains. And how I *enjoyed* that moment. I don't know how long I was there. But I felt so privileged and moved and deeply, deeply alive. *That's* what it means to enjoy creation. That's how God enjoys us.

Five: Delighting in Creation

- *Tell about a beautiful place.*
- *Tell about something in nature that captivates you.*
- *Tell about a time you felt fully alive.*
- *I wonder, if you awoke in heaven, what's the first thing you'd see.*

In two famous poems William Wordsworth captures the way the created world moves the soul. Wandering 'lonely as a cloud', he sees 'a crowd / A host, of golden daffodils ... Fluttering and dancing in the breeze'. They are having their own celebration, independent of him: 'Ten thousand saw I at a glance, / Tossing their heads in sprightly dance.' There's a whole chorus of created joy going on: 'The waves beside them danced; but they / Out-did the sparkling waves in glee.' He paused little at the time, yet it proves the sight has changed him for good, for in moments of solitude they flash upon his inward eye: 'And then my heart with pleasure fills, / And dances with the daffodils.'

Later, in his poem 'Tintern Abbey', Wordsworth returns to a place of beauty last seen five years before, and once again sees 'These waters, rolling from their mountain-springs / With a soft inland murmur.' Even though he has long been away, Wordsworth has continued to dwell on these remembered images, and in weary and lonely moments has been stirred by the way with 'the deep power of joy, / We see into the life of things'. Wordsworth equates this wondrous seeing with the anticipation of eternal life, for at such moments, he says, 'we are laid asleep / In body, and become a living soul'.

Wordsworth's delight in creation is truly enjoyment and exaltation in it for its own sake; but he also explores how the memory of that delight comforts him in his loneliness, even his fear of death, ennobles his mundane experience, inspires and animates his gestures of generosity, and gives him an insight into the life eternal, when he will perpetually have that sense of joy and ability to 'see into the life of things'.

Thomas Traherne is the great prophet of delight. He points out that ingratitude is among the worst sins of all. How should we practise gratitude and embody delight? This is Traherne's favourite subject.

> Your enjoyment of the world is never right till every morning you awake in heaven; see yourself in your Father's palace; and look upon the skies, the earth, and the air as celestial Joys: having such a reverend esteem of all, as if you were among the angels ... You never enjoy the world aright, till the Sea itself flows in your veins, till you are clothed with the heavens, and crowned with the stars: and perceive yourself to be the sole heir of the whole world ... Till you can sing and rejoice and delight in God, as misers do in gold, and kings in sceptres.

Traherne prescribes what qualities are required to be a person who can so take delight and give thanks in all things. He says:

> You never enjoy the world aright, till you see all things in it so perfectly yours, that you cannot desire them any other way: and till you are convinced that all things serve you best in their proper places ... you must have ... a clear eye able to see afar off, a great and generous heart, apt to enjoy at any distance: a good and liberal soul prone to delight in the felicity of all, and an infinite delight to be their Treasure.

And this is not simply about appreciating the creation around us. It is about one another and the ways of God. He goes on:

> Your enjoyment is never right, till you esteem every soul so great a treasure as our Saviour does: and that the laws of God are sweeter than the honey and honeycomb because they command you to love them all in such perfect manner ... God commands you to love all like him, because he would have you to be his [child], all them to be your riches, you to be glorious before them, and all the creatures in serving them

to be your treasures, while you are his delight, like him in beauty, and the darling of his [heart].

Delight is equally about detail and about awesome extent. Creation is ordered in the minutest specifics, and there is no ending to the wonder to be had in examining how intricately organisms and creatures are calibrated and how textured are the ways they relate to one another. At the same time, creation is on an unimaginable scale. We can have no idea how many universes there were before this one began 14.8 billion years ago, and how many there may be after this one comes to an end – it could be dozens, or billions. But such contemplation makes us realize that the ecological crisis is a crisis not so much for creation but for humans. Creation will find a way to absorb, transform, adapt and eventually recover: but its future may be uninhabitable for human beings. That would be a tragedy for us; but perhaps not for creation. And it would have happened because, unlike Traherne and Wordsworth, we have forgotten how to enjoy and delight, and have remembered only how to use and exploit.

Six: Participating in Creation

- *Tell about a time you were at an advantage because you knew the local conditions well.*
- *I wonder whether you're more at home in city or country, land or sea.*
- *Tell about a time you felt it didn't matter what you were doing, just whom you were doing it with.*
- *I wonder what, if we're going to enjoy heaven, we'll need to learn to live without.*

In the Old Testament story of David and Goliath, the Israelites are scared of the Philistines, when one enormous Philistine, named Goliath, steps forward to challenge the strongest Israelite. Up steps David, a shepherd boy. David sweeps aside the armour he's offered and simply takes a sling and five smooth stones. With the first one he strikes down the mighty Goliath and wins the day for the Israelites.

David's power isn't physical strength or sophisticated equipment. It's his familiarity with his surroundings and his comfort with being outdoors. He knows how to keep sheep. He knows where to find smooth stones. He knows how to craft a sling. He knows how to snare an animal, even a lion or a bear. He knows the tricks of the forest and the wilds of the woods. He challenges each of us to ask, when was the last time I felt my created nature and sharpened my wily wits by spending some time in the fields, in the streams, in the mountains? Have I so surrounded my life with gadgets and comforts that I've forgotten the exhilaration of the hillside breeze? David learns from his outdoor life the wisdom of the owl, the cunning of the fox, the agility of the wildcat, the sharp eye of the eagle. Because he's with creation, creation, when it matters, is with him.

The Bible relishes the different settings of wilderness and desert, village and pasture, town and city, lake, river and sea. It's not that one context is blessed and the others are of lesser worth; the point is how we couldn't have the whole story of the Bible without all of these settings. A life that's spent largely indoors and is restricted to the city – and an existence that's immersed in electrical gadgets and rapid forms of transport – is one that is always in danger of losing touch with the hours, the seasons, the source of food and the perils of subsistence. The eyes that never behold the stars lack a nightly reminder of the smallness of the earth in the universe.

This is known as participation. Participation is being with in its simplest form, because it sets aside awareness of different levels of skill, power, experience or ability. It just concentrates on being with one another – in this case, our being with creation and letting creation be with us. The reality that faces the world today is that the fruits of the Industrial Revolution have seriously, indeed grievously, depleted the earth's ability to sustain itself. It's hard to envisage that depletion significantly slowing, let alone being reversed. While the romantic poets enjoyed the earth, most of their successors have used it. What needs to change?

We need to learn to be with creation: to participate with creation. So much energy has been given to establishing and identifying ways in which humanity is distinct from the creation. Does humanity's uniqueness lie in its being able to talk, or to reason, or even to pray? Or is humankind's uniqueness simply that God chose to be its companion and in Christ walked the earth in human form, thus singling humanity out for bearing the divine image? So much attention in interpreting the scriptural creation accounts focuses on humans as being made in the image of God and about their subduing the earth and having dominion over it. What's lost in this emphasis is the with – humankind's being with the creation. It's as if the anxiety is always how humanity is to be with God, and the risk is that being with the creation will somehow drag humanity away from being with God. What needs recovering is the sense in which humanity is *part of* the creation – first of all not its owner or controller or conqueror, but its companion. Perhaps humanity will save the earth by being with it and becoming its companion, just as God saves humanity by becoming our companion in Jesus.

Participation with the creation thus yields confession and lament concerning the ways humanity has used rather than enjoyed the creation, especially in the last century or more. Environmental destruction is less about what some terrible people have done somewhere and more about what humankind has come to take for granted almost everywhere. Before it hastens into intercession, a congregation needs to pause and be thankful and express wonder at the many-splendouredness of creation and the privilege of humanity's being part of it. Humanity has arguably lost the moral authority to be trusted to pray for the wider creation. Thus if intercession follows, it should be from a place of being with the creation rather than a modified form of stewardship on its behalf. And it should be accompanied by humble, concrete and perhaps radical steps to change the way a congregation relates to fuel, food and transport, and not just by demands for others to be transformed.

BEING WITH

Seven: Partnering with Creation

- *Tell about a time you didn't know what to say and were glad someone said it for you.*
- *Tell about a moment when something in nature provided what you really needed.*
- *I wonder whether you've ever used something you realize you ought instead to have enjoyed.*
- *I wonder why you are or are not a vegetarian.*

Partnering with creation most obviously means moving from depleting non-renewable resources to fostering renewable ones. Creation has awesome qualities for bringing forth gifts that furnish human flourishing; but if humans use up those gifts faster than creation can replenish them, both humans and the creation suffer and the damage can be irreparable. The simple motto is look after creation and creation will look after you. This applies on global, local and personal levels.

The simplest way to think of humankind's partnership with creation is to perceive how creation invites prayer – both of praise and of intercession. The poet Gerard Manley Hopkins sees God as the giver of superabundant channels of grace: 'The world is charged with the grandeur of God. / It will flame out, like shining from shook foil.' This is an inexhaustible gift. He goes on: 'nature is never spent; / There lives the dearest freshness deep down things.' Prayer means perceiving that dearest freshness and shaking that shining foil. To pray outdoors, particularly in the fresh air of relative solitude, is to behold a heavenly host of items that can be seen as windows into God's mercy. In George Herbert's words, 'A man that looks on glass, / On it may stay his eye; / Or if he pleaseth, through it pass, / And then the heaven espy.' To pray in partnership with the creation is to pass through its glass and espy heaven.

The notion of partnership challenges any view that assumes the creation is primarily or wholly there to benefit and resource humankind. In the scriptural account of Jesus being tempted in the wilderness, we read he 'was with the wild beasts; and the angels waited on him'. More explicitly in the Old Testament, we are told of the prophet Elijah, 'The ravens brought him bread and meat in the morning, and bread and meat in the evening; and he drank from the stream.' So there's no question that animals can work with God and human beings to further flourishing life on earth. As for the wider creation, human partnership with God's action, exercised through soil and sea, is the stuff of harvest hymns: God 'sends the snow in winter, the warmth to swell the grain, the breezes and the sunshine, and soft refreshing rain'. While human beings plough and scatter seed, that land 'is fed and watered by God's almighty hand'. The analogy between God's bringing of the crops to fruition and the readying of humankind for salvation is again a theme of Henry Alford's harvest song:

> All the world is God's own field,
> fruit as praise to God we yield;
> wheat and tares together sown
> are to joy or sorrow grown;
> first the blade and then the ear,
> then the full corn shall appear;
> Lord of harvest, grant that we
> wholesome grain and pure may be.

Being with creation breeds humility not only that human life could not exist without the way the creation ministers to it, but also that the way creation experiences growth and harvest, the way life is recycled for nourishment, offers a parable of how humans face their own connectedness and death.

The irony of the ecological crisis is that, while it has been humankind's failure to be in partnership, let alone participation, with the creation that has brought the planet to the prospect of disaster, it requires an unbalanced form of partnership – with the creation doing all the 'work' – for the earth to be brought back from the brink. The ecological crisis is perhaps the most obvious case imaginable of using what should be enjoyed: what needs to change is the balance between what humankind believes is for its use and what it recognizes is simply to be enjoyed. To confuse the two is the essence of sin.

The language of participation and partnership helps clarify what's at stake in the vexed question of vegetarianism. Those who assume being with the creation means humans cannot consider eating meat pursue participation as the essence of being with. Those who believe it is justified and appropriate to eat meat regard partnership as the relevant dimension. If with is all, as for participation, eating meat is clearly out of the question; it's hard to imagine how eating an animal could be part of being with that animal. Hence people's squeamishness about eating the family cow or the domestic hen – because in such cases the with is impossible to obscure, but their relative ease in eating industrially generated meat from animals whose identity, still less personality, is entirely unknown. By contrast partnership affirms the different roles of respective parties. In this case, those different roles mean that humans eat animals but resist animals eating them. Animals, in this sense, are to be used rather than enjoyed. Again, the domestic pet is the exception – the family cat is to be enjoyed rather than used. To decide the issue of vegetarianism is to work out whether participation or partnership takes precedence.

Eight: New Creation

- *I wonder how you imagine heaven.*
- *I wonder if heaven comes to us or we go to heaven.*
- *Tell about a time when something that had been dismantled was reassembled.*
- *Tell about a time you worshipped in a way that made you feel alive.*

The last two chapters of the book of Revelation are the most vivid account of what Christians understand by glory. John sees 'a new heaven and a new earth', and 'the holy city, the new Jerusalem, coming down out of heaven from God', with 'the glory of God and a radiance like a very rare jewel'. It turns out 'the city has no need of sun or moon to shine on it, for the glory of God is its light, and its lamp is the Lamb'. A loud voice proclaims that God will dwell with humankind as their God, and they will be God's people: being with will be the nature of God's relationship with the creation. The city is a garden city, and John sees 'the river of the water of life, bright as crystal, flowing from the throne of God and of the Lamb through the middle of the street of the city. On either side of the river is the tree of life with its twelve kinds of fruit … and the leaves of the tree are for the healing of the nations.' Here is the fulfilment of creation with a tree proving the location of its healing as it was of its fall and its redemption.

Here too is the reassembling of creation arrayed around the throne of grace. This is the climax of being with the creation: that every creature, and every element of the sentient and non-sentient creation, indeed the whole universe, find its fulfilment and its ultimate role and purpose in discovering the revelation, in whatever way attunes to their level of consciousness, that God is with them. For eternal life is being with God, with one another and with the renewed creation, forever. The creation and God enjoy one another, forever.

How do we learn to enjoy and not simply to use? The principal place is in worship. In worship we reorder the world so as to enjoy that which otherwise we would simply use. Every created thing has a source and a destiny: it may be a gift to us, but we should never assume that gift is our possession; rather it's a reminder of where it came from and what purpose it serves in the kingdom. Wine comes from the grape and exists to embody Christ's blood in the Eucharist; bread comes from grain and exists to convey Christ's body.

To dwell in the world in such a spirit of worship means to exult in the sheer abundance of the world and the universe beyond. It is a form of resistance to the pragmatic, bureaucratic, utilitarian culture widespread in so much human society, and a celebration of the existence of things for their own sake. This should be the spirit of every act of worship: it is a joy to be alive, to be redeemed, to be a child of God, to be placed in such a great story, to live among such glorious dimensions of God's creation. The seventeenth-century poet Thomas Traherne captures this vocation to enjoy creation. He says,

> When things are ours in their proper places, nothing is needful but … to enjoy them. God therefore hath made it infinitely easy to enjoy,

by making everything ours ... Everything is ours that serves us in its place. The Sun serves us as much as is possible, and more than we could imagine. The Clouds and Stars minister unto us, the World surrounds us with beauty, the Air refresheth us, the Sea revives the earth and us. The Earth itself is better than gold because it produceth fruits and flowers ... By making one, and not a multitude, God evidently shewed one alone to be the end of the World and every one its enjoyer. For every one may enjoy it as much as [God].

Thus the goal of dwelling with the creation is to enjoy the world as God enjoys it.

Traherne articulates perfectly the state of mind that's missing in humanity's maltreatment of creation. There is currently plenty of lament for how humankind has lapsed into the habits that have brought about the ecological crisis. But that lament seldom comes close to Traherne's ability to convey what a right relationship might feel like. This is the aspiration of being with creation.

The calling of the church is to anticipate God's realm, to inhabit today the way it will live forever. We usually take that to mean living God's future now in social relations – to act justly, love mercy and walk humbly with God and one another, to seek a society where none are oppressed and all can flourish. But the challenge of being with creation is to recognize that living God's future now just as much means treating creation as such a society, and seeking the flourishing of the created world just as much as we do that of our fellow human beings. There was a time when Christians thought of a detached soul as abiding in God after the body had perished. But if we now believe resurrection is of the whole person, body and soul, we must at the same time realize that means a restored order of creation in which humanity will continue to take its place within and alongside, but not above, creation. Only so can it and creation flourish now and forever.

Nine: What can we do? I

- *Tell about a time someone told you you were in the wrong – and they were right.*
- *Tell about a time you realized you had to make a change – and succeeded in doing so.*
- *I wonder if there's one thing you could do differently that would affect the climate crisis.*
- *I wonder what the word 'solidarity' means to you.*

Think of a person living in two generations' time facing the extreme consequences of climate change and imagine what they'd be saying to you about what they wish you'd done differently. I'm going to set out what I suppose they might say, over this session and the next.

We begin with humility. It's the beginning of the gospel: repent. Recognize how up to your neck your life is in the practices and habits that have got us into this mess. Don't begin by hectoring the fuel extractors or denouncing the grossest emitters or berating the ozone destroyers. Accept almost all of us are immersed in a system that has made ecological depletion the inevitable fallout from human mastery of the planet. See it this way: there's humanity, the centre of the story; there's everything else that grows on or lives in or inhabits the planet; and there's limitation – be it limited length of life, or strength, or speed of movement, or comfort, or breadth of diet, or a hundred other things. For centuries now we've been playing a game, which goes like this: how can humanity use those other constituent elements of this planet in its fundamental project of overcoming its limitations? Everything – be it silicon, titanium, oil or ivory – has been corralled into this project. Almost every strategy for addressing climate change has been about working out how we can find renewable resources with which to continue this project. When will the time come when we start to question the very foundations of the project itself – the idea that we spend our time on earth seeking to overcome limitation by using those living or inanimate things with which we share our ecosystem?

BEING WITH

When I say repent, I don't simply mean 'Continue to consume at exponentially increasing rates, but be sure to check those resources are renewable.' I mean spend serious time reflecting on how much of our lives is shaped by the assumption that our mission is to make life that little bit longer, run the race that bit faster, eat food that bit more exotic, wear clothes that bit more stylish. Somebody has to pay for all these things we call progress, and further down the food chain beyond low-wage workers and unsavoury animal conditions comes the finitude of the earth and eventually life itself, of which this whole project is a denial. Humility means facing the truth that we're all invested up to our necks in this project. So we're not calling on some wicked Them to change their behaviour or parental Government to fix things for us. We're realizing that if I want the world to change, I need to let that change begin with me. And it's not about being forced to change – it's about genuinely wanting to. That's the first step: humility.

Then there's solidarity. Lying at the root of so many of the great leaps of progress was a sense of escape – that those in possession of the new technology could not only escape from the limitations of being human but could get beyond and out of reach of the great mass of humankind into a place of safety, comfort and fulfilment. Likewise at the root of much of the denial and complacency of the last 40 years has been the sense that it won't actually affect me. It may be tough on Venice, Bangladesh and the Maldives, but I'll have access to enough protective devices to seal me off from whatever damage it does. The pandemic clarified some of the issues about the ecological crisis. Covid-19 was not something you could easily seal yourself off from. It was no respecter of wealth or status. Like the climate emergency, those with resources could more often protect themselves. But the rich and fit and young died too, or were bereaved, or experienced debilitating long-term effects.

Solidarity changes our notion of the word 'we'. The pandemic exposed the absurdity of thinking any of us, individually, locally or nationally could seal ourselves away. The climate emergency is the same. Even if you're not living on a sea-level island or farming temperature-sensitive crops, the effects will reach you soon enough. There's only one 'we' now – and that's the global 'we'. The only way to address the pandemic was as a global community. What used to be charity or imperial paternalism became now simply enlightened self-interest. It's like the difference between the ethics of wearing a seat belt and of smoking a cigarette. Not wearing a seat belt endangers yourself. Smoking a cigarette endangers everyone around you. There's no individual climate crisis. It's an everybody thing. But the 'we' in the climate emergency isn't just about everyone today. It's about everyone who comes after us. 'We' now includes all future life on this planet, for hundreds, thousands, millions of years. It's a big 'we'. There's no escaping it.

We may say there's nothing especially Christian about these two steps. That's back to humility. Christians have to accept that their notion of heaven has too often been used as a form of escape that protected them while others were lost, and that their notion of salvation has too often been seen as a kind of technology that enabled their mastery over human limitation. So Christians joining the climate campaign is a form of repentance and solidarity, rather than I told you so. Sometimes you just have to accept that others are representing your principles better than you are.

Ten: What Can We Do? II

- *Tell about when another person has changed your mind by their example.*
- *Tell about a time you asked a person or organization to keep their or its promises.*
- *I wonder what you hope for, for yourself and for the world.*
- *I wonder what it means to say following Jesus and responding to the climate emergency are the same thing.*

Last week we spoke about humility and solidarity. The third response to climate change is example. What inspires? Example. What changes hearts and minds? Example. What empowers the inhibited, dismantles inertia, outflanks cynicism? Example. Let me take you by the hand and walk you, online or tangibly, round the initiatives, communities and projects around the world, and show you something that will make you change your mind. It's all in the word 'show'. We can protest, we can march, we can boycott, we can vilify, we can picket, we can sabotage, we can research, we can lobby, we can campaign, but what really changes the imagination is example. It's in the imagination that transformation really happens. A church is not fundamentally a building; it's a living example of what the Holy Spirit can do among people committed to pool their assets, work together, seek a beautiful life and open the windows to let God in. A church is built on humility, because none of us can do this alone, and solidarity, because together we can be more than the sum of our parts, we can be one body whose many members all have a vital role to play.

Let's imagine I was to ask a local congregation, 'What do you belong to?' Many would say their church. Some would say a political party or a national institution or a trade or professional body. Some would have looser affiliations, like a daily newspaper they subscribe to or a neighbourhood association they support. If we estimate how many we'd each have, there would likely be a lot of overlap, so we'll call it five. If there are 40 people in the average church, that makes 200 affiliations straightaway. Imagine we said, 'I'm going to make it my business to use all my influence to make each of those organizations an ecological example. An example of humility and solidarity – about fuel, food, waste, air quality, local sourcing of products, about all the things we all need to take for granted.' This is how a society changes. Not simply by government directives – we've all seen the complexity and inequity of that in the last 18 months – but by changing what we all take for granted, what people disapprove of but tolerate and what people no longer tolerate. It's happening about race, about gender equality, about sexuality, about online hatred. It needs to happen about ecology. You try to set an example – you fail; people point the finger – but what do you do then? You don't stop trying. You try harder. That's the transformation of example.

The next step is accountability. Accountability names the way people who generally think of themselves as powerless, or small cogs in a big machine, get to bring about large-scale change. When we're talking about governments or multinational corporations, a lot of us can feel there's little we can do. In fact what we can do comes down to three questions.

BEING WITH CREATION

We ask, 'What state do you want the world to be in in 50 years' time?' Then we ask, 'What are you going to do about it?' Then we ask, 'And have you done it?' With this third question, we're simply saying, keep your promises. We want to extract more far-reaching promises. But promises count for little if they're not kept. Accountability is the name for the way we hold people to the promises they've made.

Finally, there's hope. We approach the climate emergency with two sets of facts. One, the universe is made up of 2,000 billion galaxies, each of which has 100 billion stars. We're small beer. Two, the universe has existed for 14.8 billion years, humankind for 200,000 years, and civilization for 6,000 years. We're the blink of an eye. The universe and the earth will manage just fine without us. The climate emergency is crucial not for the planet's survival *but for ours*. Those realities should only expand our wonder at the central conviction of the Christian faith: that God chose this planet and this species with which to be in relationship, and God is invested in us however badly we get that relationship and our relationship with the planet wrong. By investing in the planet's future, we're aligning ourselves with God's investment in it and in us. God so loved the world that we might love it too. Our hope is not that we can save the world, or that God will save us whatever happens to the world, but that God in Christ will be with us whatever happens – whatever, wherever, however, forever.

Over this week and last we've talked about humility, solidarity, example, accountability and hope. We can see them as the shape of Jesus' life; in Bethlehem he humbled himself to be born as one of us, in Nazareth he lived in solidarity with us for 30 years, in Galilee he set us an example of courage and sacrifice, on Calvary he faced the accountability of the distance between us and God, and at Easter he gave us hope that nothing can separate us from him. All of which shows us that following Jesus, responding to the climate emergency and renewing our faith aren't rival projects. They may turn out to be the same thing.

BEING WITH

Commentary

This course and the one following, Being With the Other, head in a different direction from the other courses in this book because they reflect not just on the participants' experience but also on unresolved and pressing issues in the world at large. Perhaps more than any other of the ten courses in this book, Being With Creation offers an approach that differs from that available elsewhere. There are plenty of 'What you can do to save the planet' books and courses, and there are a good many Christian versions, most of which share an essentially theological approach that assumes it's all up to us and anything we do or don't do will be crucial. What these courses miss is that the planet is not what's in danger: human existence is what's in danger. The startling realization is that the planet will find a way to adapt and in due time flourish without us. So the real issue is how we understand our dependence on the planet and learn to shape our lives of faith with this dependence as a central feature. The course does conclude with two sessions entitled 'What can we do?', but these only come after eight sessions that seek to reframe the conversation from the terms in which it's conventionally configured.

The opening talk introduces the issues and frames them in the context of crisis. This is a way of creating a playing field where all participants understand and share the terms of the discussion. The second talk gradually and gently shifts the conversation from one about human survival to one about God. It's striking how little of the public debate, even in the church, is in any meaningful sense theological. This talk opens the door to what that discourse might entail. The third talk continues in this vein and explores themes of gratitude and preparation for heaven. The next five talks explore our relationship to creation through some of the eight dimensions of being with. It may be worth noting that when writing my twin books *Incarnational Ministry* and *Incarnational Mission*, I placed being with creation in the first volume, understood as an aspect of discipleship, that is, a form of being with God, rather than the second, an aspect of being with the world, because I came to realize the wider creation is principally to be encountered through the lens of worship – worship of the living God through the glory of creation – rather than of service or repair or some form of saving or rescue. Creation is the theatre for God's being with us. It's only secondarily something to assist us, or something of value independent of us. Like everything else, it's made for relationship, and the principal relationship (and the reason for the creation of all things) is God's desire to be with us in Christ. If we don't respect and honour the wider creation, God will find another way to be with us; but we will have shown God we don't cherish the chosen way for God to be with us, and thus dishonoured God and God's foundational purpose.

The course concludes with two talks on the subject of what we can do – but not in an atmosphere of panic; rather in a way that remains true to the principles and goal of being with.

9

Being With the Other

Ten Wonderings and Addresses

One: Abundance

- *I wonder what it feels like to be full up.*
- *I wonder how it feels not to have enough.*
- *I wonder how it feels to have too much.*
- *Tell about a time you turned away a gift or resource that it later turned out you needed.*

This course assumes that the fundamental reason for regarding the other as a threat not a gift is the myth of scarcity. By contrast this course assumes that God gives us everything we need. Everything we *need* doesn't always mean everything we *want*. It doesn't mean everything we need to live a long, healthy life free from suffering, disappointment, frustration or loneliness and full of achievement, recognition and contentment. These things may be welcome blessings in any human life – but they are not to be mistaken for following Jesus. Following Jesus means learning to want the limitless things God gives us in Jesus.

Scarcity assumes there's not enough information – we know too little about the human body, about the climate, about what makes wars happen, about how to bring people out of poverty, about what guides the economy. There's not enough wisdom – there are not enough forums for the exchange of understanding, for learning from the past, for bringing people from different disciplines together, and there's not enough intelligence to solve abiding problems. There are not enough resources – world population is growing and there is insufficient access to education, clean water, food, health care and the means of political influence. There's not enough revelation – the Bible is a lugubrious and often ambiguous document, locked into its time, unable to address the problems of today with the clarity required. Fundamentally, this whole assumption of scarcity rests on there being *not enough God*. Somehow God, in creation, Israel, Jesus and the church, and in the promise of the eschaton, has still not done enough, given enough, been enough, such that the imagined ends of the Christian life are and will always be tantalizingly out of reach.

By contrast, the truth is that God gives everything we need. God gives us everything we need in the past: this is heritage; and everything we could imagine in the future: this is destiny. God gives us the Holy Spirit, making past and future present in the life of the church. God gives us a host of practices, ways in which to form Christians, embody them in Christ, receive all that God, one another and the world have to give us, be reconciled and restored when things go wrong, and share food as our defining political, economic and social act. The things God gives are not in short supply: love, joy, peace, patience, kindness, goodness. Conventional accounts of our human predicament overlook, ignore or neglect those things God gives in plenty and concentrate on those things that are in short supply. In the absence of those things that are plentiful, we experience life in terms of scarcity.

Indeed if we have a problem, the 'problem' is not that God doesn't give us enough, but that God gives us too much. There's too much God. The human imagination is simply not large enough to take in all that God is and has to give. We are overwhelmed. God's inexhaustible creation, limitless grace, relentless mercy, enduring purpose, fathomless love: it's just too much to contemplate, assimilate, understand. If humans turn away it's sometimes out of a misguided but understandable sense of self-protection, a preservation of identity in the face of a tidal wave of glory.

Our encounter with the other begins therefore with a sense of our own neediness, but also a confidence that God is in the habit of giving us more than we need. What matters therefore is that we adopt appropriate ways to receive it. The parable of the good Samaritan is conventionally read as an inspiration to benevolence; we see ourselves in the kindly Samaritan, not the curmudgeonly priest and Levite. But if we identify with the man in the ditch, the story asks us to understand the Samaritan as Jesus – who brings hope and healing, restores us to life and promises to return. The question then becomes, if the Holy Spirit is offering us abundance, are we prepared to receive it in the form in which it comes? Our predicament is our reluctance to accept God's abundance because we refuse to respect or value the people through whom the Holy Spirit brings it.

Meanwhile, 'When did we see you naked?' is a question that echoes through our imaginations and our consciences. Jesus was naked on the day of his crucifixion. He was hungry and thirsty on that day too. Hence his cry, 'I thirst.' Jesus was also a stranger: hence the words, 'He came to what was his own, and his own people did not accept him.' He was sick: in Gethsemane his sweat became like great drops of blood falling down on the ground. He was led away to prison after Judas' kiss. And on each occasion his people failed to be with him. And so the irony of the six acts of mercy is their simplicity: give food, give a drink, welcome, clothe, care, visit. Not end famine, heal disease, reduce recidivism; just the simplest encounter, which requires face-to-face meeting without a solution or cure or even panacea to hand. Here's the promise: if we can have the courage and humility to open up this encounter, we will meet Jesus. Whoever bemoans scarcity has been told where to find abundance.

Being with is both the method and the goal of engagement with the other: actively being with the other, and just as importantly letting the other be with us.

Two: Rejection

- *Tell about a time you were told you weren't needed.*
- *I wonder what it feels like to be a misfit.*
- *Tell about someone you got to know because you were both left out.*
- *I wonder what it's like to be invited back into a place from which you were once excluded.*

Imagine a child going to the beach. That child can spend a half hour sorting through pebbles to find which ones look as if they would skim well. The child picks up a handful of stones and sifts through them, tossing most of them aside until finding one worthy of being hurled, flat side down, into the incoming tide.

What's it like to be those ones that are rejected? Rejection keys into our profound feelings of unworthiness, of being useless, peripheral, no more than a passenger in a world full of drivers. It makes us feel stupid, ugly and unlovable. It digs into a place that suggests, 'This would all be much better without me.' Either you fight the rejection and risk being seen as a person who just doesn't get it, or you accept the rejection and assume the identity of someone whom the world would be better off without.

A community leader once said, 'You know, we're a bunch of misfits who somehow fit together.' What he was recognizing was that, rather than rebelling against feelings of rejection, he'd found that if the community worked constructively with them, they could become something rather beautiful. People often use the word inclusion; but inclusion isn't really the right word, because it suggests there are a bunch of people in the centre whose lives are normal and sorted and privileged, and they should jolly well open the doors and welcome people in and be a bit more thoughtful and kind and generous. This is such a patronizing and paternalistic model. When the community leader said, 'We're a bunch of misfits who somehow fit together', he wasn't regarding himself as normal and secure and somehow above it all: he was one of the misfits too. He was reframing the whole idea that there was a centre and a periphery, where the centre gave kindly hospitality to the periphery, because the cost of that idea is that the periphery feels humiliated and the centre feels smug.

When Peter stands before the Sanhedrin, called to account for how he's enabled a crippled beggar to walk, he looks back into Israel's story, in which God had founded the kingdom not on any of Jesse's tall and powerful sons but on David, the youngest and weakest. Peter quotes Psalm 118, which describes the choosing of David with the words, 'The stone that the builders rejected has become the cornerstone.' And Peter identifies that rejected stone as Jesus. In his crucifixion Jesus was rejected by the builders – yet in his resurrection he became the cornerstone of God's abundant life.

The film *Pride* tells the true story of a group of lesbian and gay activists in London in 1984. They realize that the way society, media and government despise them is equivalent to the way the same forces think about the miners, who are in the midst of their titanic struggle with the Thatcher government. The lesbian and gay activists get it into their heads to reach out to a depressed mining village in South Wales. The film shows how with patience and forgiveness, grace and solidarity, and a lot of courage and resilience, prejudices on both sides are gradually dismantled and an amazing alliance grows up. The film ends with coachloads of miners coming unanticipated to join the 1985 Gay Pride march in London. It's an astonishing turnaround. Together these two groups of stones that the builders have rejected set aside bitterness and self-pity and find they've become one another's cornerstone. A bunch of misfits somehow, beautifully, movingly, somehow fit together. It's an icon of what church can be; what church should be.

The church is down in the dumps because it thinks it needs to be full of big and strong and powerful people. But Jesus was the stone the builders rejected and in his ministry he surrounded himself with stones that the builders had rejected. Jesus didn't found the church on the so-called centre – the sorted, the normal, the benevolent and condescending. Jesus assumed the church would always need the work of the Holy Spirit – the work or miracle, of subversion, of turning the world upside down. Nothing has changed, except for a lot of the intervening years the church has forgotten who Jesus was and whose company he kept.

We're not talking about a bland and affirming insight that a lot of people who have been overlooked in life turn out to have some important things to contribute. That's true, but what Peter sees is more radical than that. The stone that the builders rejected didn't find a place in the wall somewhere by being thoughtfully included like a last-minute addition to a family photo. The rejected stone became the cornerstone, the keystone – the stone that held up all the others, the crucial link, the vital connection. That's what ministry is all about – not condescendingly making welcome alienated strangers, but seeking out the rejected precisely because they are the energy and the life-force that will transform us all. If we're looking for where the future church is coming from, we should look at what the church and society have so blithely rejected. The life of the church is about constantly recognizing the sin of how much we have rejected, and celebrating the grace that God gives us back what we once rejected to become the cornerstone of our lives.

On the night before Jesus died Peter rejected him. He denied him three times. Jesus was the stone Peter rejected. But Peter became the stone, the rock on which the church was founded, and Jesus, the rejected one, became the keystone. If we see Jesus in the face of the ones we have rejected, we can let the Jesus we discover in them become our cornerstone.

Three: Identity

- Tell about a time you felt humiliated.
- Tell about a time you felt 'They don't know the real me.'
- I wonder what it feels like for someone like you finally to be recognized.
- Tell about a time when you couldn't understand why someone was working against their best interests.

In his book *The Republic*, the philosopher Plato talks about three parts of the human soul: reason, desire and judgements of worth, like pride, anger and shame. This explains why a person who is well off, and has a rewarding family and social life, can still feel fury at being humiliated, for example if for no good reason a colleague is paid more for doing the same work. Ancient societies were hierarchical. No one was thinking about identity, because their social role was determined by their age and gender. But the growth of cities and the change in patterns of ownership and production transformed aristocratic societies into democratic ones, and stratification was replaced by equality. However, not everyone was content with equality: it seems part of human nature for many to strive to be better than others – to be recognized and applauded and celebrated.

Martin Luther was the first to speak of the difference between our inner and outer selves. Authenticity names the process by which we come to identify the true character of that inner self and live into that identity, even if that makes us different in significant ways from the norms of our society. Martin Luther transformed the world from one in which the individual had to conform to the demands of society to one in which society had to conform to the truth of the individual.

The eighteenth-century French philosopher Jean-Jacques Rousseau argued that negative urges only arose when individuals encountered society. Society triggered comparison. Society is made up of rules, relationships and customs that inhibit human potential and happiness.

The nineteenth-century German philosopher G. W. F. Hegel located human dignity in the fact that human beings uniquely had a choice. They are not just governed by the impulse of their desires: the choices they make are fundamentally driven by a struggle for recognition. The French Revolution proclaimed an equal dignity for all people and thus universal recognition.

So identity for Plato is about worth, for Luther it's about grace, for Rousseau it's about disentangling yourself from society, and for Hegel it's about recognition. But from this point on, the story gets more complicated – and that's for one particular reason. Freedom sounds as if it means equal dignity for every person under the same rules. Yet it can also mean free expression of individuality and the creation of one's *own* rules. For some, that free expression is an amazing liberation and has led, for example, to the recognition of the rights of women, LGBTQ+ people and people with disabilities. For others, the opportunity to identify and define who you are has been overwhelming, leading them to take refuge in collective identity.

BEING WITH THE OTHER

Hence the rise of nationalism as individual liberty took hold in the nineteenth century and throughout the twentieth century and again today. Nationalism is driven by the desire of a group that its suppressed identity gains public recognition. It tends to arise when rapid social change undermines familiar forms of community and generates bewildering new forms of collectivity. Nationalism is fuelled by a sense of invisibility: citizens who once regarded themselves as the bedrock of a shared culture now find themselves ignored and despised by a political class that fundamentally doesn't see them. So populism grows as the reassertion of the identity of the common, collective citizen in the face of the technocratic system.

The political left used to be the traditional advocate of the collective interest of the working class and the economically exploited. But in the last generation the left has become more associated with offering recognition to and upholding the dignity of specific identity groups – groups that in many cases don't just want equality but want to change the culture in order to achieve the recognition they seek. Which is why we find the paradox that many of the voters whose economic interests would put them on the left have instead gravitated towards the right in search of validation and recognition of the dignity of lives that see identity in the mass and the imagined normal, rather than the distinctive and the different. This is how the politics of populism and the culture wars works.

Contemporary society still trusts in Rousseau's conviction of humankind's inner goodness and his confidence that our inner selves are sources of limitless potential, and that human happiness depends on its release. This assertion has led to what's been called the 'triumph of the therapeutic', by which everything comes to be evaluated by whether it affirms an individual's self-esteem. Once you decide that self-esteem is the by-product of public recognition, you reach a notion of identity that has changed from the establishment of legal equality to a culture of compulsory indiscriminate affirmation. There becomes no legitimate way to adjudicate when the needs, wants and rights of different identities conflict. Which is where we are now.

The theological language for identity rests with the communion of saints. This celebrates how God has created each one of us for a purpose, a purpose we cannot fulfil without each other, how God loves us all equally, yet loves each one of us as if we were the only one. It transforms our notion of identity by turning our attention from ourselves to God, from who we uniquely are to what God is creatively making us, from where we are specifically coming from to where we are collectively going, from where we are restless to where we find our rest in God, from our exhausting and endless quest to define our identity, to inhabiting the identity we are given as a child of God.

In the communion of saints, identity is fundamentally not a discovery to be defended but a gift to be received. Identity is in the end not about recognition by society but embrace by God. Identity is ultimately a story not about our assertion of what we are but about God's invitation to what we may become. Identity is not about the isolation of establishing there's no one else on earth like me but the solidarity of believing there's a place for each one of us at the heavenly banquet.

The communion of saints gives us something the quest for identity never can. It replaces individuality with communion; solitariness with relationship; static identification with dynamic transformation; and endless self-obsession with eternal belonging.

Four: Race

- *Tell about an encounter you've had that impacted the way you understand race.*
- *I wonder how closely race is tied to economics.*
- *I wonder what you think issues of race are really about.*
- *Tell about a person who you've seen address issues of race well.*

It's important to separate out the different things we're talking about when we talk about race. At the bottom of the evil of racism is the tendency that leads humans, in their anxiety about deprivation and death, to make themselves secure, superior and sacred, and as part of that to create hierarchies that control other humans and treat some as of lesser value. Such oppression inevitably creates antagonism. To offset the guilt of what is done and to defuse the retribution anticipated, oppressors then create a whole ideology that justifies the subjugation such action has brought about. Once that process has been going on for centuries, it becomes hard for everyone, persecutor or persecuted, to think outside the habits and language it involves. Then, when a construct has emerged, it can be manipulated in such a way that those subject to it come to be blamed for precisely the situation that was deliberately created to keep them subservient.

Beyond those general characteristics, racism today tends to focus particularly on the legacy of slavery and segregation in the US, and how African Americans today are liable to state-sanctioned violence, incarceration and murder, constituting a society-wide declaration that Black lives don't matter. While Britain ended slavery much earlier than the US, it remained, through the Mississippi–Manhattan–Manchester cotton production triangle, a central part of the slave economy. Racism is about economics before it becomes about prejudice.

But there are differences between Britain and the US. African Americans are 400-year residents who can trace their ancestors on American soil longer than the large majority of other Americans. While there have always been Black people in Britain, the presence of large numbers is largely a post-war phenomenon. Many Black Britons trace ancestry to the Caribbean and often know what it means to share their surname with that of the man who owned their forebears' bodies. But more trace heritage to Africa and have no direct ancestral legacy of slavery. Meanwhile those from the Indian sub-continent and elsewhere experience racism but are outside the Atlantic slave story entirely. The overarching story of empire that unites the Indian sub-continent, Africa and the Caribbean affirms that race and economics have long been inseparable. It doesn't for a moment mean that racism in the UK is not real, sinister and a scar on church and society. It just means we can't take a US template and transfer it straightforwardly to the UK like a Broadway production coming to the West End.

The central paradox of talking about racism is this. On the one hand racism is a construct. It's not biologically defensible. Any notion that races are clearly distinguishable, that one is superior to another, or that they're inherently at odds with each other, is nonsense. If you go back far enough, we're all related to each other. Race is not a fundamental human characteristic. On the other hand, race is everywhere: it's invoked as a battle for power, purity, identity, justice, so to discount or try to ignore race is naive, idealistic and too often part of a sinister agenda.

The world is not *racial*, in that significant differences are in our DNA; but it's certainly *racialized*, such that we can't simply relate to one another as if race was irrelevant to how we experience life. Racism is a poison that's not inherent in the world, not natural in the world, but is at large in the world. We need to pursue two approaches simultaneously: one based on addressing present racism and the legacies of oppression all around us; the other about imagining, practising and inhabiting a different world.

As to present racism, for society, while racism is damaging in any circumstance, it becomes destructive when combined with political and economic (and not just social) power. Pursuing racial equality without addressing social inequality is half a policy; seeking economic equality without addressing racial inequality is just as flawed. Plenty of people have faced racial discrimination and yet found paths to flourishing; but when you add social and economic disadvantage, you've got an even greater mountain to climb.

As to imagining differently, the church needs a radical transformation in its understanding of who God is. God is no different from the face we see in Jesus, and Jesus is not a north European white male: he's a Middle Eastern member of an oppressed race in an occupied country, born homeless, killed because his people were not protected by the rule of law, and then, in a common racial move, blamed for his own oppression. If an artist portrays a Black Jesus on the cross, it's still considered provocative – but it's closer to history than a white one. The risen and ascended Jesus asks St Paul on the road to Damascus, 'Why are you persecuting me?' The Christ made present in the Holy Spirit poses the same question to racists today.

Moving to the second approach to racism, inhabiting a different world, I want to highlight the words, 'You are a chosen race, a royal priesthood, a holy nation, God's own people.' It's a commonplace, often attributed to Rosa Parks, that 'There's only one race, the human race.' Biologically that's true, but 1 Peter makes the bold claim that in baptism Christians become part of a new race. In contrast to the distorted modern conception of race, the scriptural notion of race begins in Exodus 19, where God proclaims the Jews 'a priestly kingdom and a holy nation'. In 1 Peter 2, race is transformed from a genetic category conferred at conception to a gift bestowed to anyone who finds their home in God. Race is about God's claiming of each one of us, not our identifying ourselves or others. Race is something none of us have, all can be given and none can lose. In baptism we join a new race. The so-called race we were born into is sociologically significant. But our primary identity is thenceforth the one we receive.

That society beyond racism, that priestly kingdom and holy nation, is what 1 Peter calls church. The sad truth is that church has peddled false ideologies of racialized injustice at least as much as anyone else, and even when it's found a better vision has frequently failed to realize that vision. But by describing the church as a race, 1 Peter shows that racism isn't an unfortunate human shortcoming or an inevitable struggle to comprehend difference: it's *blasphemy* – the failing to perceive God's true nature and purpose – and *idolatry* – the attempt to impose a false form of salvation, in this case by the ostracism and oppression of others. Thus cherishing the diverse gifts of one another isn't just ethics, the ordering of our life in the image of God, it's worship, our very recognition of and response to God. If we can't reflect in our life the gift of together becoming a new race, we're not simply a sinful church: we're not really a church at all.

Five: Gender

- *I wonder what it's like to feel you're regarded or valued as lesser because of your gender.*
- *Tell about a situation from some years ago concerning gender where you might have spoken or acted differently today.*
- *Tell about a person who acted with dignity when treated without respect.*
- *I wonder what discrimination on the basis of gender is really about.*

The climax to the book of Proverbs is a poem about a wise woman. Everything before it builds up to it. It's an acrostic poem, which means that each verse begins with a different letter of the Hebrew alphabet, in order. Every word is carefully chosen and pondered and placed. It's not inherently about a good wife: a better translation of the opening phrase would say 'a woman of valour'. This isn't about the subjugation of women to circumscribed domesticity; it's about a figure who embodies the aspirations of her whole culture.

Here's the crucial sociological point that governs the interpretation of these verses. When you're trying to find a polite way to ask someone if their life is primarily centred on their growing family or if they have a regular job, the current fashionable phrase to use is, 'Do you work outside the home?' These words are carefully chosen, but they contribute to the misunderstanding of the Proverbs 31 passage. The reason is that in the post-war West, the home became the scene of domesticity: a place of leisure, consumption, childcare and internal decoration, of soft furnishings and idle pursuits. An educated middle-class woman today knows she has a mountain to climb if she's going to justify her existence to a stranger in a casual conversation by describing her life as circumscribed by these characteristics.

But the home in Palestine in the fourth century before Christ, when these words were most probably written, was a very different environment. It was the centre of economic activity. This was a pre-industrial economy. All the places where twenty-first-century people go to work – offices, factories, business parks, libraries, schools, coffee shops – none of these existed. Consider the activities the woman of valour performs through these lenses. She seeks wool and flax not to improve her own home but to manufacture goods for sale. She rises early to organize the household, especially its considerable staff team. She 'perceives that her merchandise is profitable'. That's not a bourgeois domestic idyll. She 'considers a field and buys it; with the fruit of her hands she plants a vineyard'. We're talking about a major wheeler-dealer here.

She 'opens her hand to the poor, and reaches out her hands to the needy'. This is a woman who has become the centre of public benefaction and welfare for the community. There are three results of her labours: her 'children rise up and call her happy' – in other words she's founded a considerable family business; her 'husband is known in the city gates, taking his seat among the elders of the land' – you might ask if he ever lets slip where his wealth and influence truly come from; and she becomes known not for beauty and charm, those domestic virtues, but for wisdom, strength and dignity, the qualities of a stateswoman. Listen to that last line again, now perhaps in a different frame of mind. It says, 'Give her a share in the fruit of her hands, and let her works praise her in the city gates.' In other words, credit where credit is due: this woman is the bedrock of society.

This woman takes up a role of prominent authority. She gives tasks to her servants – the word means 'legislates'. It's as if she's a local mayor. And the teaching of kindness is on her tongue. This is the most radical statement of all, because the word for teaching is 'torah', which refers to the central books of the Old Testament, and the word for kindness is the word that refers to God's disposition toward Israel, 'loving-kindness'. So she's a political and religious leader.

The notion that underscores this whole description is economics. In Greek the word is *oikonomia*, which means household management. Today the idea that economics means household management is absurd – it obviously means so much more than that. But when you read this passage it all makes perfect sense. This capable woman is managing the household the way the Chancellor of the Exchequer manages the economy. She's doing it very well. She's the engine room of the whole society. It's time she got the credit she deserves.

This is the climax to the book of Proverbs. Proverbs is a book that turns the theological claims and dramatic stories of the Old Testament into practical guidelines for living in turbulent times. It draws together insights from a variety of cultural and religious backgrounds, and it seeks renewal both individually and corporately for Israel's life with God. What's radical and remarkable is that it portrays God's perfect partner as a woman. Throughout this description of the woman of valour, the author is holding up this woman as an ideal for Israel as a whole to imitate.

In this passage we're warned that charm is deceitful and beauty is vain. But in their place, we're given here a model for both faithfulness and true happiness: a woman rolling up her sleeves to purchase wool and flax, to produce fine linen and purple, to perceive her merchandise is profitable, to buy and cultivate a vineyard, to become physically and mentally strong, to exercise authority in faith and public life, and to be a benefactor to those who are struggling. It's a daunting role model – but never let it be said that the Bible damns women with low expectations. This is a woman who inspires us all to our highest ideals, and inspires God's people to see womanhood as the epitome of what it means to be God's companion.

Six: Sexuality

- *I wonder what it's like to feel you're in the minority.*
- *Tell about a time you were in the majority and woke up to ways you'd treated people who weren't.*
- *Tell about a time you said something no one else seemed to be saying.*
- *I wonder what it feels like to receive mercy.*

The Bible has two contrasting dynamics: one in which the story is always about Israel, and everyone else is a bit part in Israel's story; and the other, in which God's mercy stretches wider still and wider, like the wideness of the sea.

Sometimes, when there's an enquiry after a public tragedy or crime, the committee can't reach a unanimous position. In those circumstances it may issue a majority report that represents its considered view and a minority report that airs the very different convictions of irreconcilable members of the group. The Old Testament has a majority and minority report. The majority report is one of a people chosen by God, which survives by wit and wile, is transformed by miracle and wonder, depends on God's providence, grows to great power, flounders in unfaithfulness and languishes in exile, before returning to the semi-dignified state we find in Jesus' time. But the minority report goes like this. God chooses Abraham, liberates and legislates under Moses and brings Israel into the Promised Land. Yet time after time Israel is challenged, saved, inspired, moved, humbled and renewed by people from beyond its bounds – by outcasts, by enemies, by gentiles.

The Old Testament is written by people who assumed the majority report. Yet it was largely compiled when Israel was exiled in Babylon, in other words at a time when Israel was discovering the wondrous truth that God seemed to be at work through people other than just the Jews.

When we turn to the New Testament, we see the ways in which the minority report starts to take over. But we mustn't assume that was a formality. You can't understand the New Testament unless you appreciate that overturning the majority report (that the story was always only about Israel) was a radical, remarkable, shocking thing to do. In the story of the Syrophoenician woman, with a mixture of symbolism and irony, Mark displays the transformation of Israel's story from the majority to the minority report.

Mark gives us several signals we're talking about a total outsider. She's a gentile, she's a woman, she seems to have no man around, her daughter's a minor and has a demon. Five kinds of unthinkable. And there's a sixth and seventh kind: the woman behaves outrageously by approaching Jesus, a man, and by kneeling at his feet, where feet are a euphemism for nether regions. Jesus' reaction is textbook majority report: 'Look, sunshine, I'm not being funny or anything, but the story's just about Israel.' Mark's not saying Jesus is mean and small-minded: he's portraying Jesus as the embodiment of Israel, in the form of the majority report. But what does the woman do? She wittily, charmingly, compellingly and irresistibly articulates the minority report by saying, 'Even if you're going to insult and demean and humiliate me, don't you see how you're still tacitly acknowledging there's a place for me in this story?' And in that one second the whole dominance of the majority report is overturned, and the truth of the minority report prevails. It's as if suddenly, astonishingly, miraculously, Israel can for the first time truly hear what God is really saying and articulate it in its own voice.

Don't miss the painful tragedy about this story and this widening mercy. For most of its history, and even today – in some respects especially today – the church has ignored this story and backed its own version of the Old Testament's majority report. Rather than see its energy in the ever-greater embrace of all God's people and the whole of God's creation in God's glorious realm of belonging and togetherness, it's said, 'This story is only about us.' And it's seen fit to exclude people just as readily as ancient Israel did, by creating its own set of gentiles whom it deemed to fall outside its self-imposed boundaries of class and race and sexuality and disability and gender. This story is a confrontational, prophetic demand that the church live into the minority report that Jesus advocates and embodies.

Here Jesus shows the church for all time that no one lies outside the wideness of God's mercy. No one.

This is obvious if you realize this passage is about turning from the majority to the minority report. It shouldn't need explaining to anyone who believes the New Testament tells how the wideness of God's mercy, which was always God's purpose, is finally unfolded in Jesus. But the tragic, horrifying, bewildering, confounding truth of our time is that it *does* need saying. A large part of our church today seems to have forgotten or ignored it and reinstated the majority report, simply replacing Israel with the church, inserting one set of exclusionary boundaries in place of another.

Which is why the call for the embrace of all God's children is such an important statement about how we read the Bible today. It's about the way the Spirit humbles God's people by the renewal that comes through those we attempt to exclude. It's about the constant, consistent call of the Spirit to see what new things God is doing among us. It's saying that just because something has been a social convention and a church assumption for generations or centuries, that doesn't mean it represents the true purpose of God or the leading of the Spirit for us today. It's calling us to the wideness of God's mercy, lest we find ourselves, to our own consternation, outside it. It's calling us into the heart of God.

Seven: Disability

- *I wonder in what way you are disabled.*
- *Tell about a time a person asked you a question that made you feel uncomfortable in a good way.*
- *I wonder whether you have a vocation to say things that otherwise wouldn't be said.*
- *I wonder in what ways you feel you're calling from the edge.*

In the book of Job, Job loses everything. What he doesn't know is that the reader is waiting to see if he will curse God. Job's friends assume the issue is a moral one and Job's losses are a result of him having done something wrong. But eventually Job dismisses them and realizes his dispute is with God alone. Job rails against God and reels off a list of quite reasonable questions that he demands that God answer. In chapters 38 and 39, God begins to respond. But God's response is not what we're anticipating. There isn't a big reveal that explains why things have turned out so badly for Job. Instead, God unfurls an overwhelming list of questions.

God's long speech covers 20 areas of the natural world and in each case God asks whether Job is capable of comprehending or conceiving of the ways of each of these creatures or phenomena. The speech covers earth, sea, morning, the underworld, light, snow, hail, storm, rain, stars, clouds, the lion, raven, ibex, wild ass, ox, ostrich, horse, hawk and falcon. The effect is twofold. Job finds himself no longer furious but awestruck, humbled by his tiny place in a colossal universe of immense complexity and deft design. Meanwhile his situation is transformed from a problem into a mystery. A problem is a straightforward deficit like a breakage or a malfunction that you can simply fix and can return to how it should be; a mystery is something unique and wondrous, which absorbs the whole of your intellect, emotion, aptitude and experience, and you can only enter, after which your heart and soul will never be the same again. Before God's speech in chapters 38 and 39, Job is saying, 'Why won't you fix this problem?' After this speech, Job is saying, 'Take me with you into this mystery.'

Those with disabilities who encounter the church tend to have two things in common. They have experience and gifts that church and society have seldom understood, rarely honoured and frequently suppressed. And they have questions that challenge the location from which theology has often been done and the subjects that theology conventionally addresses. In other words, they're looking for receptivity and belonging in church and society, and they're drawing us all into deeper relationship with God.

Perhaps most people with disabilities identify with the sense of calling from the edge. To call from the edge is to say, 'Hello, look over here will you, there's some of us on the edge, neglected, sometimes scorned and invariably forgotten by everyone else.' That meaning, while not untrue, is far from the whole truth of what's going on in this phrase.

A second meaning is to say, 'Anyone who sings the song of Mary, which speaks of God in Christ exalting the humble and meek, anyone who reads Matthew 25, which talks of meeting Christ in those experiencing disadvantage, and anyone who reads the Beatitudes, which say, "Blessed are you who mourn", knows that the edge, rather than the centre, is where the kingdom of God is to be found. So calling from the edge is calling for a renewal of church and society to be reshaped according to God's realm, a call to turn the world upside down – and those who are on the edge already are calling others to join them.'

That's getting closer to the truth. But a third meaning is to realize calling is another word for vocation. What calling from the edge means above all is the discovery that those who live with disability have a particular vocation. Only when they get together, and only when the questions they are asking take centre stage, and only when they are seen for once for what they uniquely are – precious, honoured and loved in God's sight – and not for what they are not, can that true vocation, by which God is renewing the earth and inaugurating the coming realm, truly be discovered and embodied and lived out as a blessing to everyone.

For each of us discovers our vocation when, often with the help of others, we reflect on who we uniquely are, what we alone have experienced and how wondrously we're made, and discover what we can be and do and say that only we can be and do and say. And the catch is that God has chosen to bring the coming realm not without us but through us – so if that realm is to be all God calls it to be, we must respond to our calling and play our role in realizing it on earth as in heaven.

Perhaps every disabled person has experienced others regarding them as 'that annoying person who keeps asking us to change things' or 'keeps needing us to adapt so they can participate or belong'. In other words, almost every person with a disability is accustomed to being seen as one who asks questions that invite others to live in a bigger, more complex but more wonderful world. Which brings us back to chapters 38 and 39 of the book of Job. What we discover in the book of Job is that the one who asks questions that invite others to live in a bigger, more complex but more wonderful world is called God. God is so annoying. God keeps calling from the edge, to say, 'Is your world, is your church, big enough and complex enough to accommodate me? Only if you listen to my questions and allow yourself to be humbled and inspired by the universe my questions point to will your life be as wondrous as I made it to be.'

Eight: Age

- *Tell about an older person you admire.*
- *Tell about a person who's aged in a way you find difficult.*
- *Tell about a friendship between an older person and a young person or child.*
- *I wonder what it would be like to feel ready to die.*

In 1880 a person born in the West could expect to live to the age of 40. Today, life expectancy stands at 80. Given the amount of care and research that goes into healthcare and well-being, you'd think greater longevity would be a cause of rejoicing. But it's widely assumed old age means chronic disease, a sense of obsolescence, meaninglessness, decrepitude, loneliness and a long slow retreat into death. We have a confused stereotype of old age between an image of poverty, frailty and dependence, on the one hand, and selfishness, conservatism and inflexibility, on the other. Either way the elderly seem to be a threat – so needy that society can't care for them or so dangerous that society can't withstand them.

To get to a more positive place requires one fundamental shift: to alter the almost-universal assumption that ageing is a euphemism for dying. If you see life as a relentless quest for health and wealth, ageing presents a major obstacle. That obstacle becomes a challenge; it must be either edited out of the story or medicalized and transformed into relative youth. We put our resources into ridding our later years of any ill-health or into postponing death indefinitely or into making elderly people invisible so that the rest of society can preserve the illusion of eternal youth. Ageing becomes the most apt symbol of the doomed human desire to keep control of our lives. It pushes us to ask whether there's anything to live for beyond acquisition of goods, the accumulation of experiences and the postponement of death.

We find a rich account of old age in the story of Simeon and Anna in Luke 2. Luke's Gospel begins and ends in the Temple. Luke's saying that just as the Temple was the definitive place of encounter between Israel and God, so now Jesus is all of those things. This is our first clue about old age. Youth is like a temple, a great edifice of self-important self-glorification. To grow old is to realize the folly of that temple, its inadequacy and its gradual replacement by something more beautiful, good and true. It's to turn that edifice into gentler, more abiding and more profound relationships, just as Luke portrays the turning of the covenant from the Temple into Jesus.

Simeon grasps that God has wonderful things in store. These things are not going to be achieved by or even through him, but he will witness them. He is thus the epitome of patience and humility. The popular image of old age involves neither patience nor humility. It doesn't include patience because it's so filled with people becoming exasperated with the failure of their own bodies, or so bewildered by their inability to keep pace with contemporary values or technology. It doesn't include humility because it's so filled with old codgers saying, 'I've forgotten more than you'll ever know', or, 'When you get to my age, young man ...' But an old age that's permeated by patience and humility is one that expects God to save the best till last.

The community that gathers in the Temple on the day of Jesus' presentation includes a baby, two parents and two elderly people unrelated to the parents or to one another. It's an image of the realm of God – young and old, male and female, seeking faith and blessing, finding God together. One tendency of an obsession with youth is to ghettoize elderly people in communities away from the rest of society where they can see others and be seen only by appointment. But what older people need most is the joy of interacting with all ages, and what all ages need most is the diversity and spirit of one another. Churches are one of the few places today where unrelated people of different ages relate to one another in non-contractual ways. They need to give and receive from all ages. It's often said elderly people are lonely and isolated. So are younger people. The answer lies in each other.

Simeon tells Mary and Joseph that Jesus will turn Israel's world upside down, and from him no secrets will be hidden. But Simeon also knows Jesus' mission will bring division and cause wounding pain to his parents. Simeon doesn't believe life is about avoiding conflict or simply trying to keep everyone cheerful. Some things are more important than simply staying alive. Some short lives say everything a life needs to say. But few except the old realize this.

So here are the four pillars of the wisdom of old age that we learn from Simeon and Anna. First, as we get older, we realize life isn't about attaining perfect mental and physical strength to become independent, it's about forming relationships of interdependence that grow richer with age like a good wine. Second, the patience and humility of old age affirm that we are not the centre of God's purposes, but that our greatest privilege is to witness the abundant life God brings. Third, your age isn't the most interesting thing about you. It's not good for anyone to be confined to the company of people just like themselves. A flourishing life is one spent with a diversity of ages, backgrounds and social locations. And finally, we shouldn't idealize old age: the wisdom of old age is one that sees suffering, hardship and grief but sees through them to beauty, truth and goodness.

Simeon and Anna didn't spend their lives shoring up their minds and bodies against the ravages of time or chance, or the inevitability of death. They spent them preparing for the moment they would come face to face with God in Christ. When it came, they were ready. The question for us about old age is, will we be?

Nine: Class

- *I wonder what it really means to experience poverty.*
- *I wonder what kinds of things make a person feel ashamed.*
- *Tell about a person you know who is beset by bureaucratic and practical obstacles to flourishing.*
- *Tell about a time you got something you wouldn't normally have because someone didn't want it.*

To experience genuine poverty is to face many challenges every day: in the home, the household, the place of or search for work, the bureaucratic obstacles, in transport, in health. People fall into poverty for all sorts of reasons; people remain in poverty for a bunch more; people sometimes fall into poverty again after a more stable season. But every category of poverty is characterized by one common feature: shame. Shame, because you're without most of the sources of dignity and prestige our culture prizes. All of us know what it feels like to be embarrassed, humiliated, exposed, judged, rejected, crushed – it's what we strive to avoid with all our hearts. But to experience genuine poverty is not just to feel these things – it's to feel them all the time.

The parable of the great banquet in Luke 14 comes in four scenes. In scene one, a man invites the great and the good to a grand dinner and begins to make preparations. In scene two, the dinner is served and a servant duly goes to collect the guests. But here comes the shock: one guest says he needs to inspect some land, another says he's bought ten oxen, a third says he's just got married. These people have already promised to come and make no effort to say otherwise until the food is already prepared. They're all offering excuses about things they would have been aware of plenty of time in advance.

The result is that the host is humiliated. He could be angry, vengeful, bitter and vindictive. But the host doesn't internalize the embarrassment or turn shame into anger. In scene three he pivots and says, 'Why don't we give the food to someone who wants it?' He instructs his servant to go around the town inviting those who would never normally be invited to any such gathering, because whether through their social or their physical condition they knew what it meant to experience perpetual shame. In other words, in the heat of his shame, he chose to share what he had with those who knew shame better than he did. But it turns out that even when the shamed of the town were invited there were still seats left at the table. This tells us just how many of the original guests, beyond the three whose excuses are recorded, must have turned the host down. So in scene four the host tells the slaves to go beyond the town limits and into the countryside and find the ultra-shamed, that is to say whoever is so ostracized that they're cast out from the town altogether.

See how this anticipates the story of Christ's Passion. Jesus is first tried among those whom one might expect to welcome his ministry. He's then paraded through the streets and lanes of Jerusalem and is exposed to humiliation and scorn. Finally, he's taken outside the city to the highways and byways and is put to death by the most shameful method known to the ancient world. But he doesn't internalize that shame. Instead he expresses forgiveness to his persecutors and in due course through his resurrection he turns that shame into grace. The cruelty and injustice of his tormentors he turns into hospitality and hope. The heart of the banquet story is the same as the heart of the gospel: shame and loss become grace and joy.

Let's return to our own context and reflect again on what we might call three kinds of poverty. The first is the plight of the person whose life is a struggle, whose relationships may be fragile, whose legal rights are inadequate and whose options are exhausted. The second is our own poverty. Many who aren't regarded as experiencing poverty still search for belonging, relationship, home, acceptance, or an end to prejudice, exposure, failure, humiliation or scorn. But there's a third kind of poverty – and that's what we glimpse in the parable. Jesus is saying, then and now, 'I have no home but yours. Yours is the heart where I belong. Yours is the home I long to enter. Yours is the life I long to resurrect. Yours are the burdens I long to share.' And the door is continually closed, or slammed in his face. That is the shame of God, not just on the cross but today, every day, every minute, from those from whom we might most expect there to be a welcome.

These three kinds of poverty come together in worship, where we gentiles celebrate that God's invitation went not just to God's own people the Jews but to us who were in the highways and byways; where the rejected of the world, the failures of our lives and the broken heart of God meet; where the shroud of shame is lifted and the banquet of grace begins; where a formal function becomes a playful party, and injustice, ignominy and isolation are transformed into joy.

Ten: Belonging

- *Tell about a community in which it became clear you didn't belong.*
- *Tell about a community in which you found you did belong.*
- *I wonder what it's like to feel abandoned and isolated.*
- *Tell about a meal where you felt welcomed and accepted.*

One congregation always worshipped with every member present throughout – infants, children, young people and adults. The custom was for the person presiding to kneel on the floor and present a scriptural passage using wooden figures, a felt underlay and assorted other artifacts. On one occasion the presentation concerned the Good Shepherd. The storyteller displayed the safe sheepfold, the good pasture, the refreshing water and the places of danger where a sheep could get lost.

The members of the congregation shared their experience of the church and the neighbourhood, and whether each felt like safe, good, refreshing or dangerous. One child said for him the church was like the refreshing water, because home was a place of danger. One adult said church was a place of danger, because once she and others had been pelted with stones as they left the service. Finally, attention fell upon the sheep themselves, which were made out of different kinds of wood. 'I wonder if it makes any difference that the sheep are different colours,' said the storyteller. Immediately one of the older children responded adamantly, 'It makes no difference at all – we should treat them all the same.' Not content, the storyteller pressed a little further: 'I wonder what makes them all the same.' There was a long pause. No response was forthcoming from the 30 or so members present. At last there was a quiet voice from a 6-year-old child near the back. Pointing at the wooden figure with a sheep across his shoulders, she said, 'Because they all have the same shepherd.' That's what belonging means.

At the Last Supper, Jesus addresses his Father and, speaking of his disciples, says, 'They do not belong to the world, just as I do not belong to the world.' See the tragedy of those words. God in infinite love created the world in all its myriad complexity, variety and beauty. And yet rather than freely and gladly accept its purpose, to respond in glad and grateful companionship with God, the world in great part looked elsewhere, found an alternative story, sought a different identity, inhabited another form of belonging. Stay a moment with the dismay, the injustice, the distress of that. God made a magnificent banquet – but the world breezed out and got a takeaway instead.

Now perceive what it meant for Jesus to enter that world, a world created for this very moment, for the encounter between Jesus and those God had created to be in relationship with Jesus – and yet a world that had become in so many respects a hostile environment for him. Next, ponder Jesus' drawing around himself a group of disciples, who by their association with him experienced, both during and after his time among them, the hostile environment he underwent. And once we've put these three things together – the rejection of God's purpose, the hostility to Jesus in person and the disciples' experience of this same opposition – we arrive at the true context in which we're to read these words: that is, what it feels like to feel isolated, abandoned and alone on this earth.

You can face almost anything in life if you have a deep sense of trust, respect and understanding with those alongside you. But if you lack any sense of solidarity, then the simplest task or most undemanding challenge can feel beyond you. Where do we find our belonging? Where do we find a meaningful story to live by, a narrative that makes sense of our lives and the world around us and the universe beyond and events that turn out as we wouldn't have chosen?

To be the other is to feel isolated and alone; if you sense you're different, to find you don't seem to fit in with any story that makes sense; maybe to realize that you're not the person others suppose you to be, that your identity's more complex, that your future's less clear; that it seems, in Jesus' words, you don't belong to this world. But at his Last Supper Jesus says: 'Come to me. Sit yourself at this table, and eat. The world doesn't know who you truly are. Don't be anxious about the world: it'll never understand. You aren't at all sure who you really are. Don't worry: I know you better than you know yourself. You may search in vain for belonging. You may look back and feel you've been searching a long time – maybe always. Don't despair. I dwelt here 33 years and I never found a sense of belonging either. But that doesn't mean your life is in vain. There's one thing that matters more than anything now and will matter more than anything forever. You never find it. But eventually it will find you, and when it does it will never leave you. It's only four words, but it's the most important thing you'll ever know. You belong to me.'

Commentary

The subject matter of this course is perhaps the most contentious of the courses in this book. One result of this is that the talks are a little longer than elsewhere because I'm trying to do justice to the subtleties and sensitivities around each question. But again, the potential for argument isn't something to be afraid of. As always, the message and the method are identical. Provided the method is faithfully followed, it should be possible to see divergent opinions and experiences as constructive and enriching rather than troubling, threatening or undermining. Likewise the intention of the talks is not to rehearse and replicate familiar debates frequently aired elsewhere. The course is trying to imagine how each of these issues is a stimulus to a deeper form of being with one another and the stranger. In some ways the naming of issues like race, gender or disability might be experienced as othering in itself. After all, there will likely be hardly a single participant in any conduct of this course who isn't in a 'minority' category of at least one of these kinds. I have tried to address some of this concern in the way the wonderings are framed. But in general, treating these 'sections' as subjects is recognizing that they are all points of explicit or implicit tension in society, and it's idle or naive to step over them as if ignoring that fact was a step to making the world better for everyone. The central argument of the course, as explained in the first talk, is that the church has been impoverished because it has failed to receive the gifts God has given it through those the world (and often the church) has frequently marginalized or excluded. It can't change that pattern unless it becomes aware of it, and part of such awareness is to realize that none of these categories are truly 'other' or ever have been.

The whole of the first talk is given to framing the issue in these terms, because once again it's a different way of addressing the questions from that to which participants might most frequently have been exposed. The second talk is also introductory, and moves further the connection in Christianity between being pushed to the edge and becoming the fount of renewal. The overall emphasis of the first two talks is to reframe the conversation from a tone of campaigning and advocacy to a humbler approach of receiving hitherto hidden gifts from previously suppressed sources. There's a more reflective and abstract talk on identity, but crucially it's one that relocates the whole of these debates on to theological territory. The material here is some of the most demanding in the whole book but is important for understanding the moves made in the rest of this course.

The talks then proceed through six categories, the familiar gender, race and class, the increasingly familiar sexuality and disability, and the often-overlooked old age. (I don't touch on youth because there's a whole course on being with child elsewhere.) The final talk returns to the territory of talk three and offers belonging as the goal of the whole discourse.

It goes without saying that any of the six categories could be the subject of a whole course of its own. Simply doing a course does not exhaust the ways a congregation might wish to respond – indeed, one hope would be that forms and energy for such responses might arise out of doing this course.

10

Being With Being With

Ten Wonderings and Addresses

One: For and With

- *Tell about a time someone you loved was in trouble and you didn't know how to help.*
- *I wonder what it is that drives to activity rather than sitting still.*
- *I wonder what you think makes a good life.*
- *Tell about something you learned from a time of hardship or adversity.*

Imagine a child who experiences a rare disease. Imagine a parent who investigates, demands, campaigns, litigates, fundraises and finally secures a vital, life-extending treatment, while the other parent and the other children play, watch, listen, remember – in short, walk with and abide with the sick child. Imagine the treatment extends life for only a few months, during which the campaigning parent returns to the family to find the spouse, siblings and, most of all, the child in question have become strangers – not to one another but to the heroic parent.

What has that parent done wrong? Surely all these actions are expressions of love; how can it be right to criticize such a sacrificial, selfless search for a cure? Perhaps. But that parent has become captivated by the configuration of problem and solution, and unable to conceive of how to address a problem that can't be fixed. The obsession with fixing makes the parent oblivious to what's really needed, which is the cultivation of relationships that can offer an interweaving canopy beneath the dying child, and even more importantly hint at how the child's death can become a point of family renewal and growth rather than an experience of utter loss and despair.

This parable discloses a paradox. Our culture resembles that campaigning parent. Parents want their children to do well at school, flourish at university, gain a professional training and then spend their lives fixing problems for people. We have little or no narrative for what people should do with the comfort and affluence they've attained by becoming good at repeatedly fixing such problems; except to rejoin the hamster-wheel of having children who are raised to do the same. We constantly seek, through provision of services – wealth, entertainment, health, legal, educational – to get things off the desk of delay and back into the hurly-burly of action and advance.

Our society is mesmerized by the word 'for'. What's been obscured in this valorization of *for* is the vital word *with*. The parent in the parable lost all understanding of *with*. Campaigning and fundraising were *for*, but inhibited *with*. Did the parent undertake all that frantic activity because being with the child exposed the powerlessness of encountering a problem that can't be fixed? Was it in fact easier to campaign and construct than it would have been to sit still and listen and hold hands and share last moments? By insisting that our human condition is inhibited by limitation, we miss the true purpose of living, which is relating – epitomized by the word *with*.

For is a project of endless deferral, where we provide goods, services, facilities, opportunities for others but never enter a dialogue about how we or those others should use the freedom that these extensive provisions make possible. Our culture has become like the parent in the parable, constantly delaying the moment of encounter by contenting itself with generous and self-denying preparations – preparations that never end. The rest of the child's family understand that for is missing the point; only by accepting the child's mortality and trusting relationship to be the deepest form of fulfilment can they offer the child what the child truly needs – themselves. Our culture is in danger of having myriad forms of communication but nothing to say; countless ways to overcome limitation but no way to address isolation; magnificent skills in doing things for people but a profoundly impoverished emotional vocabulary of how to be with them.

With is the final purpose of which we never speak, the true goal that we never articulate. It's not that we are unmindful of with; but we invariably diminish with by making it a means to a further end. But true relationship has no ulterior end; it's a good in itself – *the* good in itself. Profound connection is the final goal of life; faith names the ways we seek such profound connection on a transcendent, eternal plane.

A popular notion of faith is largely shaped by for. God is for us. We are in a covenant by which God provides us on a macro level with life, health and the means to flourish; on a super-macro level with peace, forgiveness and the prospect of eternal life; and on a micro level with the courage to overcome challenges, the qualities to succeed in our chosen path and the strength to withstand dangers. In return we offer a reasonable level of obedience and faithfulness. This describes a two-way relationship of for. But the God of Christianity is more truly characterized as with. God makes the universe to have creatures, especially humanity, to be with. God's covenant with Israel is a mutual commitment to be with one another. What Israel discovers in exile in Babylon is that God is with more truly than God is for – when the tangible gifts of God in land, king and temple are gone, the with is more, rather than less, apparent. The coming of Jesus isn't so much the definitive for (dying for our sins) as the ultimate with – physical, embodied with, willing to go to any lengths to be with us. Jesus' resurrection is the great proclamation that he will be with us always, despite our inclination or even determination to be without him. The sending of the Holy Spirit is the token and guarantee of Christ's promise to be with us always, to the end of time.

Thus any formation, nurture or restoration of with, in relation to self, one another or the earth at large, is an experience and disclosure of the true with that constitutes the fundamental purpose of all things.

BEING WITH

Two: Four Methods

- *Tell about a time you felt you really used your skills to the fullest.*
- *Tell about what it felt like to be part of a good team.*
- *Tell about a moment you felt really seen and cherished regardless of your accomplishments.*
- *I wonder what drives people into such heated exchanges on social media.*

How is isolation to be overcome? We can identify four ways to meet another person in the midst of their existence.

- The first is *working for.* Working for assumes that people are defined by their predicaments, and the most direct and compassionate way to interact is to use one's skills to resolve those predicaments for them. Working for requires one to cultivate and enhance one's skills and shape one's compassion to be alert for opportunities to use those skills to make other people's lives better. It is full of activity (working). But crucially it makes 'with' secondary and dispensable. It doesn't necessarily involve conversation, understanding, or mutuality. It is action without relationship.
- The second method is *working with.* Working with, like working for, is focused on active steps to overcome problems (working). But unlike the previous assumption of acting on another person's behalf, it seeks in every way to make the project a collaborative exercise, not just with the person encountered but with a wider range of people experiencing the same or a similar plight. Working with is not fundamentally about developing one's own skills to a point where one can rectify other people's problems. It's about facilitating a partnership between two or more people, where each has significant and valuable contributions to bring to the business in hand. It's about the momentum and solidarity generated through addressing a problem together.
- The third form of engagement is *being with.* Being with is different from working for because it focuses on the relationship itself (with) rather than perceiving primarily or wholly its instrumental value.

BEING WITH BEING WITH

But being with differs also from working with, because it requires a focus on enjoying the person and growing through what they truly are (being), rather than assuming the encounter is an opportunity to exercise one's agency in bringing about change. Being with thus requires a transformation of heart and mind from conventional forms of encounter. It's not about solving problems. It's about enjoying relationship for its own sake.

- The fourth kind of encounter, *being for*, isn't really a form of encounter at all, because it doesn't require you to have any actual conversation with another person. You don't need to know anything about them; instead, you judge things entirely from the perspective of a righteous observer. Like being with, you don't yourself actually bring about any tangible change. But unlike being with, neither do you develop a mutually respectful, reciprocally upbuilding relationship with a person; you simply assume you know what they are seeking and advocate their imagined cause on their behalf. Unlike working for or working with, you assume others should be called upon to bring change about. It is not for you to do so: your role is to identify what's wrong, decry the failures of the world and describe what should be done. In an information-saturated age of capturing attention by offering vivid instant judgements, it's probably the most common model of the four.

The ultimate goal of every encounter is being with. Every chance connection, conversation or collaboration offers the possibility of piercing the membrane that inhibits genuine relationship. The alternatives to relationship are many. They include estrangement, ignorance, misunderstanding, hurt, fear, scorn, discomfort, dislike and hostility. But each withholding of relationship presupposes an alternative relationship – more familiar, more trusted, more demanding, more wonderful – for whose benefit such restraint is necessary. It's not, 'I can't afford time for real connection because I've got more important things to do' – because in the end there isn't anything more important for anyone to do. But it could be, 'I can't invest in this relationship because I need to preserve my energies and emotions more fully to invest in and be loyal to these other relationships.'

BEING WITH

Being with doesn't eschew activity; instead, it sees activity as a transitional mode that can be helpful in facilitating connection. In other words, whereas working for and working with instrumentalize relationship for the sake of achievement, being with instrumentalizes activity for the sake of relationship. Thus a parent sits a young adult son or daughter in the passenger seat of a car not so much because they urgently need to go somewhere together but because it's sometimes easier to talk when looking through the windscreen rather than directly at the other person. Likewise an offer to help dig over an allotment may not arise from a conviction that home-grown vegetables are the secret of a good diet, so much as from a desire to spend time in the outdoors together in the hope that it facilitates a conversation that needs to happen. Playing sports together may be a way of keeping fit, but may more probably be a way of developing thirst for the drink afterwards where true relationship emerges.

Is being with passive in the face of a neighbour's experience of adversity or injustice? No. What it doesn't assume is that the long-term answer is working for. Being with always looks to empower the person themselves. It knows you can seldom solve someone else's problems. You can fool yourself by solving them to your own satisfaction. The best you can do is to walk alongside them while they address their own problems. It's working with if you shoulder the burden together for some of the way; it's being with if you simply commit to not running away and refuse to be scared off by setbacks or disappointments. So often working for says, 'Leave this to me', and achieves an outcome far from the needs or wants of the person in jeopardy. Equally, often working for says, 'I'll leave this with you', when it turns out such successes are hard to attain. What's really happening is that the person who is committed to working for finds it easier to transfer their attention to another person or project whose problems are easier to fix. Being with may look passive, because it doesn't leap up to fix the problem, but it understands that some problems defy solving and realizes what's needed is sheer adhesiveness, true constancy, abiding faithfulness until darkness becomes dawn – even if dawn never comes.

Three: Presence

- Tell about a time someone gave up a lot to travel to be with you.
- Tell about a relationship that had depth if not breadth.
- I wonder what it's like to be with someone who picks up your non-verbal signals as well as what you say.
- Tell about a time you gave up telling a story and said, 'You had to be there.'

Being with begins with presence. Presence is in four dimensions – height, breadth, depth and time. It is the coincidence of all four in the appearance of one person being before another. It means to be available for unmediated interaction – not a voice only, or written words only, but incorporating all the communication that occurs non-verbally. In this sense the persons of the Trinity are, without question, fully present with one another – one might even say perfectly present with one another. Here is the heart of the difference between being with and, first, working for, and second, being for. *For* doesn't require presence; *with* does. It's easy to send a message that says, 'I am with you in your suffering.' It's much more demanding to add, 'And I'm travelling to be at your side by tomorrow night.' Presence is the necessary but not sufficient condition of being with. It's a statement of one's own limitations: instead of calling all my contacts, using all my influence, pulling in favours and demanding answers, I'm going to sit beside you, stripped of all my usefulness and status and offer you nothing more or less than myself. I'm going to say, in actions rather than words, 'I'm here and nowhere else. This is the most important place in the world for me to be right now. You are the most important person for me to be with. The others can wait.' It's a statement of priorities.

By requiring presence, being with already recognizes its own limitations. Being with does have an agenda to dismantle limitation; but it does so by depth rather than by breadth. The person committed to being with knows they cannot have this depth of relationship with everyone they meet. That person also recognizes that there are appropriate limits to almost every relationship that ensure the relationship is life-giving for both parties and that respect other parties to whom each is called to be with. Being with is not a synonym for burnout or for a fantasy of having no boundaries. On the contrary, being with assumes modesty and humility. It knows it can only be present to a limited number of people. It recognizes in those encounters it must often rely on quality rather than quantity. It is aware it must sometimes be prepared to be vulnerable, whether explicitly or implicitly, and that those encounters may be costly. Being with is not a recipe for saving the world. It's an appreciation that, given one person is not going to save the world, one person can nonetheless (or all the more) embody profound relationship in the particular settings in which they find themselves, and thus portray and model what a saved world would be like.

A flawed world is precisely one in which humans experience all limitation as imprisonment; instrumentalize all relationships for the overarching project of breaking out of such incarceration; yet find on achieving their aim that their reward is isolation – since they have no one with whom to share their freedom. A healthy world is one in which humans invest in being with one another, thereby prioritizing relationship; regard limitation as a reminder of the contingency of existence; and thus find deep commonality and comradeship, such that limitation is transcended by the quality of relationship. The life of faith is simply the extension of this change of heart to incorporate being with God, wherever God is to be found, and the trust that being with God is a relationship whose quality transcends all limitation and abolishes isolation forever.

The echoing spiritual, 'Were you there when they crucified my Lord?' identifies the significance of presence. One can describe the scene in immense detail – they nailed him to the tree, they pierced him in the side, the sun refused to shine, they laid him in the tomb; but such description only enhances the conviction that one had to be there – and the only way to make up for not having been there is to be present where such suffering and glory is embodied in God's world today. 'You had to be there' is the conclusion to countless descriptions of events so wondrous or hilarious as to be beyond adequate rendition. Being there, being present, not only exposes a person to general as well as particular impressions but also means that person was there and not somewhere else – had made that place the location of their being, at least for that time. In such a way, presence implies a solidarity of wordless association and is thus the foundation of being with.

Four: Attention

- *I wonder what it feels like when someone seems more interested in their phone than in you.*
- *Tell about a time that seemed so important you disengaged from the rest of the world to get it right.*
- *Tell about a person who changed you when you became their friend.*
- *Tell about a time someone paid more attention to you than you do to yourself.*

Attention is the second dimension of being with. Attention is the practice of loving study, of noticing and remembering minute particulars, of engaging the senses to register and cherish unique and characteristic qualities, of digesting and savouring and dwelling upon appearance, gesture, texture and tenderness. Attention introduces the dimension of desire – the recognition that being in another's presence does not simply represent a numerical increase, but potentially a deepening, an enriching, an inspiring, a revealing. The mutually indwelling persons of the Trinity look upon one another with rapt attention, seeing all, aching to hear all, missing nothing, so fixed in their gaze that they absorb one another's wisdom and grace by osmosis. Presence is 'showing up'; it could be reluctant or truculent. But attention is eager, intent, sharp, poised, alert – never assuming something is about to happen, but always ready should it be so.

It is all too easy to claim presence without offering attention. Anyone who has tried to hold a conversation with a person who is at the same time captivated by a small electrical device knows exactly what that distinction means. The small electrical device is a symbol of 'elsewhere'. It's saying, 'I may physically be here, but my thoughts, emotions and interests are elsewhere.' To respond to the buzzing of such a device is to say, 'I am putting aside the demands of here for a short or long period to give myself to the elixir of elsewhere.' To pick up a device when the device is not buzzing is to say, 'I'd prefer to be elsewhere, whether because elsewhere is irresistible or simply because here is unendurable.'

Attention makes clear that being with is a vibrant, dynamic, demanding activity, rather than a passive, static one. Attention to the other need not imply, still less require, neglect of the self, but it does assume that the flourishing of the self is not the principal reason for existence or relationship. The Trinity is sometimes described as a dance: to dance requires the constant attention of each partner to each other's rhythm, energy, imagination and direction. This is the language of loving attention.

Attention has been described as the sincerest form of generosity. Building on presence, without which it cannot do its work, it's a statement that the rest of my life is on hold while I am being with you. My own well-being, my other plans, my sense of always having an alternative to fall back on or to dream of – those are no longer considerations for the duration of this passage of time. 'There's nothing more urgent, pressing, important or interesting than you.' That's what attention says. But attention also says, 'In observing, understanding and listening to you – the whole of you – I might sense or experience something you didn't realize you were communicating or intended to keep hidden. Letting me pay attention to you is no small invitation. You may never have experienced it before. It may make you self-aware in a new way. It might also make you nervous. It could be what you most crave and what you most fear.'

Attention may also have surprising effects on the person bestowing attention. There can be something gently healing about suspending one's self-preservation, self-assertion, self-centredness for a while to be wholly focused on another. And when one returns to one's own questions, anxieties and woes, they can seem less burdensome, less pressing and less significant in the light of the reality that has just been disclosed. A burden shared may halve the burden of the speaker; but it may halve the burden of the listener, too. Attention is perhaps the best form of relaxation, because it takes mind and heart completely away from the troubles of the self. To become a friend is to say to a person, 'I am allowing my life to be changed by knowing you.' Attention names the process by which this granting of permission becomes an intentional marking and validation of those changes.

The most common form of bestowing attention is to read a book. It's possible to cast one's eyes over a page, getting a sense of repeated words, length of paragraphs, density of prose; this is like presence without attention. To receive all a book can give requires sustained and deep attention, such that one becomes unaware of words spoken nearby, or dramas being enacted within arm's reach. Such attention enables the reader to pause over an especially complicated or rewarding passage, scrutinizing it for its layers of meaning or pleasing phraseology. But such attention also leaves the reader both cleansed and energized, more eager to engage the panoply of life for having delved deeply into an aspect of it.

All these qualities transfer aptly to attention in relationship to another person. Attention means dwelling upon, revisiting aspects, words, expressions. It means becoming almost oblivious to dramas or noises elsewhere, or even close by. It means emerging afterwards with a new set of lenses through which to perceive existence. And if you imagine the book being written in another language, one that takes all your concentration to comprehend, then you can imagine paying attention to another person as spending a period speaking their language and suspending your own. Afterwards you realize that other language has words and idioms your own language cannot render. Both parties are the richer as a result; tired and rejuvenated at the same time.

A term closely related to attention, which amplifies its meaning, is relaxed awareness or availability, being at the disposal of another, on all levels – physical, spiritual, practical, emotional. It's the opposite of pride, which seeks to find all its resources within itself. Availability regards the other as a *you* and not simply as a he or she. Treating others in the third person, by contrast, is regarding them as if they (or oneself) were absent. The interactions of the Trinity are the image of utter availability: vulnerable openness to the communication of the other; for which the only word is communion.

Five: Mystery

- *I wonder what it's like to feel you're a problem to someone else.*
- *I wonder what it's like to have something about you that others see as a deficit but you wouldn't want to be without.*
- *Tell about a problem you've realized you'll never solve.*
- *I wonder what things in your life you can trust will never run out.*

Being with knows it's not here to solve problems. Not just because many problems can't be solved, or because it's best for people to solve their own problems. More significantly, because some things that look strange and odd and troubling aren't best described as problems at all. A problem is something you've seen before, has a limited extent and can be addressed using a bunch of tools you already have in the satchel. You can see all you need to see from the outside. It can be fixed in practical, tangible ways. By contrast a mystery is none of these things. A mystery is unique. You've never encountered it before. You can't walk round it – you have to enter it. You have to bring all your practical experience, but also your life experience and emotional intelligence, to bear upon it. There's no question of solving or fixing a mystery. You can only enter it, abide with it, dwell among it, ponder it.

Being with looks on another person not as a problem to be fixed but as a mystery to be entered. I realize the other person is part of a web of relationships and circumstances – and it is that web, rather than simply the person themselves, that constitutes the mystery. Simply isolating the other from such a setting and context and treating her as a problem has no prospect of success. At best it creates an insuperable challenge – that of reinserting her back into her network of relationships and circumstances; more likely, it makes her existence incomprehensible.

Consider the difference between an illness and a disability. A person might say, 'I am autistic. Being autistic is part of who I am. I can't imagine not being autistic and I have no desire not to be autistic. If I were to die and go to heaven I would be autistic in heaven. The only difference would be that others wouldn't experience my autism as a negative. They would be utterly attuned to who I am and how I am.' The same person might say,

BEING WITH BEING WITH

'And I also suffer from arthritis. I realize this is a permanent condition, but it's not like autism. If you said I could be without my arthritis I would say, 'Yes, please, now and forever.' Thus autism is a mystery, whereas arthritis is a problem. Autism doesn't make life easier, but life isn't just about being easy; it can create difficulties, but properly understood those difficulties can yield a richer, more wondrous life. Arthritis, by contrast, is largely about constraint and discomfort. There is no upside. It is something one tries to withstand if not overcome; at best something with which one strives to come to terms.

It perhaps goes without saying that the Trinity is a mystery and not a problem. The persons of the Trinity can never exhaust, still less master, one another in their loving play of interaction. This explains why the Trinity can be described but never defined, for every definition is a kind of reduction. The term 'mystery' discloses two further dimensions of being with, both amply displayed in the life of the Trinity: wonder and abundance.

As to wonder, one does not wonder at a problem: one scrutinizes, investigates, calculates, hypothesizes upon, experiments on and eventually solves it. But one does wonder at a mystery. Wonder is a different mode of discourse from enquiry, description or request, from interrogative, indicative or imperative. Wonder is an invitation to an imaginative relationship, to a shared exploration of possibility and resonance, to a form of discovery where knowledge is less important than curiosity, playfulness and a willingness to be open to multiple interpretations. It is not the static settling of a problem but the dynamic unfurling of a mystery.

Abundance belongs with wonder. It is the conviction that if something is of God, there is no shortage of it; that joy lies in learning to love the things God gives in plenty, while misery awaits those who set their hearts on the ephemeral objects of scarcity; that God gives everything needed for a life devoted to faithful following. Anxiety, by contrast, perceives scarcity everywhere, and is constantly inclined to hoard or to steal, to trespass into envy or greed, and to miss the value and pleasure of what it has in the restless pursuit to protect it and acquire more. The persons of the Trinity exist in a mystery of wonder and abundance. Theirs is a wonder that goes beyond knowledge, an abundance that knows the joy of the other will never run out. It's a dynamic contentment, an inexhaustible awareness, an understanding that there is discovery without end, reward without limit, play without defeat, perception without diminishment.

Every relationship is a mystery. It's not the same as the participants' experience with others, nor identical with any other meeting of two minds and hearts. It's a garden, which needs tending, pruning and nurturing, rather than a building, which simply needs constructing and then maintaining. A problem requires skill and a trained mind; a mystery requires patience and an open mind. It's part of the nature of a mystery that it may remain always a mystery.

Six: Delight

- *Tell about a time someone recognized something in you as a good thing that others had always seen as a bad thing.*
- *I wonder what it's like to feel no one perceives your differences in a positive light.*
- *Tell about a time you enjoyed the journey so much it ceased to matter about the destination.*
- *Tell about a time the task was so all-consuming you never really got to know your colleagues.*

Delight is the perception of abundance where another might only see scarcity. Abundance is the plenitude of what is there; scarcity is the lament for what isn't there. When Adam and Eve are set in the Garden of Eden, they're invited to enjoy its superabundant joys. Yet somehow they fixate on the one thing they cannot have, the fruit of a single tree, and altogether lose sight of what they can have, which is everything else. Thus they turn delight into resentment, from which fear, suspicion, envy and anger derive; they reduce almost limitless asset into mesmerizing deficit.

If you see someone from afar, make an instant judgement and assume your role is to make their life better (in other words if you miss out presence, attention and mystery), then almost inevitably you're going to focus on their deficits rather than their assets. You see only what a person can't do or doesn't have. Whether or not the person themselves would mention this observation among the 20 most interesting and significant facts about themselves, you instantly identify it as the principal one – perhaps the only one. You define them by what they're not rather than by what they are. Thus if you walk past a person who appears to be homeless, you could make instant assumptions centred on their obvious deficit – a home. But if you'd paused and offered presence, attention and a sense of mystery, you might have found that they'd travelled thousands of miles, living on their wits, to find relative peace and comfort, having fled a country where their identity, family or convictions made life impossibly dangerous and subject to hostility. They might be highly qualified, enormously talented, deeply wise. But instead of delighting in these assets, all you choose to see is their deficit.

Delight is the habit of perceiving a person's assets and not dwelling unduly, hastily or disproportionately on their deficits. Being with a person means seeing the best in them, patiently waiting for their true colours to emerge, trusting them to be a person of unique gifts, believing them to be a person of dignity and offering opportunities for them to reveal who they really are. Delight means trusting that a person already has most of the qualities they need for their own redemption and creating a space in which those qualities may be honoured, celebrated, stretched, developed and relied upon. Hans Andersen's story of the ugly duckling is a classic tale of delight. When the other birds first see their new companion all they perceive is her deficit – that she's not, like them, a duck. Only as time goes on do they realize her real asset. She is something they could never be – a swan. Delight means seeing young swans where others see only ugly ducklings.

Delight is also about the schooling of desire. When one covets the wrong thing or fixates on the wrong person, one does not desire too much, but too little. One desires perhaps to possess, touch, own, cherish. But this is too small a yearning. One should instead pass through this mean desire to find delight in this thing or person as a wonder inviting one to take such pleasure in all things. One should yearn to enlarge one's desire, that one may take just as much glory in every creature as in the person on which one's gaze is fixed. Thus may lust or covetousness be an urge to be transcended by joy more widely expressed, more fully encompassed, making one's sensations consistently overwhelmed by the beauty and uniqueness in all things. Thus is scarcity transfigured by abundance.

Being with anticipates the communion of persons with their environment, with one another and with God who will be their joy forever. Rather than prioritizing those activities that are instrumental in bringing about such a goal, being with celebrates the goal itself by seeking to practise its habits right now. It is common for those whose whole orientation is directed towards working for or working with to be suspicious or dismissive of being with as 'doing nothing'. A counter argument is to point out how much working – especially for but also with – is an end in itself, a displacement activity rooted in fear or reluctance in the face of being with. How much is this fear truly about the elusiveness of joy? When one's life is constant work, constant deferral of the moment of reward, constant avoiding the gaze of the persons one is serving or eschewing the opportunity to name the security one is pursuing, how much of this is taking refuge in the journey because of profound doubts about the destination? Being with is not inactivity. It's activity that is seeking to be the goal itself, to be the destination, rather than perpetually regarding the destination as an unspecified, distant chimera or a prosaic, measurable quantity.

To take delight in another is simultaneously to allow the other to take delight in me. It is part of the assumption of working for that any joy the recipient may find in me is strictly limited to satisfaction in the service I perform and the results derived from it. Any further joy is not to be sought, and certainly not to be invited; it's bound to distract from, if not undermine or even discredit, the service I perform. But delight longs to be shared, or risks becoming impoverished – even perverted. Part of the self-denying character of working for is denial of the opportunity to make a genuine relationship, one in which both parties may know and express joy and delight. Yet this self-denial masks its limited perception of human flourishing. Integral to human flourishing is the sharing of mutual joy. The life of the Trinity is the mutual evocation of joy in one another, the delight taken in beholding the other equalled by the joy discovered in causing delight in the other.

Seven: Participation

- *I wonder what it's like for someone you've done a project with to become someone you want to spend time with even if there's no project.*
- *Tell about a time you spent a lot of the day with a baby.*
- *Tell about a time you kept something for yourself before realizing it had no value without being shared.*
- *Tell about a time you didn't mind someone else getting the credit for something you'd played a key role in achieving.*

The first four dimensions take us to the heart of with. Being with a person means being not-with others. It means giving them your whole being, utterly attentive to them, understanding them in the sense of genuinely 'standing under' them, allowing the mystery of who they are to displace the urge to categorize or generalize about, let alone fix or solve, them, and gradually perceiving their assets rather than glancing superficially at their deficits. The next dimension delves deeper into what it means to say being with considers a person of value for their own sake, rather than for any achievement that may be attained through or with them.

The name of this dimension is participation. Participation means with for the sake of with. Imagine meeting a person who has many engaging and likeable qualities. You might say, 'May I cook you dinner?' And so the date comes, but you have built up to it by extensive shopping, cleaning, cooking, tidying, and so when they walk through the door your home looks as good as it has ever looked, and yet you pretend all is as normal and you've just thrown together what food was to hand. If the evening goes well, perhaps they come again, and this time you suggest they come an hour earlier, and you can slice the vegetables together as you talk. If the second evening goes well, you can consider setting aside the device of the meal and just find moments to spend together, to connect and catch up and enjoy connection and companionship. The first evening is working for, the second working with, the third being with. It's a being with that says, as two lovers say to one another, 'It doesn't matter what we do – what matters is being with you.' But true friends can say such things just as well as lovers.

BEING WITH

Participation names the kinds of being with that don't always issue in profound conversation or memorable exchange. It refers to the experience, say, of being with a baby, who doesn't talk or show appreciation or disclose confidences, but still takes in presence, attention, mystery and delight. It refers to the desire to be present with someone who has experienced great loss or savage injury; when there may be nothing helpful or comfortable to say, but simply sharing in the grief is all that one can do. Participation names interdependence: 'I cannot be fully me unless you are fully you.' It has no sense of beyond: it embraces the full dimensions of now.

The Trinity displays that God is a shared enterprise. The purpose of all things is not to get to the destination quickly, efficiently, and then move on to other business; the purpose is to find ways to be (and do) with. Participation is all. There's no getting there unless all get there. Every action of the Trinity is an action of all three of its persons, and is the richer for that texture of participation. It's a commonplace to speak of athletic honour lying not in the winning but in the taking part; yet the satisfaction – and the superficiality – of athletic contests arises from the fact that life as a whole is not fundamentally made up of victory or defeat, and only becomes so if one isolates and valorizes those parts that can be so described. There is nothing of eternal value that can be achieved or secured in isolation from other beings: there's nowhere to secure the booty of such a conquest, no way to protect it from the ravages of time or the oblivion of eternity, no person to whom to entrust it for safe keeping. All that is not participation is transitory. Put more positively, all that is participation is connected to the ultimate with, the abiding being with of God the Holy Trinity and humanity restored in the new creation. Every mundane with carries a hint of that final with.

Part of taking joy in the presence and activity of others is to realize that the story is not fundamentally about oneself. To be with is to seek to be a saint and not a hero. The hero performs for the watching, anonymous crowd and for the intangible yet quantifiable glory. The saint has no sense of any watching eye beyond those whose company the saint has chosen (or been chosen) to keep. The saint is not sustained by applause or inhibited by the lack of it. The saint's presence, attention, mystery and delight are evaluated by the degree to which they are shared and translated into with. This is the extent to which they resemble the inner relations of the persons of the Trinity.

Eight: Partnership

- *Tell about a grandparent and what it meant for them to grow old.*
- *Tell about a time when you realized everyone being different was a really good thing.*
- *Tell about a time someone who seemed weak was able to help you in an important way.*
- *I wonder what it's like to find hidden gifts in yourself and others.*

It would be inaccurate and unreasonable to advocate being with to the total neglect of working with. While working with can quickly become captivated by overcoming problems, and slow to appreciate mystery, it displays a profound dimension of with: that of partnership. Partnership is a form of activity in which you bring your unique assets and I bring mine, and together we can be and do something we could never have been or done apart.

Partnership works especially closely with the dimension of delight. Every true adventure story tells of how the brave company face innumerable challenges, and each time a different one of their number has the unique quality that enables them to find a way through and live to face the next adversary. Just so in being with, to be present, attentive and so on requires different characteristics from each party, and if the story is to continue over time it may be that the respective parties develop new characteristics or lose others, so can help each other in hitherto unforeseen ways.

Most poignant can be the relationship of child to grandparent, where at the beginning the grandparent has wisdom, experience and nimbleness, but where over time, as the child gains in stature, mobility and imagination, the grandparent may diminish in those same things. And so there may develop a partnership, with interchanging gifts and contributions, in a story that continues to evolve as each grows older, where older for one means progress and for the other means regress. While being with is about participation for its own sake, it can also be discovered in the deep sharing of gifts where the goal isn't everything, but finding a way to get there together is.

The Trinity is made up of three persons entirely with one another; so with that every action of one is in some degree an action of all three – no action of one can contradict the action of another. But the three persons of the Trinity are not identical with one another; they are complementary in their diversity and creative in their difference. The life of the Trinity incorporates both the purposeless joy of participation for its own sake and the purposeful intent of partnership for the exercise and enjoyment of the diverse gifts of the respective persons. What it never has is a task so urgent or a goal so unambiguous that one member sees fit to drop the with and go it alone to get the job done.

Partnership is a development of attention in the way participation is a development of presence. That is to say, as attention notices and highlights particularities and unique qualities, so partnership translates those qualities into complementary activity. Partnership brings out the dynamism in attention: more than just noticing and registering difference, more than just tolerating difference or even appreciating it, it rejoices in difference and puts it to work.

It's important to note that being with, while it pays close regard to process and is sceptical of overemphasis on product, does not thereby exclude or denigrate activity in general or productive activity in particular. To return to the child and the grandparent, when a grandparent has had a stroke, being with, for the grandchild, does not mean the grandchild going and buying a walking frame or searching the internet for herbal remedies: these are for rather than with. There's a place for such support, but such support is not to be regarded as with, and cannot take the place of with. Instead, being with may mean sitting beside the bed in silence, perhaps holding a hand; it may mean telling stories and acknowledging fears, making plans and exploring possible therapies, watching television or listening to the radio together; or it may mean walking side by side, as the grandparent learns to walk again. These are all forms of with, and they show the ways with goes beyond participation to partnership. Participation says, 'It doesn't matter what it is, what matters is that we do it together.' Partnership says, 'If you do your part and I do mine, we can do something beautiful together.'

The significance of this is that, for the stroke victim, it's often assumed (particularly from a working for point of view) that there is no part the victim can in fact do. Yet partnership, through presence, attention and delight, comes to perceive many things the victim can do, and stays around to discover many more that the victim unearths for themselves. Partnership says, 'You've had a stroke, but you can help me with my colour-blindness, with my dyslexia, with my anger, with my depression. In fact, because you are having to take things slowly, and to set aside the thirst for productivity, I can show you those parts of myself that I wouldn't have entrusted to you before, for fear I would be wasting your precious time.' Healing is not simply taking medication or receiving physical therapy that restores lost brain and limb and speech function; healing means learning to enjoy to the full one's new range of abilities and discovering aptitudes one always had but previously had not thought relevant or necessary. This latter is a journey that depends on participation and flowers in partnership.

Nine: Enjoyment

- *Tell about a time you felt used.*
- *Tell about a person who you know well but still fills you with wonder.*
- *I wonder what things you can't do with just one hand but need both hands to do.*
- *Tell about a time you chose not to take a photograph but instead just to take it all in.*

Most important of all the dimensions is enjoyment. The reason it's most important is that it contains all the others. We may distinguish between what we use and what we enjoy. What we use we perform with one hand; it is a means to an end, it can be combined with other tasks, it comes to an end. What we enjoy requires both hands; it is an end in itself, it takes everything we are, it lasts forever.

Most relationships begin as one of use. They're professional transactions, provisions of service, or things a person's doing but we might be just as happy for a machine to do. Classmates can take a while to see one another as more than rivals, allies or distractions, and come genuinely to enjoy one another as friends. Even friendships and romantic relationships can begin as forms of use – to overcome loneliness, to provide companionship, to give advice or share information or glean gossip. But the goal of every relationship should be that it eventually graduates from use to enjoyment.

Enjoyment should include a degree of wonder. If I enjoy you, I embrace you in all your depth and glory, but part of you still fills me with wonder, still leads me almost to squeal in delight or applaud with awe, pausing my hands to wait as even more marvels are revealed. 'How do you just know what to say?' we may utter. 'I'm amazed the way you can just do that,' we perhaps add. When you call a community home, you're saying, 'Everywhere else I am used; here I am enjoyed. It's like my birthday – every other day people expect me to perform; on this day alone people are thrilled with me just existing – just being me.'

Technologically shaped existence enables human beings to undertake a fast-increasing number of activities with just one hand. The contemporary West is a culture committed to multitasking; cars, computers and telephones are designed so that one can operate them with one hand while doing something else with the other. Few things interrupt the one-hand culture: most innovation is oriented to enhancing it. One might say the things we do with one hand are those we use; those that take two hands are those we enjoy. To enjoy another person is to take them in two hands, to offer them time, to cherish their particularity and their irreplaceability – to make it clear that experiencing them requires the whole of one's attention. It is to enjoy them in the way God enjoys them, to participate in God's enjoyment of them. The persons of the Trinity enjoy one another, as it were, with both hands; there is no multitasking involved. And God enjoys the good creation with both hands.

Imagine you are climbing a high mountain. In the distance you spy a grand and rare creature – perhaps a bear. At first you are afraid. Then you realize it can't see you. Then you think to use it – to take its photograph, tell your friends how lucky and clever you are, what an adventure you're having. Finally you appreciate that you are being drawn simply to enjoy it, to be with it in the present moment and let it show you what the world beyond the fervid human microdrama is truly made of. It takes every ounce of your energy, concentration and strength to continue to gain full view without being seen. You're utterly present in that moment, fully attentive, deeply conscious of mystery, filled with delight, honoured by participation and aware of partnership. This is what it means to enjoy.

Enjoying another is a participation in God's enjoyment of that other, not an idolatrous displacement of God by that other. The other remains other and is enjoyed in their otherness – especially in their otherness – rather than made one's own creature. God remains God, and enjoys us as we enjoy the other, and enjoys the other in and with our enjoying the other. Enjoyment must always respect the with – it's always a participatory and generative, never an exclusive or consuming process. The result of enjoyment is always more, always abundance, never less, never scarcity.

The persons of the Trinity enjoy one another. To enjoy is to be in one another's presence, to bestow profound attention on the other's differences and particularities, to enter the mystery of the other and the other's relational world, to delight in one another and thus discover joy, to participate with one another simply for the sake of the with that is involved, and to see complementarities in partnership with one another. The persons of the Trinity enjoy one another with no thought to use. Enjoyment is perfect activity: it's a moment when the means and the ends so fold into one another that the distinction ceases to jar; when participants experience their activity as effortless because they cannot imagine doing anything else.

God enjoys us. Grace is the extension to the good creation of the persons of the Trinity's enjoyment of one another. God bestows upon us presence, attention, mystery, delight, participation and partnership. This is what enjoyment looks like. This is what grace looks like. Eternal life is our enjoying God in best imitation of and response to God's perpetual and utter enjoyment of us. God does not use us; we are not part of some grander plan. We *are* the plan. There's no beyond to which God is reaching that includes (and therefore uses) us. We are the beyond. God's life is shaped never to be except to be with us. God enjoys us, now and forever. That is the gospel.

Ten: Glory

- *Tell about a time someone was truly* with *you.*
- *I wonder what it's like to have a great many things but not be able to enjoy them.*
- *Tell about a time someone wouldn't do something for you so you could learn to do it for yourself.*
- *I wonder what the word 'glory' means to you.*

One dimension remains: glory. Glory is a statement that being with is not simply a healthy way to take people seriously, listen to them, withhold assumptions and show appreciation: it's actually a depiction of the life of heaven, an understanding of the character of God. In heaven there are no problems to fix, no working for to be done, no obstacles to be overcome. In heaven there will be only one (apparent) undesirable circumstance: we don't get to choose with whom we dwell. So there will be no escape into working with or working for: there will only be being with. And those who have spent today being shaped in the arts and crafts of being with will be better placed truly to enjoy heaven. Perhaps hell is not so much being denied heaven, being obliterated or being sent to a fiery downstairs; perhaps hell is being in heaven but having not the capacity or willingness to enjoy it. Being with is a practice derived from reflection upon how we shall spend forever.

Glory is a recognition that being with is the nature of God. The Christian doctrine of the Trinity portrays three persons in one substance – the perfect embodiment of being with. They have no need to fix each other, and no urgency to spend their time elsewhere; all they need is the capacity and desire to be with one another, in perpetual harmony. Being with is fundamentally a claim about the life of God.

Here is perhaps the central verse of Christian faith: 'And the Word became flesh and lived among us, and we have seen his glory, the glory as of a father's only son, full of grace and truth' (John 1.14). This verse brings together several themes: God's life is shaped to be with us; being with us is of a piece with the persons of the Trinity's being with one another; being with is full of grace and truth; and both the Trinity's being with one another and the Trinity's being with us in the Word made flesh are best described as – indeed become the epitome of – glory. God being with God and God being with us are what we mean by the term 'glory'.

In his high priestly prayer in John 17, Jesus says, 'Father, glorify me in your own presence with the glory that I had in your presence before the world existed.' Here Jesus affirms that glory consists fundamentally in the persons of the Trinity being with one another, but he implies that this glory can exist in the presence of human beings, as is about to happen in his own Passion. Then he says, 'Father, I desire that those also, whom you have given me, may be with me where I am, to see my glory, which you have given me because you loved me before the foundation of the world.' Here Jesus connects the notion of being with to the ultimate revelation of glory. Glory precedes the foundation of the world. Being with was the purpose of God from before creation. Glory thus becomes the theme that connects the relations of the persons of the Trinity, the purpose of God in founding the world, the presence of God among human beings, and the notion of being with.

Perhaps most vividly, Jesus portrays the compelling quality of being with. If one takes the traditional shape of his ministry, he spends perhaps a week in Jerusalem working for us – dying and rising for the sake of the world. He spends perhaps three years in Galilee working with us – empowering disciples, teaching about the kingdom, demonstrating the ways of God. But he spends fully 30 years simply being with us: the hidden years, largely in Nazareth. The percentages – 1 per cent working for, 10 per cent working with, 90 per cent being with – reveal God's priorities. Those who follow Jesus must surely say, 'These are my priorities, too.'

This transforms almost every conventional notion of God. No longer is God fundamentally for us. No longer do we become frustrated or refuse to believe in a God who consistently fails to do the things we demand, plead or entreat that God do – to heal, relieve suffering, distribute justice, bring sun or rain. Now God is revealed as the one who is truly, utterly, unendingly with us. With us even to the point of becoming flesh with us. With us even to the point of being crucified with us. With us even to the point of being raised from death, never to be parted from us.

And we can glimpse that glory: every time we enter, explore, discover, deepen, restore and celebrate the wonder of being with. For every moment of with is a window into the heart of God.

Commentary

This course is obviously different from all the others. It came about in response to those training to be hosts and storytellers who asked to understand the eight dimensions of being with without needing to read *A Nazareth Manifesto* or the other related books. After two introductory talks that describe the context in which being with becomes a significant concept, the remainder of the course walks through the eight dimensions in turn, giving equal weight and treatment to each one. This course is most appropriate for an extended training programme either for those leading courses or for those seeking to understand and implement being with as an ethos for a whole community or parish.

References and Further Reading

W. H. Auden, '1939, 'Stop all the clocks, cut off the telephone', *Another Time*, Faber & Faber.
Rachel Carson, *Silent Spring* (Boston, MA: Houghton Mifflin, 1962).
George Herbert, 'The Elixir', *George Herbert and Henry Vaughan*, ed. Louis L. Martz, The Oxford Authors (Oxford: Oxford University Press, 1986).
Gerard Manley Hopkins, 'God's Grandeur', ed. Catherine Phillips (Oxford: Oxford University Press, 1986).
David McKee, *Not Now, Bernard* (London: Andersen Press, 1980).
Donald Nicholl, *Holiness* (London: Darton, Longman and Todd, 1981).
Thomas Traherne, *Centuries of Meditations* (London: Bertram Dobell, 1908).
Samuel Wells, *Act Justly: Practices to Reshape the World* (Norwich: Canterbury Press, 2022).
—— *A Cross in the Heart of God: Reflections on the Death of Jesus* (Norwich: Canterbury Press, 2020).
—— *A Future Bigger than the Past: Catalysing Kingdom Communities* (Norwich: Canterbury Press, 2019).
—— *God's Companions: Reimagining Christian Ethics* (Oxford: Blackwell, 2006).
—— *Hanging by a Thread: The Questions of the Cross* (Norwich: Canterbury Press, 2016 and New York: Church Publishing, 2017).
—— *The Heart of it All: The Bible's Big Picture* (Norwich: Canterbury Press, 2019).
—— *How Then Shall We Live? Christian Engagement with Contemporary Issues* (Norwich: Canterbury Press, 2016).
—— *How to Preach: Times, Seasons, Texts and Contexts* (Norwich: Canterbury Press, 2023).

—— *Humbler Faith, Bigger God: Finding a Story to Live By* (Norwich: Canterbury Press, 2022).

—— *Improvisation: The Drama of Christian Ethics* (London: SPCK and Grand Rapids, MI: Brazos, 2004; 2nd edn, Grand Rapids, MI: Baker, 2018).

—— *Incarnational Ministry: Being with the Church* (Norwich: Canterbury Press and Grand Rapids, MI: Eerdmans, 2017).

—— *Incarnational Mission: Being with the World* (Norwich: Canterbury Press and Grand Rapids, MI: Eerdmans, 2018).

—— *Learning to Dream Again: Rediscovering the Heart of God* (Norwich: Canterbury Press, 2013).

—— *The Moment of Truth: Reflections on Incarnation and Resurrection* (Norwich: Canterbury Press, 2023).

—— *A Nazareth Manifesto: Being with God* (Oxford: Wiley-Blackwell, 2015).

—— *Speaking the Truth: Preaching in a Pluralistic Culture* (Nashville, TN: Abingdon Press, 2008); rev. edn, *Speaking the Truth: Preaching in a Diverse Culture* (Norwich: Canterbury Press, 2018).

—— *Walk Humbly: Encouragements for Living, Working, and Being* (Norwich: Canterbury Press and Grand Rapids, MI: Eerdmans, 2019).

—— *With: Thoughts One Can't Do Without* (Milan: Juxta Press, 2020).

William Wordsworth, *Poetical Works*, ed. Thomas Hutchinson (Oxford: Oxford University Press, 1969).

www.ingramcontent.com/pod-product-compliance
Lightning Source LLC
Chambersburg PA
CBHW060556080526
44585CB00013B/582